CYCLE TOURING
IN SWITZERLAND

D1555821

Cycling in Switzerland?
You must be joking!

About the Authors

Judith and Neil Forsyth are both Lancastrians and learned to cycle at an early age. Their trusty bicycles were much used, until they stopped cycling in their 20s.

Judith worked as a teacher in Manchester for 20 years before moving to Germany to marry Neil. He had left Britain some years earlier to work for a German engineering company. He was reintroduced to cycling by a group of colleagues who had formed a weekend touring club. Once in Germany Judith, too, learned the delights of continental cycling. Together they explored much of southern Germany, eastern France and Switzerland by bicycle. They gained a reputation for British eccentricity with their neighbours when they cycled over the Alps from Heidelberg to Brissago on Lago Maggiore. This was further reinforced by Alpine cycling on Brompton folding bikes. They are both very fond of Switzerland, especially its superbly laid out and signposted cycle routes.

Chance late career moves into technical editing gave them enough courage to try to write a guide book. Now retired they have published six guides about Germany and Switzerland under the Bergstrasse Bike Books imprint. This is their first guide for Cicerone.

CYCLE TOURING IN SWITZERLAND

by

Judith and Neil Forsyth

2 POLICE SQUARE, MILNTHORPE, CUMBRIA LA7 7PY
www.cicerone.co.uk

First edition 2008
ISBN-13: 978 185284 526 1

All the photographs, maps and text are by the authors.

A catalogue record for this book is available from the British Library.

Acknowledgements

We would like to thank the employees of Veloland Schweiz for their work in designing and organising a superb cycle route network, and for their patience in answering our innumerable questions. In addition thanks are due to the staff of the Tourist Information Offices in Switzerland that we visited and again posed difficult questions. Sam Cage not only regularly let us use his living room as a base camp, but was a valuable source of information about Switzerland and local cycling routes. Klaudia and Edwin Ebi were very helpful both sharing their experience of cycling in Switzerland and offering us accommodation. As ever our friends Katja Maibauer, Reinhard Gleisner, Cindy Vargo and Chris Mitchell gave us their support and practical assistance.

Advice to Readers

Although the authors have made every effort to ensure the accuracy of this guide-book, readers should note that the weather, roadworks, forestry operations to name but a few can all cause unexpected route changes. The touring cyclist should always be prepared to listen to and accept local advice. The authors would be grateful to hear of any changes – please send them to the publisher.

Front cover: Cycle art near Meiringen (Swiss National Cycle Routes 8 and 9)

CONTENTS

The Swiss National Cycle Routes

(Based on information supplied by Veloland Schweiz)

FRANCE

Basel
Liestal
Aara
Saignelégier
Solothurn
Biel/Bienne
Neuchâtel
8
BERN
Sarne
Fribourg
5
Vallorbe
Thun
Lausanne
9
Interlaken
Eig 39
▲
Jungfrau 4158
Montreux
Gstaad
Nyon
Aigle
1
Brig
Sion
Genève
Martigny
Matterhorn 4477
▲
Mont Blanc 4807
▲
Monte Rosa 4633
▲

7

Route Key

1 Rhône **2** Rhein **3** North–South **4** Alpine Panorama

GERMANY

chaffhausen

olenz

Winterthur

2

Romanshorn
Rorschach

Zürich

St Gallen

St Margrethen

Appenzell

Zug

AUSTRIA

Luzern

Schwyz

Glarus

Stans

4

Chur

Scuol

Grindelwald

Thusis

6

Andermatt

Gletsch

3

St Moritz

▲
*Bernina
4049*

Locarno

Bellinzona

ITALY

Chiasso

Mittelland   **6** Graubünden   **7** Jura   **8** Aare   **9** Lakes

The route gets wilder beyond Montbovon (Route 4, Stage 7)

Map Key

∙∙∙∙∙∙∙∙∙∙∙	Main route (where it follows Swiss National Route)
∙∙∙∙∙∙∙∙∙∙∙	Route diversions/extensions
∙∙∙∙∙∙∙∙∙∙∙	National boundary
⅄	Pass
▲	Mountain
● ○	Town/village
R4 →	Route label
∼	River
⬭	Lake
Lowland Hilly Mountainous	Lowland Hilly Mountainous

Pragelpass summit with goats (Route 4, Stage 3)

INTRODUCTION

Cycling? In Switzerland? At your age? Surely that's only for the über-fit, the super rich or the foolhardy? We hear this from relatives and friends and have prepared a whole host of earnest reasons for hopping on our bikes. These include the environmental, keeping fit and getting-to-know-the-country-better arguments.

However none of these really explains why we prefer to travel by bike. The honest truth is that cycling is fun. And there is no other country in the world quite like Switzerland. It has four official languages. It has been a democracy for centuries. It has many of Europe's highest mountains, glaciers and azure lakes with white steamers gliding gracefully about like swans. It is the home of Grindelwald, the Eiger and the Reichenbach Falls where Sherlock Holmes disappeared and Moriarty met his end; Davos where international business people gather for conferences; little bright red trains; palm-fringed subtropical promenades in Ticino; Heidi and Grandfather; superb chocolate; good cheese; cowbells; yellow Postbuses and cities small enough to cycle through easily. It also offers the contrasting landscapes of the Jura, the Mittelland and the Alps.

For over a hundred years Switzerland has been a paradise for walkers and climbers though perhaps less visited by cyclists, other than the Tour de Suisse competitors who power over the high passes annually. Recognition of this fact led to the establishment, in 1995, of Veloland Schweiz (The Cycling in Switzerland Foundation), whose aim was to create a national Swiss cycle network. Between 1998 and 2006, 40 million CHF was invested in planning and signposting cycle routes and today there are nine Swiss National Cycle Routes (referred to in the guide as R1, R2, etc), which form the basis of the first nine routes described in this guide. The Swiss have a long tradition of marking paths, reflected in extremely reliable cycle signposting, with distinctive and clearly legible maroon signs, removing the need to check guide, map, compass or GPS at every junction. The overall aim is to guide cyclists onto quiet roads and cycleways. Where sections of the official, signed routes are unsurfaced, detours have been suggested within each itinerary for riders of narrow-tyred road bikes, although they may require you to use unsignposted routes and face heavier traffic.

The Swiss cycle network now covers most of scenic Switzerland, wherever roads or trails exist. All the national and several regional routes are described in this guide. In addition, some as yet unmarked and signposted variations are suggested, in Central Switzerland, the Berner Oberland, Graubünden in southeastern Switzerland, and in and around Andermatt, The Alpine Star – three strenuous routes which take in the Susten, Nufenen (Passo di Novena), Furka, Grimsel, Oberalp and Lukmanier (Lucomagno) Passes. You may choose to ride the routes end-to-end or 'pick and mix', depending on fitness or weather and put together a personalised tour high in the mountains or around the shores of various lakes. You will meet other cyclists but rarely in vast numbers. Many routes set the heart racing but you should be able to look forward to a clean bed and a decent meal every evening, even at 2000m (although it is possible to camp or bivouac if you prefer), without breaking the bank.

There are some hard routes for experienced cyclists (such as the Alpine Star), but there are also pleasant easy routes for families (in particular, the Rhein Route after Disentis, the Mittelland, the Aare from Meiringen and Lakes Routes and the tours in the Berner Oberland from Interlaken). Many of the trans-Alpine roads – like the San Bernardino Pass, built around 1820 – were built for horse-drawn traffic long before the invention of the car. Cyclists can be grateful for horses' preference for gentle gradients, which give you time to inspect wild flowers or basking lizards by the roadside. But if it all gets too much public transport is excellent, with almost all trains and lake steamers and even some buses accepting bicycles.

This book is a cycling guide which leaves Swiss history and culture, and full information on the towns and cities that you will pass through, to other sources. Completing the research and riding the routes has been challenging, sometimes cold and wet, frequently spiritually uplifting and it involved enjoying a lot of food and the odd beer. The physical backdrop was our constant companion, but a great bonus was the people we met: fellow cyclists, folk on

trains, people we stayed with. Travellers need a friendly wave or a helpful train conductor to remind them that, beyond the route or the dirt on the bike, the real world goes on.

AN OVERVIEW OF THE ROUTES

All of the Swiss National Routes (R1–R9) are signposted in both directions and the modifications that we have suggested to Routes 1, 4 and 8 can also be cycled in reverse. The routes suggested based on Swiss National Routes 2, 3 and 6 will not be signposted completely for cyclists in either direction, although you should have no difficulty navigating by Swiss road signs. The aim was to offer a weave of routes so that not all east–west routes, for example, are described in the same direction, to make it easier for the reader to combine routes into longer tours. Where the topographic features of a reverse route are such that it is inadvisable, this is highlighted below.

Estimated cycle times are based on a leisurely progress on touring bicycles with baggage and no sag wagon (backup vehicle), allowing time to smell the flowers and look at the scenery, especially on uphill stretches. The grades are the subjective judgments of the authors, ranging from 'easy' to 'exceedingly strenuous'. Where two grades are given, the first indicates the difficulty of the route without public transport in the direction first described and the second the difficulty if the tougher stretches are bypassed by taking a bus or train. All routes are suitable for road bikes or touring bikes.

1: The Rhône Route, R1
(difficult/easy)
Distance: 318km
Cycling time: 30 hours

The route starts in Andermatt high in the Alps and ends in Genève on Lac Léman. The first stage is a 'difficult' climb over the Furka Pass, which can be bypassed by Postbus or train. During the next easy stages the cyclist descends through the Rhône Valley with good views of snow-capped peaks. Later the route reaches the shores of Lac Lèman with its *mondaine* resorts and ends in Genève. The route would be almost as satisfying in the reverse direction, but the climb over the Furka at the end of the route would become 'strenuous'. The route passes through or close by many charming towns. **Brig** has a quaint Old Town. At **Visp** keen cyclists can climb to **Zermatt** to look at the Matterhorn. **Sierre** is a sleepy little historic town with a wine museum and **Sion** has a cathedral and fascinating Old Town, with a major art gallery and museum complex (Fondation Pierre Gianadda) nearby at **Martigny**. You also cycle past **Château de Chillon** and upmarket **Montreux** (which has a youth hostel, all the same). **Vevey** offers memories of Charlie Chaplin, a bungalow designed by Le Corbusier and the headquarters of the Nestlé Company. **Lausanne** is an elegant, vibrant, cultural hub, and very hilly although the youth hostel is down near the lake. **Nyon** has a Roman history museum and is interesting to football fans as the home of UEFA. **Genève** has a fine old town, the United Nations, some good museums and an airport offering cheap flights to the rest of Europe.

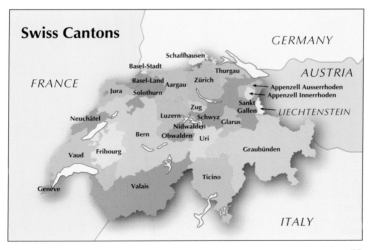

Swiss Cantons

2: The Rhein Route, based on R2

(moderate/easy)
Distance: 486km
Cycling time: 45 hours

This route too starts in Andermatt, climbs to near to one of the sources of the Rhein and then follows the river to loop round the Bodensee and on to Basel. The first stage over the Oberalp Pass is 'moderate', but afterwards the route is 'easy'. It is eminently suited to cycling in reverse although it is a long climb from Chur to the Oberalp summit. Initially the scenery is Alpine with windswept meadows, then rolling along the valley floor between snow-capped peaks. The northern shore of the Bodensee is delightfully rural until the return to the Rhein Valley proper. The river and the cycle route run mainly through wooded, undulating landscapes. The route visits **Disentis** with its monastery, **Chur** with its Old Town and cathedral and **Liechtenstein** with its castle and art gallery. At **Lustenau** there is a fascinating museum about controlling the Rhein, including little steam trains out into the delta. Crossing into Austria, **Bregenz** hosts open air operas on the lakeside in summer, more art galleries and you can take a cable car up Mount Pfänder for a fine view of the Rhein delta. **Lindau** has an Old Town, Bavarian beer and an interesting harbour. **Friedrichshafen** is home to the Zeppelin Museum which is well worth a detour, as well as a low cost carrier airport. **Konstanz** has yet another interesting Old Town, and a fine minster. **Stein-am-Rhein** has some striking painted houses.

Schaffhausen offers an Old Town, churches large and small, a fortress and the Rhein Falls nearby. There is an excavated Roman city called Augusta Raurica in **Kaiseraugst**, just outside Basel and **Basel** itself has an amazing range of museums, art galleries, a cathedral and some good pubs.

3: A North–South Route, based on R3

(strenuous)
Distance: 578km
Cycling time: 60 hours

This is a tough modification of the Swiss National Cycle Route 3, with more altitude to climb, and is intended for the really able cyclist. The start is in Basel and the end in Bellinzona with a last quick run up into the wooded hills of the Megadino into Italy with views of Lago Maggiore, before returning to Bellinzona. (It can also be cycled in reverse but this means starting with the harder climbs rather than warming up to them.) There are serious hills and passes to cross every day. Initially the route runs through hill farm country and the countryside gradually gets wilder until reaching the Italianate south. **Basel** has many museums and art galleries and decent restaurants. **Aarau** is an interesting small town with magnificent painted gables. **Luzern** has the famous bridge, an exceptional Old Town, lake steamers and the Swiss Transport Museum. **Altdorf** has a statue of Wilhelm Tell, **Disentis** a baroque monastery and the route finishes in **Bellinzona** with its castles and a lively Old Town.

4: The Alpine Panorama Route, R4

(strenuous)
Distance: 483km
Cycling time: 50 hours

This is a tough route with magnificent views as the name suggests. It starts or finishes in St Margrethen in the northeast corner of Switzerland and eventually reaches Aigle in the southwest of the country. The hills are fierce either way. The route passes through the forests and small farms of Appenzell, running into the Linth Valley, and then climbs over the Klausen Pass above the treeline. It drops to the edge of the Vierwaldstätter See (Lake Lucerne) and then, after a ferry crossing, climbs past several small lakes. After another pass you arrive in Sörenberg to fine views of the Brienzer Rothorn group of mountains. A series of small hills brings you to the edge of the Thuner See, followed by yet another climb to Fribourg and finally over hill and dale to a fantastic drop into Aigle's wine growing country. There are few major towns along the way. **Appenzell** has a village atmosphere. **Thun** has a medieval double-decker shopping street in the Old Town and views of the Eiger, Mönch and Jungfrau and castle high above the town. **Fribourg** is an elegant city with narrow streets, a cathedral, a printing museum and good art galleries. It is known as Freiburg in German and sits astride the linguistic border between French and German speakers, the official language changing as you cycle across the river.

5: The Mittelland Route, R5

(moderate/easy)
Distance: 374km
Cycling time: 30 hours

This is an ideal route for families or those returning to cycling after a period of inactivity, although there is a 'moderate' climb at the start. Route 5 runs from Romanshorn on the Bodensee to Lausanne on Lac Léman across the Mittelland, the plateau lying between the Alps and the Jura Hills. The route can be cycled in the other direction. Leaving Romanshorn – which sits in a major fruit growing area – the route then runs through thick woodland, then swings around Zürich International Airport to reach the Aare Valley. The wide, rather ponderous, river is followed until the Lac de Bienne where the route crosses a vast market gardening area to reach the Lac de Neuchâtel and meanders through fields and forests to Yverdon les Bains. Eventually you face a gentle climb and descent to reach Lausanne. The first major city on the route is **Winterthur** with its excellent museums. **Zürich** with the Swiss National Museum, the Bahnhofstrasse, one of the most expensive shopping streets in Europe and several interesting churches is just off the route. Also well worth a stop is **Solothurn**, a baroque treasure, and **Lausanne** (see chapter 1).

6: An Engadine Circuit, and beyond, based on R6

(strenuous)
Distance: 531km
Cycling time: 50 hours

This route is for keen cyclists. National Cycle Route 6 runs south from Chur with a branch over the San Bernadino Pass to Bellinzona and another to St Moritz and Martina on the Austrian Swiss border. The Engadine Circuit follows Route 6 from Chur to Splügen, crosses the Splügen Pass into Italy and climbs to St Moritz to reach the Albula Pass. It then follows the Landwasser Valley up to Davos, climbs over the Flüela Pass to reach the Inn Valley and Martina and swings up into Nauders to cross the Reschen Pass into the Südtirol (Italy). Next it climbs back through Santa Maria over the Ofen Pass to reach Livigno and then climbs over the Forcola di Livigno. Finally it drops to reach the Passo di Bernina road, climbs over a final pass and drops through Pontresina to reach the Albula Pass road again and return to Chur. Although the scenery and the climbs may be the main attraction there are many other things to see. **Chur** has a medieval Old Town and a cathedral. **Bellinzona's** castles are a UNESCO World Heritage Site as is **Santa Maria's** monastery. Cycling this route the other way round is not to be recommended, particularly because of the extremely tough climb from Chiavenna to Splügen.

Snowsheds and roadworks by the Reschensee (Route 6, Stage 5)

7: The Jura Route, R7

(strenuous/moderate)
Distance: 275km
Cycling time: 25 hours

This route runs from Basel and along the French-Swiss border to Nyon on Lac Léman. The Jura are hills rather than mountains. The ascents and descents tend to be short and steep. The countryside is wooded and interspersed with fields at the start and then high bare limestone country with swallow holes, dry valleys and limestone pavements. Teenage children should be able to manage this route in the direction suggested, with some support from public transport or by splitting a stage into two. In the reverse direction, the long slog up to the Jura tops may put off even the hardiest soul. The only major towns along the way are **Basel** with its Old Town, museums and cathedral and **Nyon** with its Roman museum and lakeside promenade.

8: The Aare Route, R8

(easy to moderate)
Distance: 281km
Cycling time: 25 hours

This route is ideal for families and returning cyclists. It starts in Koblenz on the Swiss German border near Waldshut and follows the Aare to Meiringen. It begins very near the wooded hills of the Black Forest and ends in the Berner Oberland at the foot of the Alps. The reverse direction can also be cycled. On the way you pass through **Solothurn** with its baroque treasures and computer museum and through **Bern**, the Swiss capital, with its Alpine Museum, the famous bear pit and romantic Old Town. **Thun** offers medieval double-decker shops. **Interlaken** is the gateway to the Berner Oberland. **Meiringen** has excellent cake shops and connections to Sherlock Holmes.

9: The Lakes Route, R9

(moderate with good
public transport support)
Distance: 497km
Cycling time: 45 hours

This route runs from Montreux in south-western Switzerland to Rohrschach in the northeast and can be cycled in both directions. It not difficult and, with judicious use of public transport, would be a good route for a family with teenage children. It climbs steeply through

woods above Montreux to reach the cow-filled fields of Gruyère country before climbing through a long Alpine valley to descend to Interlaken and the Berner Oberland. Once over the low Brünig Pass the route drops in a series of steps to the Vierwaldstätter See and Luzern. It follows the River Reuss to Zug and then climbs over high moorland to descend to the Zürichsee and thence to the fjord-like Walensee to reach the Rhein Valley and the Bodensee. The towns along the way are interesting: **Montreux**, **Vevey**, **Gruyères**, **Gstaad**, **Interlaken**, **Meiringen**, **Luzern**, **Zug**, **Einsiedeln** and **Liechtenstein**.

10: The Berner Oberland

(easy to strenuous)
Total distance for all seven tours: 451km
Cycling time: 40 hours

This is a group of of day tours, either circular or out and back, which would make a leisurely week's cycling, especially with use of the excellent public transport facilities in the area. A week based here would make a good family holiday. **Thun**, **Interlaken**, **Luzern**, **Spiez** and **Meiringen** are well worth visiting.

11: The Alpine Star

(exceedingly strenuous)

These three tours are suggested only for active, well-trained cyclists and, with climbs of up to 3000m per day, they demand a considerable level of fitness.

HOW TO USE THIS GUIDE

This section contains general information for a cycle trip to Switzerland, including:

- Swiss traffic laws and navigation aids
- how to travel there with a bicycle and how to get to the start of your tour
- choice of bicycle and what (and what not) to take
- the landscape
- the weather and the best times to go
- where you can stay without breaking the bank, and
- what you can expect to eat and drink.

The next section – 'The Routes' – describes nine routes based on the Swiss National Cycle Routes, followed by a series of tours radiating from Interlaken (The Berner Oberland) and, finally, in The Alpine Star, a trio of tours for the very fit. (Note: The National Cycle Routes are referred to as R1–R9, and the routes in the guide as Route 1, Route 2, etc.) The routes are graded from 'easy' to 'exceedingly strenuous'. The 'easy' routes are normally flat or climb imperceptibly and are suitable for families and returning or new cyclists. The 'moderate' routes have stages that are short and climb a maximum of 800m. The more challenging route stages – 'difficult' or 'strenuous' – normally involve between 800 and 1500m climbing. The 'exceedingly strenuous' routes described in the Alpine Star chapter are over 100km long and feature climbs of 3000m. Each individual route is broken down into a series of stages, rather than days. Sometimes it may be possible to cycle two stages in a day.

For each route, full information is provided, in a series of tables on: distance, climb and grade overall and for each stage; additional maps; links to other routes; public transport options; facilities en route and contact details for local tourist information offices. A short overview of the route is also given, along with detailed directions for road and touring bikes (where different) for each stage. The facilities table indicates whether places on the route have a camp site, youth hostel or backpackers' hostel, a B&B, hotels, a railway station and a bicycle shop. More than four hotels in a settlement is considered to be 'many'. The majority of villages also have grocery shops and/or bakers, cafés and banks or cash machines (ATMs).

The appendices provide useful websites and information sources (Appendix 1), a selection of recommended accommodation (Appendix 2) and a bicycle glossary (Appendix 3).

STAYING ALIVE: SAFETY AND ROUTE FINDING

Emergency telephone numbers:

- Swiss ambulance: 144
- Swiss fire brigade: 118
- For the EU (Austria, France, Germany, Italy): 112.

Cyclists really are welcome in Switzerland. The country's politicians, traffic planners and tourist authorities plan and provide fully for the traveller, tourer or commuter by bike. Veloland Schweiz – an organisation which is recognised and supported by the federal government, all the cantons, Swiss motoring organisations, the Swiss Tourist

Office and Swiss Railways as well as many others – has played a uniquely valuable role in opening up cycle routes in Switzerland. Their national guides to individual routes are excellent but not yet available in English. Their website does, however, have an English version which is well worth visiting: www.cycling-in-switzerland.ch. Local authorities maintain signpost networks and report dangers or diversions. On some routes it is possible to arrange baggage transfer in summer, along with hotel bookings and other services. There is wide recognition of the services provided by Veloland Schweiz and the transport providers and hoteliers now work together to attract cyclists.

The rules of the road

It is assumed that cyclists will ride responsibly and obey the rules of the road, such as riding on the right-hand side. The regulations are fundamentally the same as for the rest of Europe, except for the colour of road signs – blue for ordinary roads and green for motorways. (If you are concerned, you can buy a *Handbook of Swiss Traffic Regulations* from Swiss bookshops.) Bike lanes, traffic lights and overall provision for the cyclist are better than in many other countries. Helmets are not legally required, although cyclists are encouraged to wear them by road safety campaigns.

Signs and symbols: Cyclists from outside continental Europe may be taken by surprise by the *priorité à droite/ Rechtsvorfahrt* law. This says that, if no road priority is shown, the traffic coming from the right *on a road of equal value*

has right of way. Priority is shown by the symbol that looks like a square fried egg on the main road or the arrow sign for a particular junction. Minor roads are indicated by the conventional international 'Stop' and 'Halt' signs.

Be warned that a lot of European drivers do not look left when approaching a junction where they have priority. They just drive out. At the same time, use your common sense. If you technically have priority but an 18-wheeled juggernaut is dropping down over a hill towards the junction, it's better to let it pass. Swiss heavy goods vehicle drivers are generally considerate of cyclists but a lot of the vehicles on Swiss roads come from other countries, so don't push your luck.

One distinctively Swiss sign is the Postbus priority sign. This is found high in the mountains and means that after this point Postbuses have absolute priority. Their drivers use this privilege and swing wide round hairpins. There are sections where the road is only as wide as a Postbus, so when you hear the Posthorn get well over to the side of the road.

Autobahns, motorways or expressways are indicated by white lettering on a green background, unlike the familiar blue signs of the rest of Europe. Cycling is forbidden on these. There are often separate cycleways over bridges built to carry these highways over rivers or other landscape features (safe but rather noisy and you will be glad to escape after a few hundred metres). Other major highways are designated by white letters on a blue background. Traffic on these is usually heavy and they are not recommended for cyclists, although occasionally they may be the only option for

Postbus and priority signs

short distances. Road signs in black on a white background usually indicate quiet routes and are recommended for cyclists, though they may be busy on high days and holidays.

Signs specifically for cyclists are dark red with white lettering and include a bike symbol. National route numbers are clearly indicated in white on a blue square, incorporating a tiny Swiss flag. At important route junctions there is often a Veloland Schweiz information board with a regional map and other points of interest, though this may not have information in English. Local and regional routes (many) use bike symbols on red or other backgrounds. A mountain bike route symbol indicates routes even narrower or more vertical, not recommended for touring or road bikes. Some of these cycle signposts also include distance or altitude information.

Excellent signposting (Rhein embankment, near Buchs)

On main routes diversions may be signposted during floods, tree-felling or some other emergency, although local routes are occasionally just blocked without warning. Hazards such as steep climbs (or descents), narrow paths alongside rivers or above cliffs are usually indicated but Veloland Schweiz and regional planners take the view that cyclists are able to assess risks for themselves. Inexperienced riders or headstrong youngsters may need guidance.

Yellow signposts with black lettering are for walkers and usually indicate

21

Hazard warnings

time taken to reach a destination. Some of these routes are also used by cyclists but you should take care passing walkers, who have priority use. If necessary, push your bike on these sections. Signs for walkers often include altitudes, which can be useful in determining how much further you need to struggle to the top of the pass.

Urban cycling
Dedicated cycleways may be provided, indicated by red tarmac or bike pictogram. Cyclists can often move into a box ahead of traffic at traffic lights, and, in some cases, may turn right on red, as indicated by small traffic lights for cyclists. Routes in cities often select quieter roads parallel to the main arteries, although even in Switzerland parked vehicles may block the way. In bigger cities, like Basel or Zürich, trams are a special hazard for those unused to them. They are quiet, use lines almost designed to unseat the unwary rider and have priority over most other road users. Watch out, take care and walk your bikes through busy crossings if you are at all uncertain. Accidents involving cyclists and trams are infrequent, although wet tram lines can be treacherous.

One way streets and pedestrian zones: Cyclists are allowed to cycle some one way streets in the wrong direction, as indicated by a bike pictogram beside the word 'frei' or 'excepté'. Bus and taxi lanes are also open to cyclists. In pedestrian zones, bicycles are often permitted if ridden at walking pace and with consideration for walkers. Riding through busy streets, markets or festivals where

people are eating, drinking or dancing is clearly inadvisable, although not specifically forbidden. Special care is needed near transport interchanges because there are often lots of people, many local cyclists heading to work or home who know exactly where they are going, tram lines, bus stops, underpasses, steps and ramps and those who insist on blocking narrow spaces, to say nothing of taxis, buses, trams and light railways.

On railway stations, do not ride along platforms, even though you may see locals doing this. It is illegal and you risk a hefty fine. Shout or wave to attract train staff attention if you are late for a train. Usually they'll wait, for a microsecond at least.

Special hazards
There are some hazards peculiar to Alpine cycling, which are worth mentioning. The biggest is the problem of encountering other road users on narrow mountain passes. Particularly at weekends, you may encounter large groups of motorcyclists or, worse, quad bikers, who may pass you too closely, just when you are negotiating a steep drop. The sheer noise associated with bands of 20 bikers roaring past may give you a shock and so it is best to avoid the passes at weekends, especially in summer. Coaches too can cut things rather fine. Most motorists are not aggressive, although some do pass on blind corners. It is a good idea to make eye contact and smile at oncoming road users if possible.

The pass routes are mostly on regular roads, blocked by snow for part of winter. Frost action plus clearing by snow plough damages the surface, not

Snowshed (Passo del Bernina)

enough to notice on the slow crawl uphill but hazardous when freewheeling down at over 50km an hour, so take care. Where streams flow they can shed gravel or pebbles onto roads after heavy rain, making skidding and falls a possibility. Remember too that heavily laden bikes will handle very differently. Minor mishaps occur through not concentrating because there's no apparent danger.

Tunnels and snowsheds on mountain roads can be long and so noisy that you cannot tell which way a vehicle is coming or how far it is away and so they need to be approached with care. They are safe as long as you can be seen, and although tunnels are often equipped with street lights you need to make sure that drivers, suffering from the contrast with bright sunlight outside or peering through steamy windows, can see you. The tiny blinking LEDs often used by weight-conscious cyclists are not enough. They have their place in addition to a battery or dynamo lighting systems. We smother ourselves, bikes and bags in reflective strips and piping. You will also see much better if you take your sunglasses off as you enter a tunnel. Another unexpected hazard can be cows congregating in snowsheds during the heat of the day.

Major floods happen in the Alps quite frequently leaving lasting scars long after the water has gone. Bridges, landslides and rockfalls on roads are usually replaced or cleared very quickly but cycle trails along river valleys may be open but almost impassible for weeks or months. Check on the Veloland Schweiz website before you set off from home for news of recent floods, and, if storms are forecast, think twice before setting off.

Motorcyclists in hot pursuit (Splügenpass Swiss side)

Washed-out route near Klosters

Material in the road: The sign showing boulders falling onto roads (*Steinschlag*) is a fairly frequent one in Switzerland where roads may be carved through rocks. Casualties caused by rockfall are relatively rare and the sign really means: 'beware rocks on road'. In the Jura, weak shales release a rain of small rock chunks from exposed banks. They would not hurt if they hit you but could cause a skid or even a fall on touring bikes. The cows leave the other main deposit on roads: cattle dung, best avoided in the rain and at high speed on descents. Towards the end of September cattle (and horses and goats) are brought down from high pastures in the Alps to winter quarters in village barns. If you are looking foward now to a picturesque *transhumance*, cattle bedecked in flowers and crowns, small children in *Tracht* and farmers wearing their best checked shirt, think again. It can be a traffic holdup even on major roads and then a messy ride onwards. However, you should be able to overtake all the 4x4s, coaches and motorcyclists to get a good view of the procession.

Cattle grids: Cattle grids are extensively used on minor roads, indicated by either *Viehrost*, *Querrost* or the more guessable *Bovi Stop*. In addition, on tracks used as parts of the national routes there are novel solutions to allow riders through areas of animal husbandry. Many fields are divided using electric fences, including gates where an insulated handle can be unhooked to let a cyclist through. Cattle with young calves

Cows block bridge on Grimselpass road

may protect them aggressively so the advice is to give them a wide berth. Heifers or bullocks may be inquisitive and not move from gateways, which can be intimidating. It's up to you to decide whether to risk going on or turning back. A different option encountered in the Jura for bypassing an electric fence was a narrow metal bridge, barely passable with a laden bike.

Ticks: Despite occasional press reports of wolf or bear incursions, there are no large dangerous animals in Switzerland that you are likely to encounter. However there is a slight, increasing risk of tick-borne diseases. Two diseases are carried: Lyme Disease and Tick-Borne Encephalitis. The first usually responds to antibiotics. The second is more dangerous and the only way of reducing your chance of getting it is to seek immunisation before leaving home. Consult your doctor and take advice. Cover your legs and shoulders when cycling through grass and check for ticks at the end of each day. Local pharmacies can supply tick forceps for their removal. (www.masta-travel-health.com/tickalert provides more information).

Bicycle shops

There are many bicycle shops in Switzerland. Tiny Meiringen has three bike shops. Most, but not all, close on a Monday. If you need a spare part or a repair on a Monday check to see whether a local shop is open or ask at the tourist office. Sometimes the owner lives over the shop and can be persuaded to replace the odd item in an emergency.

Base touring

Moving on daily can be doubly tiring because of always packing and unpacking bike panniers, always travelling through new places and not having time for domestic tasks like washing or shopping. Some of the nine national routes are quite short and perhaps lend themselves to completing in a week or less, like the Jura R7. Others involve climbing over 7700m in 483km (Alpine Panorama R4) so will take most people somewhat longer.

As an alternative, many people choose to base themselves in a region such as the Berner Oberland and make tours from a centre. A veteran American cyclist, Norman Ford, developed the concept of base touring. A base is chosen, lodgings booked for two, three or more nights and then routes explored from there. This works excellently with Switzerland's public transport network. Main luggage can be left at the billet. You can follow circular routes or use public transport at the beginning or end of the day. Route finding back to base becomes easier as you get to know your area, as does coping with public transport and it gives you time to catch up on the washing, showering and postcard writing. The Berner Oberland chapter in this guidebook describes day routes from Interlaken. Most of the communities where two or more routes cross can provide several interesting single day tours, for example: Aarau, Andermatt, Bulle, Lausanne, Meiringen, St Margrethen, Sarnen or Buchs, Stans and Thun.

GETTING THERE AND GETTING ABOUT

By air

There are airports in Friedrichshafen (Germany), Genève, Zürich and Basel.

- *From Friedrichshafen:* Follow the signs to the centre of Friedrichshafen (*Stadtzentrum*) by following the exit (*Ausfahrt*) signs from the terminal and turning right along the main road once out of the airport. Once in Friedrichshafen there are excellent cyclepaths. Follow the signs to Fähre, Hafen or Romanshorn. From Hafen (harbour) the cyclist can follow the Bodensee Radweg to Konstanz or Lindau, or take the car ferry across to Romanshorn, Switzerland.

- *From Genève:* Leave the terminal building at its western end to pick up the cyclepath along the Route de l'Aeroport. Follow it east then TR over the motorway. Follow unnamed road to meet Chemin du Jonc. TR. TL into the second left road (Chemin des Corbillettes). TR onto Chemin de Joinville. TL along Chemin de Sapins. TR along Chemin Terroux. TR along Chemin des Corbillettes. SO into Avenue Trembley. SO into Rue Pestalozzi. RF into Rue Chabrey. RT into Rue Hoffmann. LT into Rue de la Servette. LT by Notre Dame church to reach Gare de Cornavin (railway station) to pick up R1.

- *From Zürich:* The airport is on Route 5 and there is a signposted route to the main railway station in Zürich.

- *From Basel:* This is the least convenient. It is in France, just north of the city, and has only a bus connection meaning that access with a bike by public transport at busy times might be problematic. However, there is a cycleway from the airport to Basel, via the French village of St Louis.

From the UK and Ireland: There are direct flights from most airports in the British Isles to Switzerland. For example, Swiss Air offer flights from London, Birmingham, Manchester and Dublin and British Airways offer flights from London, Manchester and Edinburgh.

From North America: There are direct flights from a number of North American cities to Genève and Zürich, although it is often cheaper to fly via another European hub such as Frankfurt, London and Paris.

From Australia and New Zealand: There are no direct flights to Switzerland from Australia and New Zealand. You will need to change at one of the major Asian hubs such as Singapore, Hong Kong and Mumbai.

By train

From the UK: Overland travel to Switzerland from Britain by train with a bicycle is possible. Take an early Eurostar to Paris, then transfer from Nord to Est station (300m) to take a train to Basel (Bâle). Unless your bike is a folding bike, you will need to send your bike the day before on Eurostar, or pack it half dismantled in a bike bag (available from most bike shops). You should arrive in the early evening.

Bikes on Postbus, Meiringen

From other European countries: Rail travel with an accompanied bicycle from other European countries should be easy but you will need to reserve a place for your bike on the international express trains that carry bicycles (of which there seem to be fewer and fewer). It should be noted that the German ICE and Italian-Swiss Cisalpino trains do not take unfolded bicycles but some of the French TGVs do. Excellent background advice on travelling in Europe by train can be found at www.seat61.com. Information about travel by train to Switzerland can be found on the Swiss railway website www.sbb.ch, where you can download a pdf file detailing all the international express trains that carry accompanied bicycles.

If travelling a long way, it is worth checking out trains with sleeping cars.

For example, the overnight CityNight-Line (www.citynightline.ch) will transport passengers and bicycles directly from Amsterdam to Basel or from Copenhagen to Zürich, whereas during the day the same journey would need three or four changes.

By car
Switzerland is about a day's drive by car from the English Channel ports. Once you are there moving about is fine, but it can be an expensive nightmare to park the car once you stop.

Getting about
Swiss public transport is the best in the world. The key is integration of all public transport, whether state, regional or privately owned, and making all of it highly bicycle-friendly. There is a single website

29

GETTING TO THE START

Chapter	Based on National Cycle Route	Start/Finish	How to get there
1 The Rhône Route	1	Andermatt	Good rail connections from Basel, Bellinzona and Zürich changing at Göschenen. Access via E35 autobahn.
		Genève	International airport. Rail connections from SW France and Paris.
2 The Rhein Route	2	Andermatt	See Route 1.
		Basel	Good direct rail connections from Brussels, Frankfurt, Milan, Paris and Vienna. Excellent road links via E35 autobahn.
3 The North–South Route	3	Basel	See Route 2.
		Bellinzona, Chiasso	Good rail connections from northern Switzerland (Basel/Zürich), Italy (Milan) and from Germany (Frankfurt/Stuttgart). Excellent road links from north and south via autobahn.
4 The Alpine Panorama Route	4	Aigle	Rail access via Montreux. On autobahn Montreux – Martigny.
		St Margrethen	Good rail links from Munich via Lindau and Bregenz and from Austria via Bregenz. On Bodensee lake steamer routes. Road access via E60 autobahn.
5 The Mittelland Route	5	Lausanne	Good high speed rail links from France (Paris) and the airport at Genève. Good autobahn connections.
		Romanshorn	Ferry link from Friedrichshafen (airport) and on Bodensee lake steamer routes.
6 An Engadine Circuit, and beyond	6	Chur	Rail connections from Paris and Hamburg. By road via E43 autobahn.
		Bellinzona	See Route 3.
		Martina	Postbus from Austria (Landeck/Nauders).
7 The Jura Route	7	Basel	See Route 2.
		Nyon	Served by lake steamers and Genève – Basel, Bern, Zürich express trains. On autobahn between Genève and Lausanne.
8 The Aare Route	8	Koblenz (Hochrhein)	Train to Koblenz (CH) or Waldshut (D). Excellent road links via E35 autobahn.
		Meiringen	Train from Luzern or Interlaken.
		Gletsch	Postbus from Andermatt, Oberwald or Meiringen.
9 The Lakes Route	9	Montreux	Good high speed rail links from France and the airport at Genève.
		Rorschach	Good rail links from Munich via Lindau and from Austria via Bregenz. On Bodensee lake steamer routes. Road access via E60 autobahn.
10 The Berner Oberland		Interlaken, Luzern	Good rail links from all parts of Switzerland. Good autobahn connections.
11 The Alpine Star		Andermatt	See Route 1.

which provides comprehensive travel information for all means of surface transport: www.sbb.ch. (There is also a good deal of information about bicycles and trains in Switzerland at http://mct.sbb.ch/mct/en/reiselust/freizeit /velo_bahn.htm, with a map of public transport routes that will take accompanied bicycles.)

By far the majority of trains take bicycles, costing a single adult fare up to 10 or 15CHF, above which you can buy a day ticket for the bicycle. Stations have ramps and lifts to help you get your bike up to the platform and, should you need further assistance, even smaller stations are manned. Ticket machines are multilingual: English, French, German and Italian.

Postbuses took bicycles at a charge of 6CHF per bus trip in 2007. Theoretically you should to book a bicycle place on a bus the day before but outside high season this is not necessary. In their own interests, the drivers will help you secure your bike, on hooks on the back of the bus or on trailers.

There are various travel passes available: Swiss Pass, Swiss Card and regional tickets that offer you free or reduced price travel. The Swiss Card offers you free transport to your destination from the border crossing point and half price travel after that but if you intend to spend most of your time in the saddle then paying the full price as you go along is probably the best option. Swiss Tourism has more information (www.myswitzerland.com).

Some tips from experience:
- The easiest way to buy a ticket is to use a machine, so make sure that you have enough small notes or coins. Although these machines do take Euro notes they only give change up to 20CHF.
- In rural areas, buses replace branch line trains often after 20:00. These buses do not take bikes and do not always stop directly at the stations.
- At some small stations, trains will not stop unless someone wants to get off or you (waiting on the platform) push a button next to the ticket machine. Once on the train check whether you should push one of these buttons to tell the driver

SOME USEFUL TRANSPORT TERMS TO RECOGNISE	
Ausgenommen	Except
Bahn/bahnhof/hauptbahnhof	Railway/railway station/main railway station
CFF/SBB/FFS	Swiss Federal Railways
CH	Switzerland
DB	German Railways
Eau non potable/ kein Trinkwasser/ aqua non potabile	Not drinking water
Frei/excepté/gestattet	Allowed
SNCF	French Railways
Stazione/staziun	Station

that you wish to alight. Be ready to dismount, standing by the door, once the train stops.

- If disaster strikes and you need to make a complicated journey, check where you need to change trains before making the journey, otherwise you may end up having to spend 55 minutes at a deserted halt.

Getting on and off trains: You may well only have two minutes to get your party and the bikes on the train. Be prepared. There are marked areas on trains reserved for bicycles and the stations often have blue posters showing where to put your bikes on the train. These special compartments are indicated by a bicycle logo on the window. On the double decker trains these are at one end only. Check the blue posters or ask station staff to find out where they are

likely to be. (Staff usually speak some English.)

Take luggage off the bicycles before trying to manoeuvre them and check you've got it all with you again before the train leaves. Leaving your bar bag behind, with your camera and passport, can quite spoil your day. If you are struggling, get one member of the party to lean on the open door button. The train cannot leave with a open door. There is often a button on automatic doors for disabled passengers, which means that the door stays open longer. Use it!

Walking through the double decker trains clutching a bike is difficult, especially up and down narrow stairs. There is no access on one level from carriage to carriage along the train. If you find you are in the wrong place it is quicker to run with your bike along the platform, rather than getting on quickly and attempting to

Brienzersee ship

move once the train is in motion. It is likely that you will need to hang your bikes from a hook. If you travel on a train with a baggage car, the staff will help you get your bikes on the train, but expect you to hang them up yourself.

Lake steamers: Lake steamers take bicycles. A crew member will show where to put your bike. It is a good idea to have a bungee with you to fasten the bicycle to the mainbrace or similar.

MONEY

Switzerland's currency is the Swiss Franc (CHF) with 10, 20, 50, 100, 200 and 1000CHF notes and one, two and five franc coins. Each franc can be divided into 100 centimes (c) in French-speaking areas, Rappen (Rp) in German-speaking areas and centesimi (c) in the Italian-speaking South. The exchange rates from other major currencies at the time of writing are: US$: 1.16CHF, EUR: 1.7CHF, GBP: 2.4CHF. These are, naturally, subject to change.

Normal banking hours are 08:30 to 16:30, but in the countryside these hours can be restricted. All banks are closed on the following public holidays: Good Friday, Easter Monday, 1 May, Ascension Day, Whit Monday, Corpus Christi, 1 August, 15 August, Christmas and New Year.

Credit cards are widely accepted – in supermarkets, bigger hotels, youth hostels and by the railways, even in some ticket machines, however you may have difficulty using them in village shops, smaller hotels and B&Bs and at unstaffed railway halts.

WHAT TO TAKE

The bicycle
Almost any bike can be used for touring in Switzerland. For many years the standard Swiss Army bicycle was a single gear monster weighing over 22kg which recruits still managed to cycle over Alpine passes. People cycle over passes on folding bikes, recumbents, tandems and recumbent trike tandems but the ideal bike is robust, has wider tyres, mudguards, a good bottom gear, enough gears to allow small step changes and luggage carriers. Gear should be carried on your bike and not on your back because heavy rucksacks are hot and tiring to carry and raise your centre of gravity to dangerous heights. Mudguards are essential in wet weather. It does rain in Switzerland quite often producing a layer of oil, mud and water which, without mudguards, will be sprayed all over you and your bike.

Racing bikes are not recommended largely because they are too delicate for many of the official routes and difficult to cycle on the unsurfaced tracks. (The proportion of unsurfaced track can be as high as a third (Route 6) or almost zero (Route 4).) Alternatives to the unsurfaced sections of route are suggested for tarmac lovers, but this does involve leaving well-signposted routes. Racing bikes also rarely have lugs to attach bags, carriers and mudguards.

You will also see a lot of mountain bikes in Switzerland. They are just as fashionable there as they are elsewhere. However, although they offer a good range of gears, they too may not have luggage carriers or mudguards and have wide tyres with a high rolling resistance.

Wide-tyred bikes can cope with rough stuff (Route 6 in Inn Valley)

Most of the research for this guide was done on a pair of Dahon TR folding bikes with DualDrive gears with a sufficient range (509 per cent) from the lowest to the highest gear to winch us up hills and let us belt down the other side. Their balloon tyres meant the bicycles floated over cattle grids, tramlines and the odd patch of unsurfaced road. Folding bicycles also give you the flexibility to travel on any train in Europe and are as good as a dog for making friends, especially as you wrestle your metal origami on a railway platform.

Cycling clothes and baggage

Above all, aim to be comfortable. On a bike you stretch arms, legs and back, delicate parts of the body can suffer chafing, hands and feet work hard in contact with handlebars and pedals and you're usually travelling much faster than walkers. Some modern materials are good at being flexible, breathable, second or third skins, and wicking sweat away, while others act as crucial windbreakers and waterproofs. It is worth buying technical cycling shorts or trousers. There are few more miserable conditions than saddle soreness with 50 miles to ride, so find space for padded pants and talc. Flapping wide trousers are a real danger if they catch in the chain on a fast downhill. Cycle shirts with rear pockets for maps, money or snacks work really well. In Switzerland most people are quite happy to look like cyclists and there is no stigma to being 'Lyrcra-clad'.

Only general suggestions can be made here. First, many of our routes involve high altitude sections where

Layers and windproof for descents

35

temperatures, winds and precipitation can be extreme. Whatever the weather forecast a windproof and waterproof outer layer is a must – it could be a life saver. Even in fine weather, cycling fast downhill can be very chilly. Waterproof overtrousers can also be used to protect against the wind. To avoid sunburn, lightweight cover-ups, vests or long-sleeved shirts are essential. If you don't use clip-in cycle shoes, choose trainers that are stiff enough to use on pedals. Padded half gloves protect the hands from wear and tear and help reduce numbness, whilst lightweight windproof full gloves make downhill stretches enjoyable. Whether you wear a helmet for safety is up to you. Arguments about their benefits continue to rage in the cycling press.

Cyclists are welcomed in Swiss hotels. No one minds if you turn up on a bike, looking a bit warm or cold and dripping wet. Hoteliers do assume, however, that you'll have a cleanish change of clothes and that, after your shower, you'll emerge looking more or less like any other tourist. In the warmer months your hastily washed cycling kit should be dry by morning but you may want to carry a second set. Carry a tube of detergent paste.

Trailer, panniers, saddlebags, front bags?

Weight counts, especially when cycling in the mountains and going downhill – heavily laden bikes are much harder to control. Campers may need to consider the various trailer options but otherwise panniers should suffice. There are many relatively waterproof and lightweight panniers for both rear and front racks now, especially combined with the seal-able polythene bag, or compressor. Our advice is to try to limit yourself to rear panniers or a saddlebag and a handlebar bag. The latter is very handy for maps and valuables because you can quickly detach it and take it with you. A stretch net with hooks is useful to stuff water-proofs into on those days when the weather can't make its mind up, and also for making picnic and other items quickly accessible.

Repair kit

Switzerland is well equipped with bike repair shops, even in small villages. We have always been helped and sent on our way quickly when unable to fix things ourselves. Some routes pass through thinly populated areas so a few basic spares, tools and a little knowhow can save hours and long walks. Have your bike checked before you leave home, especially the tyres, brakes and cables. Then gather the necessary inner tubes, puncture repair kit, tyre levers and a multitool (screwdriver, chain breaker and spanner, available from bike shops) together with the essential piece of rag and hand cleaner. Plastic garden ties make excellent substitute screws to hold together mudguards, bits of luggage or even clothing at a pinch. Five metres of duct tape can be fastened round a screwdriver. A small amount of lubricating oil in a leak-proof container can help keep you rolling after rain. Have a pump that works and connectors to a variety of tube valves. Put everything in a plastic container in an accessible location.

Maps

Basic sketch maps of individual routes are provided in this guide, but the sign-posting combined with the itinerary descriptions should be adequate. (Local place name spelling is used throughout, for example Bodensee (not Lake Constance) and Luzern (not Lucerne), because that is what you see on the signs.) However, it is sensible always to have a proper map because routes do get blocked or diverted and you may end up being taken a long way from your original route. Swiss maps are wonderful – works of art and precision instruments combined – so they are expensive. A particular favourite is the 1:301,000 scale Kümmerly & Frey Switzerland Tourist Cycling Map with all of the Veloland Schweiz and other routes and GPS data (ISBN: 3 259 00533 1). In addition, the 1:200,000 Michelin map 551 Suisse Nord covers almost all of Switzerland except the extreme west, south and east (for about £5 in 2007). Companion maps 552 and 553 cover the 'gaps' with lots of overlap. These are certainly adequate for planning and even have some city maps of cities such as Zürich and Luzern.

For those who want more detail, Swisstopo (Swiss Federal Office of Topography) 1:100,000 Composite maps that cover the routes are listed in each route description. Experience shows that only the 1:100,000 maps for the immediate local area are easy to buy locally, so if you decide that the maps are essential, you should buy the maps beforehand. They are stocked by Stanfords in the UK and cost £14.50 each (www.stanfords.co.uk), by omn-imap.com in the US at US$23.95 (www.omnimap.com) and by Swiss Topo at 28CHF (www.swisstopo.ch).

First aid kit

Being able to clean wounds, stick a plaster or paint on a bit of new skin does wonders. We don't move far without a small bag of basics. Trusted over-the-counter remedies for muscle stiffness, headaches, colds and stomach upsets are to be recommended, but for anything else consult a pharmacist (*apotheker/pharmacie/farmacia*) or a doctor. If you need to take prescription medicines, keep all the details with you, in case of (unlikely but possible) checks at customs posts or the need to obtain something similar if you lose them or run out.

Insurance

Although Switzerland is not a member of the European Union, there is provision for EU citizens to use their European Health Insurance Card (EHIC) to receive treatment in emergencies. Consult the relevant body in your home country for details. In any case it is a good idea to invest in holiday health insurance. Policies vary widely in terms of age restrictions, length of stay and activities covered so do some research before you commit yourself. Non-EU citizens should equip themselves with health and accident insurance before they leave their home country. Switzerland's ambulance, health and police services are well up to western European standards with staff usually able to speak English competently.

Other documents

Naturally, you need to take and safe-guard passports, credit cards, airline or rail tickets and all the usual paraphernalia of modern life. For cyclists, border controls tend to be low-key. Some of the routes cross uncontrolled international borders relatively frequently, often on tracks or quiet roads, but there is a legal requirement that a) you are qualified to pass from one country to the other, b) that you can prove your identity if checked and c) it is daylight. Otherwise passports are more usually required by hoteliers, particularly Swiss ones. However you don't need, as a visitor, to register your bicycle or pay a licence fee, unlike the residents of Switzerland.

Mobile phones

Mobile phones are used extensively in Switzerland. If you wish to take a mobile phone with you, check with your mobile phone company whether your phone will work in Switzerland and enquire about charges. Do not use it while cycling unless you have a hands-free system. If you are caught using a mobile phone while cycling by the police you are likely to be fined 20CHF on the spot.

LANDSCAPE

Switzerland is small, roughly twice the size of Wales. For the cyclist the 220km distance north to south and about 350km east to west make it look like an ideal destination for a week long tour. However, scenery, gradients, accessibility and facilities en route are all factors to be considered in planning a particular cycle trip. Little of Switzerland's scenery is entirely natural and it has been shaped by centuries of human influence.

The Jura

The Jura extend along the northwest frontier of Switzerland and into France. These hills are complex parallel ridges and valleys of sedimentary rocks, mostly limestones combined with clays and shales. Limestone is fractured, allowing rainfall to drain underground and dissolve the rock. Clays and shales are impermeable and so carry streams and rivers. The Jurassic geological period, made famous by the film 'Jurassic Park', derives its name from here. The mountains, at below 1500m, are much lower than the Alps, and lack dramatic glacial features and pointed peaks. The Jura were completely covered by ice during glaciation. No glacial deposits mask the rocks, allowing their structure to show clearly.

The passes or cols, frequently used in road races, are sometimes steeper than Alpine equivalents and offer exciting challenges to the sporting rider. An individual Alpine pass may be the entire day's route, but Jura routes winding over several cols in a 70km day may result in a greater total climb than over the Oberalppass. Jurassic folding occurred late in the Alpine earth movements when soft sedimentary rocks were squeezed into folds on top of a hard crystalline layer. The hilltops are often broad plateaux formed by upfolds. There may be limestone crags, waterless karst regions similar to the English Pennines, or amazingly green pastures for cattle. All the best-known limestone features including swallow holes are to be found.

Cattle on limestone ridge near Mont Soleil (Jura)

Deep wooded valleys run along the downfolds and shelter springline settlements, like Vallorbe. A notable river is the Doubs, which heads north and then cuts gorges from one parallel valley to the next near St Ursanne, its waters eventually flowing into the Rhône. The eastern edge of the Jura is marked by a tremendous escarpment, forming the junction with the Mittelland and followed by Routes 5 and 8.

Some guidebooks describe the Jura as 'natural' or 'wild' landscape but settlement began before the Romans. It is a cultural landscape, changing slowly as economies evolve. Forests are long-term crops and on the high plateaus open pastures provide grazing for sheep, cattle, goats and horses. It is a hard life so many remote farmsteads are abandoned, as young people get jobs in towns.

Agricultural industries are important. Most settlements are small and tourism plays a part in the economy, although specialised medical instrument-making or high technology activities have developed, using similar skills to the traditional watch-making. Older settlements like St Ursanne have attractive ancient cores with castles and half-timbered houses but there are plenty of modern residential and industrial developments too.

The Mittelland or Central Plateau

This region between the Jura and the Alps has subdued relief, once below sea level in a giant forerunner of the present-day Mediterranean. Lengthy deposition occurred in lakes, in saltwater deltas, or even in desert regions as the Alps rose and were eroded. Enormous thicknesses of pebbles, gravels and sands, called

39

Lac de Neuchâtel from above

Molasse, were deposited and became rock. Rivers flowed north from the rising Alps cutting valleys, creating spurs and ridges. This entire landscape was then completely altered by Ice Age glaciers, which first bulldozed routes across hills and valleys, then filled valleys with gravels or plastered boulder clay into drumlins. In interglacial periods the ice melted leaving moraines behind, sometimes damming lakes, and outwash plains of sand spread away from the ice sheets.

Finally, the present river patterns were created. Ice on the Alpine north side moved northwestwards, as the Aare valley shows downstream of Lake Thun. The Jura diverted ice northeastwards, gouging out the basins of Lakes Neuchâtel and Biel and determining the Aare's route near Solothurn and Olten.

This region cannot truly be described as either low or flat. From a cyclist's viewpoint it is distinctly lumpy. Hills extend out from the edge of the Alps, providing sites for Fribourg, Zürich and Winterthur. Ridges are forested, valley sides and floors farmed for crops or grazing for cattle. Rivers have cut river terraces above flood plains, or created incised meanders as at Bern. Lower land was originally peat marsh, large areas around Lac du Biel having since been drained to form rich agricultural land. This is by far the most densely populated part of Switzerland, with the highest density of roads and traffic. There is good provision for cyclists, even in capital city Bern. Industry is important, so expect to see many factories. Contrary to popular myth, the Swiss do not depend just on tourism, high finance and chocolate.

Closer to the Alps slopes steepen and the Alpine panorama begins to unfold. Even along a river route like the Aare there are ridges or short steep climbs over drumlins to raise your pulse rate. The Mittelland route following river valleys and lake shorelines climbs 1400m in 374km, which some may regard as strenuous.

The Alps

This part of Switzerland is awe inspiring and offers the biggest challenge to the cyclist. The actual landscapes of the Alps are extremely varied, since their geological history, rock types and structures cover huge time ranges and have involved mind-boggling upheavals and huge climate changes. Details are beyond the scope of this guide but a little explanation may be useful.

The Alps are fold mountains, the movements starting 96 million years ago, just after the Jurassic period. Evidence suggests that marine sediments accumulating between Africa and Europe were squashed and pushed northwards. This process continued, sometimes violently with earthquakes and volcanic outbursts and sometimes much more slowly. Now the whole zone has been reduced by about 50 per cent. Massive sections were torn from their base and forced over newer rocks, without even being folded. Old sea floor chunks and even bits of the African continent are now in Central Europe. The force resulted in steeper south facing slopes making it usually easier to cycle from north to south, as our descriptions indicate. Immediately uplift began surfaces were weathered and eroded, forming peaks and valleys.

Glacier-scraped rocks on St Bernadino Pass (Route 6, Southern Leg)

Eroded material was transported north and deposited in the Mittelland. Southwards it ended up in Italy.

River patterns were modified by glacial advance and retreat over the last million years. Freezing water expands, meaning that glaciers occupy a larger volume than a river. Glacial erosion produces a characteristic U-shape, as the Lauterbrunnen Valley shows. Debris-laden glaciers can flow uphill and cut straight-sided valleys. Where two glaciers join erosive power increases creating rock steps. Cycling down mountain passes, like the San Bernardino southwards or Graubünden's Ofenpass is like being on a roller coaster as the initial steep drop flattens out, followed by further hairpins to the main valley floor. The highest mountains remained ice free, but stuck out like fangs, constantly exposed to freezing temperatures. Some make pyramidal peaks, like the Matterhorn, others rotting pinnacles, depending on the rock type, and many are directly visible from the cycle routes. Where glaciers scraped over granites or gneisses, as on the San Bernardino Pass, scratched rock sheets remain, impressive but not beautiful.

Beneath many glaciers debris-laden rivers flowed, able to be siphoned uphill and to cut deep vertical gorges, like the Aare gorge by Meiringen. In between ice advances were interglacial periods, often warmer than today when rivers reoccupied the valleys. In geological terms, glaciation occurred very recently so its imprint on the landscape is very fresh. The present glaciers are tiny, shrinking remnants of the last advance. Rising temperatures over the last hundred years have resulted in exposure of new rocks below the Rhône glacier's snout, seen on the Furkapass and Grimselpass routes. Most pass routes give glimpses of glaciers, seeming very close when a wind sends a chill breath downhill.

As rivers returned they formed waterfalls over hanging valley edges, then meandered down the wide U-shaped sections. Frost-shattered loose rocks slid into streams and were carried away in floods, or rolled and broken into sand. Where glaciers had scooped out depressions, lakes like the Bodensee or Thunersee formed. Many others have disappeared naturally or been drained.

Small landslides happen frequently in the mountains as loose debris succumbs to gravity. Melting permafrost may also be making an impact. In 2006, motorists were crushed by rockfall on the Gotthard autobahn. Most major landslides have occurred in sedimentary rocks surrounding the Aare granite massive. Catastrophic landslides causing destruction are rare but have resulted in some spectacular landforms, such as the Rhein Gorge near Flims encountered on Route 2 between Ilanz and Bonaduz. This happened about 14,000 years ago with no historical records of either landslide or the subsequent floods that created the gorge. In spring 1991, 30m^3 of rock crashed down close to Randa, down valley from Zermatt. The massive glistening slide is especially spectacular viewed from bike level. Throughout the mountain routes you'll see evidence of avalanches and minor landslides. Villages may relocate to apparently safer positions. Increased traffic, deforestation

Avalanche remains on St Gotthard approach (Route 3, Stage 5)

Delta formation in Lago Maggiore taken from near Alpe di Neggia (Route 3, Stage 7)

and even occasional earth tremors accelerate natural downslope movements.

The Alps are not just a winter or summer playground. Stone is quarried, gravel extracted, cattle and goats provide milk for cheese, grazing on summer pastures near the treeline. Transport routes are constructed, hydroelectricity is produced and small-scale industry is encouraged. The Swiss prefer their countryside to be a living entity, with services provided to their rural communities as in the cities, rather than keeping them as museums. Some Alpine activities may disfigure the landscape from the tourist's viewpoint but they may provide jobs, water or electricity to keep a settlement going.

Lakes and rivers

Switzerland and its neighbours have some of Europe's largest lakes, such as Lac Léman (Lake Geneva), where erosion exploited weak structures and glaciers scoured out basins. Many like the Walensee, fed by streams from glaciers which carry fine rock dust, are an eye-catching turquoise colour especially in sunny weather. These same streams, often grey or milky in colour form deltas at lake inflows, like the Aare near Brienz or the entire drainage into Lago Maggiore by Locarno. Flat deltas make good sites for towns, farmland and a wonderful contrast to uphill struggles for cyclists. Many artificial Alpine lakes supply water or hydroelectricity and some are great scenery enhancers, though the Grimselpass lakes, thick with grey debris, have an unearthly appearance.

Post-glacial rivers Rhein and Rhône rise in the Alps, close to each other – the Rhein flowing to the North Sea and the Rhône to the Mediterranean. Both rivers are followed by bike routes as well as railways and roads over some of the high passes. The Ticino, Aare, Reuss and Thur rivers, little known outside Switzerland have wonderfully scenic Alpine valleys. Many smaller watercourses like Thur tributary Sitter, from Appenzell to Bischofszell, or Aare tributary Limmat, flowing out of Lake Zürich, make excellent cycle routes, sometimes uphill over moraines even when cycling down river. Over in Graubünden, the Inn or En flows to the Black Sea from near St Moritz. The Jura's River Doubs is not the only surface stream, but well-known because of its strange course.

Present-day Alpine river flow varies rapidly, following late spring snowmelt, tiny trickles quickly become torrents, hazardous perhaps to early bird cyclists. Summer flash flooding after thunderstorms or persistent rainfall is a much greater danger. Streams overflow carrying rocks, undercutting tracks and roads and sweeping bridges away. Cycle routes then take time to repair.

WEATHER

The Germans say 'There is no such thing as bad weather just the wrong choice of clothing'. You may not agree. It is possible to experience drought and 30°C temperatures in March, but also snow in May and even August. Deluges are swiftly followed by jungle humidity. Although modern bikes and protective clothing now make it possible to cycle in almost every weather likely to be thrown at you in the warmer months in Central Europe, some conditions can be uncomfortable, tiring or even dangerous. Switzerland's weather is complicated by the southwest/northeast Alpine chain but an excellent system of weather stations feeding information directly into national and cantonal weather offices keeps forecasts fairly accurate.

Cyclists with access to TV can view city or mountain top conditions every morning between 07:30 and 09:30, and

Weather you hope for: (Route 4 near Sörenberg)

CLIMATE CHARTS

GENÈVE											
	Jan	Feb	Mar	Apr	May	Jun	Jul	Aug	Sep	Oct	Nov	Dec
Av. temperature (min)	-2	-1	2	5	9	13	15	14	12	7	3	0
Av. temperature (max)	4	6	10	15	19	23	25	24	21	14	8	4
Wet days	11	9	9	9	11	11	9	11	10	10	11	10
Av. rainfall (cm)	6.3	5.6	5.5	5.1	6.8	8.9	6.4	9.4	9.9	7.2	8.3	5.9

LUGANO											
	Jan	Feb	Mar	Apr	May	Jun	Jul	Aug	Sep	Oct	Nov	Dec
Av. temperature (min)	-2	-1	3	7	10	14	16	15	13	8	3	0
Av. temperature (max)	6	9	13	17	21	25	27	27	23	16	11	7
Wet days	7	7	9	11	15	13	11	12	10	10	10	9
Av. rainfall (cm)	6.3	6.7	9.9	14.8	21.5	19.8	18.5	19.6	15.9	17.3	14.7	9.5

ZÜRICH											
	Jan	Feb	Mar	Apr	May	Jun	Jul	Aug	Sep	Oct	Nov	Dec
Av. temperature (min)	-3	-2	1	4	8	12	14	13	11	6	2	-2
Av. temperature (max)	2	5	10	15	19	23	25	24	20	14	7	3
Wet days	14	13	12	13	14	15	14	14	12	12	12	13
Av. rainfall (cm)	7.4	6.9	6.4	7.6	10.1	12.9	13.6	12.4	10.2	7.7	7.3	6.4

SÄNTIS (1)											
	Jan	Feb	Mar	Apr	May	Jun	Jul	Aug	Sep	Oct	Nov	Dec
Av. temperature (min)	-11	-11	-9	-6	-2	1	3	3	1	-3	-7	-10
Av. temperature (max)	-7	-7	-4	-2	3	6	8	8	6	2	-3	-6
Wet days	16	15	14	16	16	19	18	18	15	13	13	15
Av. rainfall (cm)	20.2	18	16.4	16.6	19.7	24.9	30.2	27.8	20.9	18.3	19	16.9

Av. = Average
(1) Located at 2500m in eastern Switzerland.

summaries of temperature (°C), precipitation (ml), wind direction and force on SF1 (Swiss German TV). Failing that, newspapers, found in hotels or cafés, usually show weather charts and local forecasts. Many hotels and youth hostels also post internet meteorological information on noticeboards (easy to follow with a few words of French, German or Italian). The Swiss Met Office website also offers weather information and forecasts (in English) for the whole country (www.meteosuisse.admin.ch). Recorded weather information in French, (High) German and Italian is available by dialling 162 within Switzerland, but to get more detailed information you need to be able to pronounce a language correctly enough for voice recognition to work!

Rain is produced by fronts within low pressure systems or by thunderstorms from convection in summer. Cyclonic rain can be prolonged if the depressions become jammed against the Alps, instead of dispersing after 24 hours or so. Then Alpine streams can flood rapidly. Convection rain can also be dramatic but may only affect a small area. Changing destination to the next valley or over a mountain range may provide a ride in dry conditions. Temperature falls with elevation by roughly 1°C per 100m so valley rain turns to snow by the top of a pass, and this is usually mentioned in weather reports (snowfall boundary at so many hundred metres). Passes reach over 2000m so there is also less oxygen. A few people may experience altitude

Weather you can also get, Brienzersee (Route 9, Stage 4)

Looking back at weather you've just endured, river in spate, Splügen (Route 6, Stage 1)

sickness, headaches and shortness of breath. If affected, descend carefully as soon as possible.

High pressure brings settled weather, with much hot sun in summer and daytime temperatures often in excess of 30°C in lowlands and valleys. Cyclists should drink plenty of liquid when riding and top up in the evenings. Cover exposed skin with loose clothing or high protection factor sunscreen, especially in the Alps where UV levels are high. In spring and autumn, anticyclonic weather may cause morning or evening frosts and persistent mist in valleys. Above the cloud level, cycling can be extremely pleasant, so route choice is important.

Headwinds can be more tiring than hill climbs so if winds settle in a particular direction the wise cyclist takes bus or train and rides in comfort. One particular wind is frequent in the Alps: the Föhn wind caused when pressures and temperatures vary greatly on the north or south side of the Alps. Winds blow downhill, compressing the air and causing rapid rise of temperatures, like the Chinook in the Rocky Mountains. Riding downhill with the Föhn at your back in the upper Rhein valley is fast and exhilarating. Riding uphill against it is a real struggle. The Föhn also causes rapid snowmelt, avalanches and is yet another cause of flooding, but it does bring views. Upvalley winds in the Rhein and Rhône valleys can be a nuisance.

The weather north of the Alps may be different from that on the southern slopes, so the two regions are treated separately in weather forecasts. The south has milder spring and autumn temperatures, more thunderstorms and hotter summers. The northern slopes are generally wetter and have more frequent rain, with temperatures slightly lower than in the south on any given day. Again, judicial use of public transport over or through the Alps can rescue a cycle tour from a deluge in Uri or boiling temperatures in Ticino.

Seasonal conditions

Although some cyclists are prepared to battle snow and winter chills, most of the Alpine passes are closed from October to May, the high Jura is snow-bound and the Mittelland muddy. Touring in the warmer months is preferable. There are very pleasant conditions in spring and autumn – cool mornings and evenings, but shorter days.

Monthly rainfall figures show that Switzerland has more rain in summer than in winter, because of its Central European location. Most summer rain results from violent thunderstorms, often very localised and short lived, with sun returning quickly afterwards. August has frequent storms, high temperatures and humidity, so the months either side of August may give more settled periods without excessive rain.

Long-term climate data for Genève (representing the Jura), Säntis (the High Alps), Zürich (the Mittelland) and Lugano (the south) is shown here (source: BBC weather website). This data should be treated with some caution, however. A wet day is defined as one on which more than 0.025cm (0.01") falls, so a light shower before breakfast followed by a dry sunny day will count as a wet day. Temperatures may also vary up and down from those shown here.

What a surprise! Snow in late May, near Sörenberg (Route 4, Stage 4)

ACCOMMODATION

This guide does not include a comprehensive list of accommodation options. Just about every Swiss community offers accommodation of some type, as shown in the Facilities table for each stage, and information about accommodation and booking are easily available on the internet. Check out in addition www.myswitzerland.com to find links to all the local tourist offices in Switzerland. Swiss tourist offices will bury you in printed material if requested. The addresses and websites of the relevant regional, cantonal or local tourist offices are given in each stage description. In addition, Appendix 1 gives the postal and web addresses of national tourist organisations outside and in Switzerland and most of the regional tourist offices. Appendix 2 has a list of recommended accommodation.

No matter where you stop in Switzerland you and your trusty bike will be made welcome. Swiss hosts have long recognised the cyclist's valuable contributions to the economy, whether in a 4-star palace or a simple farmhouse. Modern tourism originated in Switzerland, so hotels range from the top end, where you are likely to rub shoulders with international politicians, pop stars and racing drivers, to simpler hotels or guest houses, youth hostels (YH), backpackers (BP) and bed and breakfasts (B&B).

The Veloland Schweiz website has a list of partner hotels with a wide price range. Velotel – an association of hoteliers – offers accommodation for

Emil's room in the old stable in Neuchâtel

cyclists, which are value-for-money but not always cheap. Although both organisations guarantee somewhere secure to leave your bike under cover overnight, even the most basic accommodation will offer some sort of bike storage.

Budgeting

Our budget estimates assume: 10CHF daily to spend on extras like a visit to a museum, a cup of coffee, a visit to an internet café and/or the odd postcard (if only to write home asking for more cash!); a picnic at lunchtime and an evening meal. As elsewhere, singletons may pay more.

On this basis, you should expect to spend per person per day:

- about 45CHF for camping
- about 60CHF (sleeping 6 to 8-bedded rooms) or 80 to 90CHF per person (for double rooms with en suite showers) in youth hostels
- about 80 to 90CHF (including a beer or a glass of wine with the evening meal in the youth hostel or in a small pub) in b&bs
- about 190CHF (sharing a double room, with a light lunch and large evening meal) for a mid-range hotel
- up to 650CHF (eating very well at both lunchtime and dinner) for a 4 or 5-star hotel.

Wherever you hang your hat, a cup of coffee or a hot drink will cost about 3CHF in cafés (in 2007).

When you book a hotel room specify that you want a low-priced room and ask for half board, even if you are just stopping one night. Rooms without en suite facilities are cheaper. Swiss hotels are often expensive compared to neigh-bouring countries. On the Rhein Route and in Engadine you are only a stone's throw away from Austria, Germany or Italy where hotels and restaurants are cheaper. Follow the Rhein Route (chapter 2) during the day in Switzerland and then cross the border each evening and it will save you money.

On the other hand, the Swiss tourist authorities have now recognised the problem of Swiss hotel prices, compounded by high exchange rates for the Swiss Franc, and do offer a number of 'affordable' hotels that can be booked by telephone in Switzerland (0800 1002 0030) or on the internet (www.myswitzerland.com/affordable).

Also Swiss youth hostels no longer have an age limit and are superb value for money. Most of them cost about £25 a night per person for half board in a double or family room. This makes them popular to book in advance online at www.youthhostel.ch. The website has instructions about finding each hostel. It is worth downloading and printing these instructions out. The hostels are open during the day, so if the weather is bad you don't have to lurk nearby. Austrian and German youth hostels (with Bavarian hostels as an exception) will also take older people. We have heard that the Bavarian hostel in Lindau (Bodensee) might take older people out of season.

Tourist offices also have lists of holiday flats and B&B. We have also had good experience with accommodation offered through Bed and Breakfast Switzerland. If you cannot find any through this organisation, check out www.tourisme-rural.ch for B&Bs in the

French-speaking areas of Switzerland or the local community's website, via www.myswitzerland.com, and look for words like 'tourisme, Tourismus, Hebergement, Unterkunft', then 'B&B, Gite, Privat-Zimmer'. Villages offer cheaper accommodation than cities, particularly if they are off the main tourist trail, so plan your trip to stop overnight somewhere quiet and visit the tourist destinations during the day. You can camp but this means carrying a lot of gear. Fresh air fiends could check out the farms that offer Schlafen im Stroh ('sleeping in the hayloft'). You will need to take a sleeping bag and a torch. If you do decide to stop in these farmhouses, be warned that they are often outside villages and it can be a trek to the nearest restaurant.

You could check out the package holidays in Switzerland for a fixed base stay and hire a bike for day trips. Various organisations, including Veloland Schweiz (www.veloland.ch), organise touring holidays with accommodation, baggage transport and bike hire. For base touring, holiday flats are a sensible choice, cheaper than a hotel and more convenient if you wish to make early starts. Our Berner Oberland and Alpine Star chapters reflect this approach.

It is possible to tour and not book ahead. It is quite exciting not knowing whether you are going to stop in a 4-star hotel or a B&B and it can be comforting to know that if the weather turns nasty you can stop in the next village. However, it is advisable to start looking by 16:00, which means you have fairly short days on the bike. If there are more than four people in your group then booking in advance, at least by phone at lunchtime, is probably the only way.

Languages

Switzerland has four official languages. French is spoken in the west of the country. Italian is spoken in the south. Romansh, a Latin dialect, is spoken in Graubünden (Grisons) in the southeast and German is spoken by 67 per cent of the total Swiss population in the centre and north of the country. Most people in Graubünden seem to understand German. Swiss French and Italian are the mainstream versions of those languages and as such can be understood by foreigners. Swiss German is not easily understood, even by native speakers of German, but educated Swiss can, on request, speak High German (Buchdeutsch), albeit sometimes unwillingly.

The better the hotel, the better the chance of being able to communicate in English. Youth hostel wardens and some B&B owners also speak English. However, some knowledge of one of the languages spoken in Switzerland will help you enjoy your holiday much more.

FOOD AND DRINK

Food

Food in Switzerland is influenced by its neighbours. The northeast has dishes that would not be out of place in Germany or Austria. South of the Gotthard Pass restaurants offer spaghetti and Milanese veal dishes, while to the west the food becomes very French. The Swiss eat out a lot and are prepared to pay for quality.

Forget portion control

If your budget is restricted check out what is available. Read the menus outside restaurants before making your choice. You need not eat where you are staying if you fancy somewhere else. Unfortunately the most economical option – special lunch menus – does not suit cyclists. It is uncomfortable to cycle on after a heavy lunch and better to picnic at lunchtime and eat a main meal in the evening.

Local dishes if available are rarely disappointing. It can be difficult to pronounce dishes like 'Schwynigs und Cheschtenä', so keep an eye on what other guests are eating and point. Cheeses vary from place to place. A plate of rösti with bacon, cheese and a fried egg goes down well after a day in the saddle. Bündnerfleisch is a deep red,

dried beef, served in wafer thin slices, or used to flavour soups. There are also barley-based recipes in Graubünden, polenta from maize in the Alps or Ticino and risottos in the Italian-influenced south. Most of the large lakes provide trout-like fish, which are grilled and served with steamed potatoes, a slice of lemon and a side salad. Mouth-watering!

Portions can be generous so, if you find you are struggling to finish, ask for a pensioner's portion next time. Hotel staff are used to the strange ways of tourists and usually oblige, whatever your age. Child-friendly menus are often available, with smaller portions. Chips are almost ubiquitous, as is pasta and tomato sauce, should your children be conservative in their diet. If the worst comes to the worst, you can also find

53

international burger bars in Switzerland. If you are really hungry, go for the 'menu' option in a restaurant, which will generally include soup or starter, a main course and perhaps dessert.

In both the Jura and the Alps, settlements are sparse, so stock up on picnic supplies before heading out of town. The routes often bypass towns, so you need to plan for shopping or café stops. If your overnight accommodation does not include an evening meal, ask for the nearest restaurant when you arrive. Most people will offer at least bread and cheese if all the local places are closed or too far away, but, if in doubt, try and check as you book.

Breakfast is usually some variation of ham, boiled eggs, cheese and jam with bread, croissants and rolls. The bread is usually freshly baked. Tea and coffee are generally good, the latter stronger and the former weaker than Britons are used to. The extent of the breakfast choice depends upon the size of the hotel or pension, but you are unlikely to go hungry. Lunch is available in most towns or villages. Swiss *Konditorei* or tea rooms (confectioners) make delicious cakes and pastries for afternoon tea time. Later in the summer, you will see tartlets filled with chestnut purée, topped with whipped cream. These alone are worth a trip to Switzerland! Evening meals can be found in larger places to suit all tastes and pockets, but in small settlements it is probably best to go for local or known dishes. Generally you get a better deal if you choose the set menu rather than à la carte. If you stop in a youth hostel and would like an evening meal, make sure you say so when you book.

Groceries

People from European Union countries have got used to paying relatively little for their groceries, and so Swiss prices can come as rather a shock. Most Swiss reckon that they could not survive without Coop, Denner or Migros, the major supermarket chains. Some also have restaurants where you can eat lunch or an early dinner at reasonable prices. In Switzerland, shops are closed on Sundays and public holidays, although shops at railway stations are open for provisions, at a price. In small towns and villages, shops often close between roughly 12:00 and 14:00, just as you may be getting peckish, so buy in advance. Do not forget chocolate. Everyone knows that the Swiss make chocolate, but the range is far wider than most of us realise, so try something new. A bar of chocolate makes good emergency rations. The Swiss themselves eat about 10kg each every year.

Wine

Wine is produced all over Switzerland and is eminently drinkable. Close to Basel, Blauburgunder (Pinot Noir) wines are prominent. The main wine-producing region lies further south, close to Lac Léman, where Switzerland's most famous wine, Fendant, a delicate white, is made from Chasselas grapes. There is another source of Rhein wine around Maienfeld. It appears that the Swiss also like their wine. Consumption per head of population is among the highest in the world and little is exported. The easiest way to try Swiss wine is to visit the country.

A glass of Fendant is a refreshing accompaniment to a cheese or meat platter, but beware the strict drink/drive regulations. A bicycle counts as a vehicle in Switzerland and the Swiss alcohol limit for being in charge of a vehicle is 50mg per 100ml of blood, rather than 80mg in the UK. Swiss traffic fines are heavy and may be payable on the spot by non-residents.

South of the Alps in Ticino, the usual wine produced is Merlot, and you would be unfortunate to find a poor specimen. House wines are available by the glass in most bars or restaurants, at reasonable prices (about 3 to 4CHF per glass). It makes sense to ask about the local tipple if you fancy a glass of wine with your meal.

Beer and other drinks

Swiss beer is good and additive-free since the breweries have a voluntary Reinheitsgebot (beer purity regulation). The usual measure is a 0.5l glass (price about 6CHF), but one glass is the limit if you are going to continue by bike. The beer is about five per cent alcohol. A shandy (beer/lemonade mixture) is called a *panache* in Switzerland and a *Radler* in Germany.

Cola and lemonade drinkers can expect to find their favourites. International brands have just about driven out local soft drinks, with one exception: Rivella, a soft drink made as a by-product of the dairy industry in Switzerland. It most resembles Lucozade and is available in a variety of flavours: red with sugar, blue sugar-free and green with green tea. There are also mineral waters and fruit juices. *Apfelsaftschorle* – a mixture of apple juice and sparkling mineral water – can

Drinking fountains abound (Route 5 near Bischofszell)

Milk machine at farm, Kaltbrunn (Route 5)

be found just about everywhere. Ovomaltine – a malted milk drink taken hot or cold – is most fortifying in cold weather or in energy crises.

The Swiss buy immense amounts of mineral water, but not for safety reasons. They just prefer the taste. Tap water is of good quality and Swiss public water fountains in the centre of villages and small towns normally deliver high-purity drinking water. However keep your eyes open for the sign 'kein Trinkwasser' or 'l'eau non potable' in the west, or 'acqua non potabile' in Ticino – meaning 'not drinking water'.

Special dietary requirements

If you are a diabetic or have to follow a strict dietary regime, then you need to book ahead and check out whether your requirements can be met. If you are a vegetarian, then all major hotels and restaurants serve some vegetarian dishes, albeit often rather limited and unimaginative. Most large supermarkets have 'health food' sections where you can stock up on sugar-free products, non-gluten biscuits, organic products and the like, but the little village store and bakery will only stock more mainstream products. If you are concerned, get advice from Swiss Tourism or from an advisory body in your own country, before you set off.

Tipping

Swiss restaurant prices include both a service charge (10 to 15 per cent for the waiter) and tax, so what you see is what you pay. You need not add a tip. However it is considered polite to round up to the next CHF for the waiter or waitress.

In the descriptions of each route which follow, as much information as possible has been tabulated for quick reference on the move. The tables work as follows:

For each route:

- Route summary – gives the overall distance (including, in brackets, the number of kilometres of that distance that are unsurfaced) and the climb and grade (with and without public transport, and, where available, in either direction). In some cases, the recommended route varies for road bikes and touring bikes, and separate figures are given for each. Where not otherwise stated, the distance quoted is the distance for the touring bike route.

- Summary of stages – gives a breakdown of distance, climb and grade for each stage (without taking the public transport options).

- Local maps – publisher, number and title of local maps covering the route (at a larger scale than the 1:301,000 Kümmerly & Frey Switzerland Touristic Cycling Map).

- Links to other routes – shows the places along the route where other Swiss national routes could be picked up and where they lead.

- Public transport backup – gives more detail about the public transport options available along the route, in case of bad weather or exhaustion!

Police escort for the Tour de Suisse near Scuol

For each stage:
- Itinerary – provides directions and the distance between, and (in most cases) the altitude at, key points.
- Facilities – shows accommodation, railway stations and bike shops at key points.
- Tourist information – gives the contact details of tourist information offices for the regions cycled through.

Abbreviations used in tables	
RB	Road bike
T	Touring bike
TO	Tourist office
VSIB	Veloland Schweiz Information Board
LF/RF	Left fork/right fork
LT/RT	Left turn/right turn
TL/TR	Turn left/turn right

THE ROUTES

Swiss cycle routes have excellent signposting (Rhein embankment near Buchs)

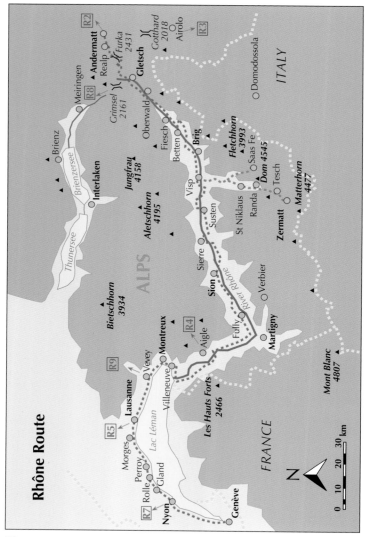

Rhône Route

1 THE RHÔNE ROUTE, R1

ROUTE SUMMARY					
From/to	Distance (km)	Climb (m) with public transport	Climb (m) without public transport	Grade with public transport	Grade without public transport
Andermatt/ Genève	**RB:** 309 (0) **T:** 318 (30)	420	**RB:** 1390 **T:** 1710	Easy	Difficult
Genève/ Andermatt		730	2710	Moderate	Strenuous

SUMMARY OF STAGES (WITHOUT PUBLIC TRANSPORT)				
Stage	From/to	Distance (km)	Climb (m)	Grade
1	Andermatt/Oberwald	38	980	Difficult
2	Oberwald/Sierre	**RB:** 85 **T:** 94	**RB:** 140 **T:** 460	**RB:** Easy **T:** Moderate
3	Sierre/Montreux	92	20	Easy
4	Montreux/Genève	94	250	Moderate
Total	**Andermatt/Genève**	**RB:** 309 **T:** 318	**RB:** 1390 **T:** 1710	

LOCAL MAPS	
Swisstopo 1:100,000 Composite	
101	Thunersee–Zentralschweiz
105	Valais–Wallis
108	Gruyère–Le Léman

This route can be cycled in both directions. Our description starts in Andermatt high in the Alps, climbs in a southwesterly direction over the Furkapass and down into the Rhône Valley through Brig, Sierre, Sion and Martigny to reach Lake Léman near Montreux. It then skirts along the northern shore of the lake through Lausanne to reach Genève.

Hard riders looking for thigh-busting excitement will find the trip over the Furkapass amusing, but the rest of the route will not offer them much, unless they climb up into the tributary valleys around Sierre and Sion. They should consider either turning north in Gletsch to follow the start of the Aare Route (chapter 8) over the Grimselpass, or east over the Nufenenpass towards Airolo and the St Gotthard or south in Visp towards Saas Fe and/or Zermatt. More relaxed tourists could consider taking a bus to the Furka Summit or Gletsch, before gently drifting down the Rhône Valley. The official language changes from German to French in Sierre.

Below Oberwald on the banks of the young Rhône (Stage 1)

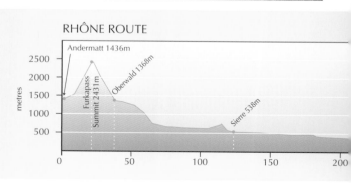

RHÔNE ROUTE

LINKS TO OTHER ROUTES		
Location	**Route/s**	**To**
Andermatt	R2: Rhein Route	Chur, Bodensee, Basel
Andermatt	R3: North–South Route	North: Luzern, Basel South: St Gotthard Pass, Lago Maggiore, Chiasso
Gletsch	R8: Aare Route	Bern, Koblenz
Aigle	R4: Alpine Panorama Route	Thun, Luzern, St Margrethen (Bodensee)
Montreux	R9: Lakes Route	Gstaad, Luzern, Rorschach (Bodensee)
Lausanne	R5: Mittelland Route	Biel/Bienne, Aarau, Romanshorn (Bodensee)
Nyon	R7: Jura Route	Vallorbe, Basel

PUBLIC TRANSPORT BACKUP		
Section	**Service**	*Comment*
Andermatt – Oberwald via Gletsch	Postbus	*June to October*
Andermatt – Oberwald	Train	*Tunnel!*
Oberwald – Genève	Train	
Montreux – Genève	Ship	*Spring, summer, early autumn*

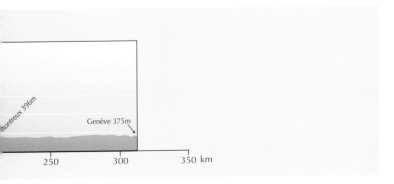

Stage 1: Andermatt – Oberwald
38km; 980m; difficult

Looking back up the Furka at the remnants of the Rhône Glacier

Andermatt is a good victualling and starting point, with hotels, B&B, a bike shop, cafés selling large cream cakes and a supermarket. Most people visit Andermatt for the superb mountain views, rather than its architecture, although the old rough chalets have a distinct charm.

The climb to the Furkapass summit is just under 1000m in 21km, mostly after Realp. You ascend a series of hairpins at first, followed by some straight sections, before a couple of wiggles bring you to the summit café. Avoid the weekend if possible since this pass is also a favourite for motor cyclists. There is a short level section at the top followed by a death-defying drop past the shrinking Rhône Glacier to Gletsch, a hotel and station, the present terminus of the Furka Steam Railway, which does not take bicycles. (Visit the glacier before it disappears.) There's a wonderful downhill section to Oberwald, sometimes past rusting narrow gauge railway lines awaiting restoration, so that steam trains can reach Oberwald again. In Oberwald, another chalet village, magnificent mountain views right down the Rhône Valley can be enjoyed.

In bad weather, take the train to Oberwald through the tunnel or book the Postbus from Andermatt the day before (officially).

ITINERARY		
Distance (km)	Location	Directions
0	Andermatt (1436m)	TO on corner by station. Stay on R1/R3 through village centre to road to Hospental. Take any RT across railway line to follow a much quieter road left to Hospental station.
3	Hospental (1452m)	RT at roundabout signposted Realp, Furkapass (R1).
8	Realp (1538m)	Climb main road (R1).
21	Furkapass summit (2431m)	Descend. Enjoy!
38	Oberwald (1368m)	

FACILITIES							
	Distance (km)	Camp site	YH/BP	B&B	Hotel	Station	Bike shop
Andermatt	0	✓		✓	Many	✓	✓
Hospental	3		✓		Many	✓	
Realp	8	✓			3	✓	
Tiefenbach	16				1		
Hotel Belvedere	23				1*		
Gletsch	31				1*		
Oberwald	38				Many	✓	✓
* only open in summer							

TOURIST INFORMATION			
From/to	Name	Address	Telephone/Website
Andermatt/ Tiefenbach	Tourist Info Uri	Tellspielhaus Schützengasse 11 Postfach CH-6460 Altdorf	+41 (0)41 872 04 50 www.uri.info
Gletsch/ Oberwald	Obergoms Tourismus	Furkastrasse altes Pfarrhaus CH 3999 Oberwald	+41 (0)27 973 32 32 www.obergoms.ch

Stage 2: Oberwald – Sierre

RB: 85km, T: 94km; RB: 140m, T: 460m; RB: easy, T: moderate

A lovely start on rough trails by the young Rhône, followed by a helter-skelter plunge on the road into Fiesch, but beware poorly placed grids, especially when wet. Thence by a breathtaking serpentine section after Deisch, where the Rhône has cut a deep gorge, past the cable car station for the Aletsch Glacier and along the riverside into

Centre of Brig: trains to Zermatt

Brig. Those unhappy about cycling in traffic should consider taking the train from Lax or taking R1 from Ernen via Ausserbinn, Grengiols and Bister to Brig. Rock hounds would enjoy climbing through Ausserbinn to beyond Binn to sift through the mine spoil for Bergkristal and other minerals. There is a short climb from Susten to Varen.

In bad weather or for a day off, take the train.

ITINERARY		
Distance Location **(km)**		**Directions**
0	Oberwald (1368m)	Follow R1 signs out of the village to avoid a tunnel on the main road. Poor surface, puddles and corrugations, **RB** take right bank tarmac road.
5	Obergesteln (1355m)	**RB** Carry SO by station and follow main road down towards Greich. Tourists can take R1 (partly unsurfaced) on the other side of the Rhône to Lax or Mörel.
T: 41 **RB: 34**	Lax /Greich (1039m/760m)	Main road towards Brig.
T: 49 **RB: 42**	Naters/Brig (684m)	Do not take road into Brig but TL before roundabout. About 200m rough stuff then smooth promenade to Brig. (TL over river, under railway to station and town. TO in station.) SO on minor road.
T: 59 **RB: 52**	Visp	Cross river twice.

T: 67	Raron (637m)	LT in village.
RB: 60		
T: 82	Leuk/Susten	Leave R1 to follow minor road through Varen and Salgesch
RB: 75	(731m/624m)	(130m climb).
T: 94	Sierre (538m)	
RB: 85		

FACILITIES							
	Distance (km)	Camp site	YH/BP	B&B	Hotel	Station	Bike shop
Ulrichen	6	✓		✓	4	✓	
Münster	10				Many	✓	
Reckingen	13	✓			Many	✓	
Ernen	24	✓		✓	Many		
Fiesch	27	✓	✓	✓	Many	✓	✓
Brig	50	✓			Many	✓	✓
Visp	60	✓			Many	✓	✓
Raron	67	✓			3		
Susten	82	✓			4	✓	
Sierre	94	✓			Many	✓	✓

TOURIST INFORMATION			
From/to	Name	Address	Telephone/Website
Ulrichen/ Sierre	Valais Tourism	Rue Pré Fleuri 6 PO Box 1469 CH-1951 Sion	+41 (0)27 327 3570 www.wallis.ch

Stage 3: Sierre – Montreux
92km; 20m; easy

This is a flattish section where the language changes from German to French. On clear days the mountain views are fantastic as the route weaves along the Rhône banks with small towns and steep vineyards above. Sion is delightful. At its Friday market the really hungry can eat *raclette* for breakfast. The more energetic can take a slightly hillier route through the vineyards along the edge of the valley. Approaching Martigny there's a hard RT through a narrow, often windy defile. Near Evionnaz is the biggest maze in the world.

Close to St Maurice, there is an exciting swoop along the road with a sharp right exit back into farm lanes. The gorge is guarded by a fort which, in typical Swiss manner, is now open to visitors. To leave the town head for Monthey on an elevated road.

Mountains and vines in the Rhône valley

Further cruising between the almost vertical rock walls is rewarded by the view across Lac Léman. There are extensive patches of giant cow parsley in this area. **This plant should not be touched.** It can cause severe blistering.

In bad weather or for a day off, take the train.

ITINERARY		
Distance Location (km)		Directions
0	Sierre (538m)	Follow R1 over the Rhône. RT along the river.
18	Sion (499m)	In town centre ride through bus station and head left round the post office to exit town. **RB** Follow regional route through vineyards to Conthey, Vétroz, Chamoson. TL in Leytron to rejoin main R1. **T** Stay by the river on R1 to bypass Martigny.
45	Martigny (461m)	Follow signs for Montreux. Short stretch on road after Evionnaz, but follow the Rhône towpath to Villeneuve.
88	Villeneuve	Follow cycle route into Montreux
92	Montreux (396m)	

FACILITIES							
	Distance (km)	Camp site	YH/BP	B&B	Hotel	Station	Bike shop
Sion	18	✓	✓	✓	Many	✓	✓
Martigny	45	✓		✓	Many	✓	✓
St Maurice	60				2	✓	
Bex	62			✓	Many	✓	✓
Monthey	64				2	✓	✓
Aigle	72	✓		✓	4	✓	✓
Villeneuve	88				3	✓	✓
Montreux	92	✓	✓	✓	Many	✓	✓

TOURIST INFORMATION			
From/to	Name	Address	Telephone/Website
Sion/ Monthey	Valais Tourism	Rue Pré Fleuri 6 PO Box 1469 CH-1951 Sion	+41 (0)27 327 3570 www.wallis.ch
Aigle	Aigle Tourisme	Rue Colomb 5 CH-1860 Aigle	+41 (0)24 466 3000 www.aigle.ch
Villeneuve/ Montreux	Office du Tourisme du Canton de Vaud	Avenue d'Ouchy 60 Case Postale 164 CH-1000 Lausanne 6	+41 (0)21 613 2626 www.lake-geneva-region.ch

Stage 4: Montreux – Genève
94km; 250m; moderate

If unhappy in traffic you may want to take a ship or a train to St Prex from Montreux. Without access to detailed maps, the route planning cyclist might be forgiven for thinking that navigation and cycling are easy today – just keep the lake on your left and settle into a high gear. However, much of the route avoids the developed lakeside to wind over glacial debris and up and down various tiny river gorges on quiet roads and cycle tracks.

All the same, the lake and the Alps to the south are ever present – an unforgettable day, through historic villages and vineyards, the climbs nicely balanced by satisfying high speed descents. On Sundays, families are underway on bikes and the boulangeries offer coffee, bread and pastries. The autobahn service station at Gland is accessible to cyclists too. The 'castle' in Bénex is a water tower. The lake shore in Nyon is slightly off route, down a steep hill. The official route is very narrow and rough for a short distance after Nyon. The final noisy section into Genève was protected and well signposted, but we found the cyclists aggressive.

In bad weather, take a train or ship.

Farm festival near Geneva

ITINERARY		
Distance (km)	Location	Directions
0	Montreux (396m)	Follow the promenade road with the motorists until after Clarens.
7	Vevey (396m)	Back on the road until Cully.
17	Cully (391m)	Cycleway and road to Ouchy (Lausanne).
26	Lausanne (374m)	Cycleway and quiet road.
38	Morges (374m)	Busy road.
43	St Prex (392m)	Busy road, then up and down through the vines on cycleways and quiet roads. Short stretch of unpaved track after Allaman (399m) followed by a steep climb to Perroy (418m).
69	Nyon (378m)	Short nasty narrow rough track beyond Nyon station.
94	Genève (375m)	Cycle track along major highway. Beware local cyclists overtaking from all sides. Well signposted to railway station.

FACILITIES							
	Distance (km)	Camp site	YH/BP	B&B	Hotel	Station	Bike shop
Vevey	7	✓		✓	Many	✓	✓
Lausanne	26	✓	✓	✓	Many	✓	✓
Morges	38	✓		✓	Many	✓	
St Prex	43			✓			
Allaman	48			✓			
Nyon	69			✓	Many	✓	✓
Genève	94	✓	✓	✓	Many	✓	✓

TOURIST INFORMATION			
From/to	Name	Address	Telephone/Website
Montreux/ Genève	Office du Tourisme du Canton de Vaud	Avenue d'Ouchy 60 Case Postale 164 CH-1000 Lausanne 6	+41 (0)21 613 2626 www.lake-geneva-region.ch

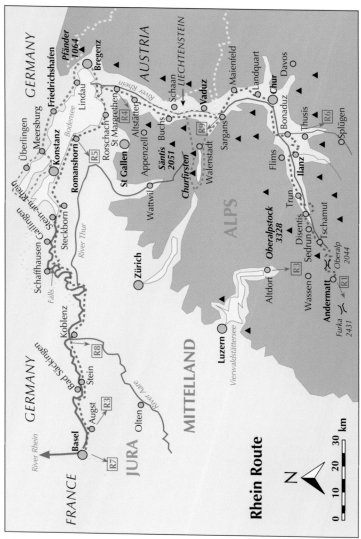

2 THE RHEIN ROUTE, BASED ON R2

ROUTE SUMMARY					
From/to	Distance (km)	Climb (m) with public transport	Climb (m) without public transport	Grade with public transport	Grade without public transport
Andermatt/ Basel	486 (80)	1150	2070	Easy	Moderate
Disentis/ Basel	452 (80)	860	1450	Easy	Easy

SUMMARY OF STAGES (WITHOUT PUBLIC TRANSPORT)				
Stage	From/to	Distance (km)	Climb (m)	Grade
1	Andermatt/Disentis	34	610	Moderate
2	Disentis/Chur	64	580	Moderate
3	Chur/Buchs	48	270	Easy
4	Buchs/St Margrethen	41	0	Easy
5	St Margrethen/Lindau	25	0	Easy
6	Lindau/Konstanz	101	120	Easy
7	Konstanz/Gailingen	36	70	Easy
8	Gailingen/Koblenz (Hochrhein)	66	340	Moderate
9	Koblenz (Hochrhein)/ Basel	71	80	Easy
Total	Andermatt/Basel	486	2070	

LOCAL MAPS	
Swisstopo 1:100,000 Composite	
101	Thunersee–Zentralschweiz
102	Basel–Luzern
103	Zürich–St Gallen
110	Vorderrhein–Hinterrhein

This is an ideal route for families with small children, especially if you start from Disentis rather than slog up the Oberalppass and/or cycle east along the steeply dropping road from the summit. Some modest descents continue after Disentis with one climb before Bonaduz. For this reason the stages are short. However there is nothing to stop you combining or cutting stages to make longer or shorter versions. The route can also be done in reverse, starting from Basel. The grade is similar to the downhill version with the exception of the end when the Oberalppass is 'difficult'.

Looking down on Andermatt (Stage 1)

An excursion is suggested based on the *Rund um die Churfirsten* (Churfirsten Route) from Buchs to Sargans via Wattwil and Walensee for road bikers or braver touring types.

Our main route follows R2 from Andermatt to the Bodensee but then crosses to the northern shore running into Austria near Bregenz and on to Germany, near Lindau,

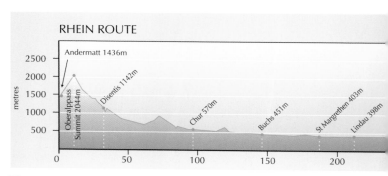

then through Friedrichshafen, Meersburg and Überlingen to Konstanz. The northern bank of the Bodensee has tremendous views across the lake to the Alps although the waymarking is only just adequate. In addition Bregenz has Austro-Hungarian flair and opera on the lake in summer. Lindau, Meersburg and Konstanz are medieval jewels. Friedrichshafen has a superb Zeppelin Museum. The Austrian, German and Swiss shores all have very pleasant summer resorts. Every community has lakeside swimming beaches or pools.

The tour rejoins R2 to reach Stein-am-Rhein. Between the Bodensee and Basel the route is delightful despite approaching a major industrial region.

Although the official language on this route is German, it switches to German and Romansh at the top of the Oberalppass, before reverting to German in Maienfeld.

LINKS TO OTHER ROUTES		
Location	**Route/s**	**To**
Andermatt	R1: Rhône Route	Martigny, Montreux, Genève
	R3: North–South Route	North: Luzern, Basel
		South: St Gotthard Pass, Lago Maggiore, Chiasso
Chur	R6: Graubünden Route	Bellinzona, St Moritz, Inn Valley
Sargans	R9: Lakes Route	Luzern, Gstaad, Montreux
St Margrethen	R4: Alpine Panorama Route	Luzern, Thun, Aigle
Romanshorn	R5: Mittelland Route	Zürich, Biel/Bienne, Lausanne
Koblenz	R8: Aare Route	Bern, Gletsch
Augst	R3: North–South Route	Luzern, Andermatt, St Gotthard Pass, Lago Maggiore, Chiasso
Basel	R7: Jura Route	Vallorbe, Nyon

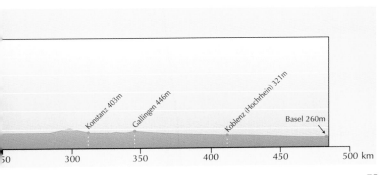

PUBLIC TRANSPORT BACKUP	
Route	Service/Comment
Andermatt – Chur	Train
Chur – Sargans – St Margrethen	Train
St Margrethen – Bregenz – Lindau – Friedrichshafen – Konstanz	Train
St Margrethen – Rorschach – Bregenz – Lindau – Friedrichshafen – Meersburg – Überlingen – Konstanz	Ship *Spring, summer, early autumn*
Meersburg – Konstanz	Car ferry
Friedrichshafen – Romanshorn	Car ferry
Konstanz – Radolfzell – Stein-am-Rhein – Schaffhausen	Train
Konstanz – Radolfzell – Stein-am-Rhein – Schaffhausen	Ship *Spring, summer, early autumn*
Schaffhausen – Basel	Train

Stage 1: Andermatt – Disentis
34km; 610m; moderate

Snowsheds and train at Oberalppass summit

Andermatt is a good victualling and starting point, with hotels, B&B, a bike shop, cafés selling large cream cakes and a supermarket. Most people visit Andermatt for the superb mountain views, rather than its architecture, although the old rough chalets have a distinct charm.

There is a 600m climb up the Oberalppass which is not that difficult. At the summit you reach a hotel, so cyclists getting to Andermatt at lunchtime could stock up on essentials, ascend the pass, stop overnight in the hotel at over 2000m and then start next day with an 800m drop into Disentis. If you feel the climb is excessive take the train from Andermatt up the pass.

After the pass, R2 drops through high moorland and tiny Tschamut to reach Sedrun whose most interesting feature is a hole in the ground – a shaft for the new railway tunnel (scheduled to open in 2015) with an exhibition (closed Tuesdays). Disentis has a massive baroque monastery church with regular sung masses.

In bad weather or for an easier day, take the train to Oberalppass or Disentis.

ITINERARY

Distance (km)	Location	Directions
0	Andermatt (1436m)	TO on corner by station. Follow R1/R2/R3 then TL at roundabout to climb R2 on road over Oberalppass. Dark snowshed near summit.
11	Oberalppass (2044m)	Follow R2 on road through Sedrun (1404m) to Disentis.
34	Disentis (1142m)	

FACILITIES

	Distance (km)	Camp site	YH/BP	B&B	Hotel	Station	Bike shop
Andermatt	0	✓	✓ Hospental (3km)	✓	Many	✓	✓
Oberalppass	11				1	✓	
Tschamut	18				1	✓	
Rueras	23	✓			2		
Sedrun	25				Many	✓	
Disentis	34	✓			Many	✓	✓

TOURIST INFORMATION

From/to	Name	Address	Telephone/Website
Andermatt/ Oberalppass	Tourist Info Uri	Tellspielhaus Schützengasse 11 Postfach CH-6460 Altdorf	+41 (0)41 872 0450 www.uri.info
Tschamut/ Disentis	Graubünden Vacation	Alexanderstrasse 24 CH-7001 Chur	+41 (0)81 254 2424 http://ferien. graubuenden.ch/en

Stage 2: Disentis – Chur
64km; 580m; moderate

The official route from Disentis turns right below the descent into town and leads past the railway station down to the valley floor. Next there is a climb uphill a similar distance, followed by an undulating gravel track through Surrein to Trun, a road crossing and an extremely rough section of track into Danis. During the week, unless very nervous in traffic, cyclists should follow the conventional road via Trun, as far as Danis, then turn off right along an unsurfaced but reasonably smooth road to Ilanz, with its fine medieval centre. R2 then crosses the young Rhein, climbing steeply alongside the Ruinaulta, a narrow canyon, through an ancient landslip. The Ruinaulta can be seen by train through the gorge from Ilanz station or joining a river rafting trip to Reichenau. (Contact the tourist office in Ilanz (www.ilanz.ch) for more information.)

Shortly afterwards R2 reaches Bonaduz, where there is now a Sushi bar! Mountain bikers who enjoy some steep climbing and rough stuff might try an interesting unsignposted route (20km/600m) from Tamins up the valley side over the Kunkelspass to Bad Ragaz.

Chur is a major city and the capital of Graubünden with an ancient centre and a superb cathedral. However, it is possible to bypass the city if you wish do so.

In bad weather or for a day off, take the train to Chur.

ITINERARY		
Distance (km)	**Location**	**Directions**
0	Disentis (1142m)	**RB** TL at bottom of long hill past abbey church to follow Road 19 to Trun. **T** TR then TL to pass the station, cross the Rhein and the climb to a hamlet to follow an undulating rough track to the tarmac in Cumpadials and Surrein to Trun (or TL after the abbey church following the RB on 19 to Trun).
13	Trun (852m)	**RB** Stay on tarmac on Road 19 to Ilanz. **T** Cross the road and climb away to return to the roadside soon and be directed up a steep, muddy track. Those persevering will reach a tarmac road and Road 19 at Tavanasa. The signposted track off to the right is unsurfaced but smooth.
29	Ilanz (698m)	Follow the minor road south of the Rhein up the hill to Versam (908m) and then down to Bonaduz.
51	Bonaduz (655m)	**RB** Take care after Bonaduz because the route follows the approach roads to the autobahn. TR in Reichenau towards Domat/Ems and Chur. **T** Follow the minor road through Reichenau and Tamins, then right along an unsurfaced track via Felsberg and an Army practice area into Chur.
64	Chur (570m)	

FACILITIES							
	Distance (km)	Camp site	YH/BP	B&B	Hotel	Station	Bike shop
Sumvitg	9	✓				✓	
Rabius	10				1		
Trun	13				2		
Ilanz	29	✓			Many	✓	✓
Valendas	36	✓		✓	1		
Versam	41				1		
Bonaduz	51				2	✓	✓
Rhäzuns (off route)	53			✓	1		
Reichenau – Tamins	53				1	✓	
Felsberg	59						✓
Chur	64	✓			Many	✓	✓

TOURIST INFORMATION			
From/to	Name	Address	Telephone/Website
Disentis/ Chur	Graubünden Vacation	Alexanderstrasse 24 CH-7001 Chur	+41 (0)81 254 24 24 http://ferien. graubuenden.ch/en

Stage 3: Chur – Buchs
48km; 270m; easy

This stage leads you through the Maienfeld hills where Johanna Spyri set *Heidi*, the famous children's book. One can drink 'Heidiland' mineral water and buy Heidi souvenirs by the ton. It is surprising not to find a Heidiburger Bar. Delightful as the books are, one can only take so much sweetness and light, and the advantage of bicycle touring is that you can't carry too much.

You are soon out of Maienfeld. Malans, Jenins, Maienfeld and Fläsch make up a major wine-producing area. For serious wine tasting stay in a local hotel rather than test the drink/drive laws. The church in Fläsch is home to 1100 bats. Pushing the button to the left of the screen by the church provides live infrared pictures of the creatures. It is a pity that R2 bypasses Bad Ragaz because the sulphurous spring waters in the thermal baths there are renowned for helping rheumatism sufferers and would surely benefit aching cyclists. (If you wish to avoid Heidi and company, and visit Bad Ragaz, you can stick to the Rhein after Zizers and travel through Landquart to Bad Ragaz on an unsurfaced track.)

Vines in Heidi country

After this, the main route stays with the Rhein on the flat. Follow the combined R2/9 towards Buchs and St Margrethen. As you pass the turn-off to R9, Liechtenstein is on the other side of the Rhein. Soon afterwards the sinister towers of the castle in Vaduz appear. Unless you are an art fan wanting to see world class art collections, a stamp collector or wish to do some serious banking, Liechtenstein does not have much to offer over Switzerland except for a pleasant youth hostel in Schaan. Cross into Liechtenstein over the covered bridge.

Buchs is a pleasant little town and a good victualling stop. Just beyond and not really separated from Buchs is Werdenberg, the smallest town in Switzerland with 60 inhabitants and certainly worth half an hour of your time. Follow R2/9 out of Buchs and then the signposted left turn into the car park.

In bad weather or for a day off, take the train to Buchs.

In case you have a day or two to spare at Buchs, a description is also given here of the Churfirsten Route, which can be done as an excursion, with or without public transport to make it less challenging. The options include taking a Postbus from Buchs (451m) to Wildhaus (1060m) or the railway from Wattwil to Ziegelbrücke.

ITINERARY		
Distance (km)	Location	Directions
0	Chur (570m)	Return to R2 from in front of the station or carry on to bypass Chur and follow R2 towards Malans.
20	Malans (568m)	Up and down on a minor road through Jenins, Maienfeld and Fläsch. Cross the Rhein to cycle along a flood dyke to the turnoff to Sargans (R9).
32	Sargans (483m)	Follow R2 along the Rhein flood dyke. Liechtenstein lies across the river over a covered bridge.
48	Buchs (451m)	

FACILITIES							
	Distance (km)	Camp site	YH/BP	B&B	Hotel	Station	Bike shop
Untervaz Station	9				1		
Landquart (off route)	15	✓				✓	✓
Malans	20			✓	1		✓
Jenins	22				1		
Maienfeld	25			✓	1	✓	
Bad Ragaz (off route)	27	✓			Many	✓	
Fläsch	28			✓			
Vilters (off route)	32				3		
Sargans	32				1	✓	✓
Buchs	48	✓	✓ Schaan (2km)		Many	✓	✓

TOURIST INFORMATION			
From/to	Name	Address	Telephone/Website
Chur/ Maienfeld	Graubünden Vacation	Alexanderstrasse 24 CH-7001 Chur	+41 (0)81 254 2424 http://ferien. graubuenden.ch/en
Bad Ragaz/ Buchs	Ostschweiz Tourismus	Bahnhofplatz 1a CH-9001 St Gallen	+41 (0)71 227 3737 www.ostschweiz.ch

Excursion: *Rund um die Churfirsten (Around the Churfirsten)*
101–116km; 200–800m, moderate to difficult

This excursion is moderate to difficult not so much because of the hills, although the first climb is challenging, but because of its length. Families would be well advised to take the bus and stop somewhere overnight. In bad weather or for an easier day, take the train from Wattwil via Ziegelbrücke and Sargans to Buchs.

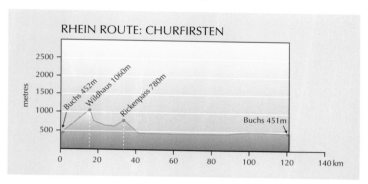

RHEIN ROUTE: CHURFIRSTEN

			ITINERARY
Distance without bus	**Distance with bus**	**Location**	**Directions**
0	0	Buchs (451m)	Save the 600m climb to Wildhaus by taking the Postbus from Buchs railway station, from June to October. You need to reserve a place for your bike at least an hour before, although out of season it is not necessary. If not taking the bus follow R2/9 out of Buchs to Grabs. TL in Grabs towards Wildhaus and climb!
15	0	Wildhaus (1060m)	Follow the *Rund um die Churfirsten* route on roads through Alt St Johann (890m) to Neu St Johann.
32	17	Neu St Johann (759m)	Follow minor road through Ebnat–Kappel (647m) towards Wattwil. TL near Ulisbach.
43	28	Ulisbach (625m)	Follow R4 over the Rickenpass (780m) towards Ziegelbrücke.
67	52	Ziegelbrücke (423m)	Follow R9 to Sargans. Two short hills and cycle tunnels.

| 101 | 86 | Sargans (483m) | Follow R2/9 along Rhein dyke. |
| 116 | 101 | Buchs (451m) | |

FACILITIES (LISTED CLOCKWISE)							
	Distance (km)	Camp site	YH/BP	B&B	Hotel	Station	Bike shop
Grabserberg	4			✓			
Wildhaus	15	✓			Many		
Alt St Johann	19	✓		✓	4		
Neu St Johann	32			✓	2		
Ebnat–Kappel	39			✓	1		✓
Wattwil	45					✓	✓
Gommiswald	52				1		
Kaltbrunn	54			✓	1	✓	✓
Weesen	70				Many		
Filzbach	73		✓		4		
Walenstadt	88	✓			3	✓	✓
Mels	100				1	✓	

TOURIST INFORMATION			
From/to	Name	Address	Telephone/Website
Grabserberg/ Mels	Ostschweiz Tourismus	Bahnhofplatz 1a CH-9001 St Gallen	+41 (0)71 227 3737 www.ostschweiz.ch

Stage 4: Buchs – St Margrethen
41km; 0m; easy

The official route from Buchs to St Margrethen is pleasant through the fields with about 5km of untarred but reasonable track. It leaves the Rhein to meander across to Altstätten and on to St Margrethen. You could also cycle on tarred maintenance roads along or behind the Rhein flood dyke either staying in Switzerland (especially road bikes) or nip over to Austria and follow the other bank of the Rhein. The signposting on both banks is superb.

However, in 2007 the Rhein flood dyke was being strengthened giving rise to diversions. You rejoin R2 in St Margrethen. Those interested in narrow gauge railways and civil engineering should try to visit the Internationale Rheinregulierung (Rhein control) museum (Rheinschauen) in Lustenau (Wednesday, Friday to Sunday afternoons). Steam trains run from there out into the Rhein delta.

In bad weather or for a day off, take the train to St Margrethen.

Farmhouse garden decorations near Altstätten

ITINERARY

Distance (km)	Location	Directions
0	Buchs (451m)	**RB** Return to Rhein towpath and TL at Rhein. Continue all the way to St Margrethen/Lustenau. **T** Follow R2/9 through Grabs to Oberriet.
23	Oberriet (421m)	**T** Follow R2/9 via Altstätten to St Margrethen.
41	St Margrethen (403m)	

FACILITIES

	Distance (km)	Camp site	YH/BP	B&B	Hotel	Station	Bike shop
Grabs	2				3		✓
Oberriet	23				3	✓	✓
Altstätten	30		✓		3	✓	✓
Lustenau	40	✓	✓		3	✓	✓
St Margrethen	41	✓			1	✓	✓

TOURIST INFORMATION

From/to	Name	Address	Telephone/Website
Buchs/ St Margrethen	Ostschweiz Tourismus	Bahnhofplatz 1a CH-9001 St Gallen	+41 (0)71 227 3737 www.ostschweiz.ch

Stage 5: St Margrethen – Lindau
25km; 0m; easy

From St Margrethen cycle along the delta edge into Austria and then cross the Rhein towards Hard and Bregenz. If you have time, follow the Bodensee Radwanderweg to Gaissau and turn off right on the edge of the village to follow R2/9 across the delta. Beyond the restaurant and camp site take the top of the dyke for superb views of the mountains, the bird life and the reed beds. Don't miss the concrete halfpipe for skate boarders and inline skaters in Hard. In Bregenz in sunny weather it seems that half the population of Austria is out and about on bikes or on foot, especially near the back of the railway station and the steamer pier. Notice the large opera stage on the left for the Bregenz Festival. The city, shops, art gallery, internet cafés and coffee shops are across the tracks to your right. During the Festival in August rooms are scarce and more expensive than usual.

If you have time take a cable car up Pfänder with your bike. The bike goes free for an hour in the mornings. There is some good cycling beyond Pfänder. The ticket office has a brochure with routes.

Four kilometres after Bregenz, the cycle signs change and you are in Germany, Bavaria to be precise. The Bavarians are famous for a relaxed attitude to life and their bicycle signposting is less comprehensive than the Swiss signposting. Lindau, yet another medieval jewel, is a good place for a beer or *Kaffee und Kuchen* (coffee and cake – a mid-afternoon calorie bomb). Don't worry about putting on weight. According to a popular Bavarian saying, 'a man without a paunch is a cripple' ('ein Mann ohne Wampe ist ein Krüppel').

If you are short of time then follow R2 west along the Swiss bank to Kreuzlingen and Konstanz. In bad weather or for a day off, take the train from St Margrethen to Bregenz or Lindau.

ITINERARY		
Distance (km)	Location	Directions
0	St Margrethen (403m)	Follow R2 along Rhein to road bridge and cross Rhein toward Hard in Austria. Follow signs to Bregenz on surfaced and unsurfaced tracks. Nice little bridges supply the only up and downs.
14	Bregenz	SO on the edge of the lake between railway and lake to cross into Germany.
25	Lindau (398m)	In Lindau follow the Lindau–Insel signs off to the left to reach the medieval town and harbour.

FACILITIES							
	Distance (km)	Camp site	YH/BP	B&B	Hotel	Station	Bike shop
Bregenz	14	✓	✓	✓	Many	✓	✓
Lindau	25	✓	✓	✓	Many	✓	✓

TOURIST INFORMATION			
From/to	Name	Address	Telephone/Website
Bregenz	Vorarlberg Tourismus	Bahnhofstrasse 14 A-6901 Bregenz	+43 (0)55 7442 5250 www.vorarlberg.travel
Lindau	Internationale Bodensee Tourismus GmbH	Hafenstrasse 6 D-78462 Konstanz	+49 (0)75 31/90 9490 www.bodensee-tourismus.com

Stage 6: Lindau – Konstanz
101km; 120m; easy

The Bodensee Radwanderweg (Bodensee Cycle Route) is one of the most popular routes in Germany, unfortunately, so keep your eyes open for other cyclists, inline skaters and walkers. Friedrichshafen has much more than an airport to entertain visitors – the Zeppelin Museum, a wonderful baroque church, an elegant promenade and a ferry back to Switzerland. Magnificent Meersburg with its castle and half-timbered market place (Marktplatz) is rightly thronged by tourists.

A short cut on the car ferry to Konstanz avoids much climbing around the western Bodensee. However, consider making a 12km return trip to Unteruhldingen to the impressive Pfahlbauten, replicas of Bronze Age houses on stilts in the lake before taking the ferry. The island of Mainau, north of Konstanz, is famous for its gardens – rather expensive but wonderful. Konstanz offers history, medieval architecture, a cathedral, a harbour, a quick way back into Switzerland and the scurrilous but amusing Lenkbrunnen on Auf der Laube Street.

In bad weather or for a day off, take the ship or train to Konstanz. For a shorter day, take the ferry from Meersburg to Konstanz.

ITINERARY		
Distance (km)	Location	Directions
0	Lindau (398m)	Next to the post office there is a cycleway and pedestrian route that follows the railway out of town to a reasonably signposted, mildly hilly route through Wasserburg and Langenargen to Friedrichshafen. Part of the route is unsurfaced but adequate. In Friedrichshafen TL towards the

		Hafenbahnhof and Zeppelin Museum. There are covered bike racks, toilets and shops.
24	Friedrichshafen	Cycle round the old town and follow the cycleway along the inland side of the park and towards the Ducal castle and church to run parallel to the very busy B31. After the Dornier factory take underpass into Immenstaad. TO down hill on right.
34	Immenstaad	Follow Hagenau Bodensee signs to Hagenau. TL to reach lake shore. Follow the track to Meersburg.
41	Meersburg	Go through the lower old town to the car ferry to Konstanz (every quarter of an hour). Cycle on a rough, rapidly improving track to Unteruhldingen. Minor roads between Unteruhldingen and Überlingen, some unsurfaced.
53	Überlingen	Towards Ludwigshafen. SO towards Bodman, then on the cyclepath next to the lake. At end ignore cycle route signs across fields and TL towards T-junction. TR at T-junction along minor road following Konstanz. TL at junction signposted Liggeringen. In Liggeringen towards Langenrein, Dettingen, Wallhausen and Dingelsdorf. **T** Take unsurfaced track across fields to Dingelsdorf. **RB** Stay on road. Follow minor roads along lakeside through Litzelstetten past Mainau to Egg.
101	Konstanz (403m)	Follow *Konstanz Zentrum* signs to centre.

FACILITIES

	Distance (km)	Camp site	YH/BP	B&B	Hotel	Station	Bike shop
Wasserburg	6	✓		✓	Many	✓	
Langenargen	16			✓	Many	✓	
Friedrichshafen	24	✓	✓	✓	Many	✓	✓
Immenstaad	34	✓		✓	Many		✓
Meersburg	41			✓	Many		
Unteruhldingen	46	✓			4		
Überlingen	53	✓	✓	✓	Many	✓	
Ludwigshafen – Bodman	63	✓	✓	✓	Many	✓	✓
Konstanz	101		✓		Many	✓	✓

TOURIST INFORMATION

From/to	Name	Address	Telephone/Website
Lindau/ Konstanz	Internationale Bodensee Tourismus GmbH	Hafenstrasse 6 D-78462 Konstanz	+49 (0)75 31/90 9490 www.bodensee-tourismus.com

Stage 7: Konstanz – Gailingen
36km; 70m; easy

The route follows R2 from Konstanz, then on to Steckborn and Stein-am-Rhein. There is a good network of well-signposted cycleways in Canton Thurgau stretching inland between Arbon and Diessenhofen (www.thurgau-touristinfo.ch). Stein-am-Rhein's Old Town, with its painted houses, will stop you in your tracks. Gailingen in Germany is a good place to stop overnight (www.gailingen.de). The prices are low and the food in the Hotel Hirschen is excellent.

In bad weather or for a day off, take the train to Diessenhofen (just south of Gailingen).

ITINERARY		
Distance (km)	Location	Directions
0	Konstanz (403m)	Follow *Schweiz* signs and TR after Rhein bridge at end of Bodensee along left bank (Rheinsteig). TL (signposted) across road and down Schottenstrasse, later Schützenstrasse to Döbele Platz. Swing left then TR into Emmishofer Strasse. Cross into Switzerland and TR along R2 (Tägemoosstrasse).
1	Kreuzlingen (403m)	Follow R2 along a tarmac cycle path, then a quiet road and treated track to Ermatingen. More unsurfaced but good quality path (4km) follows to Berlingen and Steckborn. After Mammern there is a slight climb on unsurfaced roads to Obereschenz followed by a drop to the Rhein. Cross the river to Stein-am-Rhein.
28	Stein-am-Rhein (400m)	**RB** Leave via arch at end of main street to Hemishofen. SO to Ramsen. TL and follow the Gailingen road over a small pass (500m) into Germany. **T** TL in Hemishofen then TR following R2 signs on a track that climbs and gets rougher. Follow the walkers' signposting as well to Gailingen.
36	Gailingen (446m)	

FACILITIES							
	Distance (km)	Camp site	YH/BP	B&B	Hotel	Station	Bike shop
Kreuzlingen	1	✓	✓		Many	✓	
Ermatingen	8				Many	✓	
Steckborn	17	✓			3	✓	
Stein-am-Rhein	28	✓	✓	✓	Many	✓	✓ (Wagenhausen)

| Ramsen (off route for tourists) | 37 | ✓ | | 1 |
| Gailingen | 36 | | ✓ | Many |

TOURIST INFORMATION			
From/to	**Name**	**Address**	**Telephone/Website**
Konstanz/ Stein-am-Rhein	Internationale Bodensee Tourismus GmbH	Hafenstrasse 6 D-78462 Konstanz	+49 (0)75 31/90 9490 www.bodensee-tourismus.com
Gailingen	Tourist Information Gailingen	Hauptstrasse 7 D 78262 Gailingen am Hochrhein	+49 (0)77 3493 0320 www.in-gailingen.de

Stage 8: Gailingen – Koblenz (Hochrhein)
66km; 340m; moderate

You can pick up the R2 either by dropping down the hill towards Diessenhofen or cycling on towards Büsingen on a quiet road past a mini shopping centre full of Swiss saving money by shopping in Euroland. Büsingen is a German enclave in Switzerland and has two postcodes, two telephone boxes side by side – one Swiss, one German – and Swiss Francs as working currency.

Schaffhausen has a well-kept old town, good museums and art galleries, fine churches and an interesting bicycle builder at Velowerk, Fischerhäuserstrasse 18a (www.velowerk.ch) near the river before the old town. The Rhein Falls, one of the most famous features of Schaffhausen, is actually downstream in Neuhausen. The Rhein, 150m wide at this point, pours over a 23m high step. It is spectacular, especially after heavy rainfall, and well visited. If you want to see to the Falls, go through the castle grounds after climbing up in Laufen on R2. In many ways it is better to make a separate excursion from Schaffhausen on the right bank, where you can see more.

As you pass by Rheinau look down at the monastery, now a wine cellar, and take a good look at the 'historic' tower on the city walls. It is actually a WWII bunker. Rheinau sticks up into Germany and is surrounded on three sides, so it was a well-defended strong point.

R2 runs on down river towards Zurzach with its thermal baths, good for aching legs. From Koblenz you can cycle over the bridge into Germany and visit Waldshut, with painted houses similar to those in Stein-am-Rhein but feeling less like a museum. Accommodation on the German side of the river is cheaper.

In bad weather or for a day off, take the train from Diessenhofen or Schaffhausen to Koblenz.

Quiet flows the Rhein in Büsingen

ITINERARY		
Distance Location (km)		Directions
0	Gailingen	Rejoin R2 by Diessenhofen bridge or follow quiet road to Büsingen.
9	Schaffhausen (390m)	Follow R2 along right bank of Rhein. Cross over to other bank. TR and follow unsurfaced path (2km) by Laufen. Push bike up short rough rise. Access to Rhein Falls. R2 surfaced to Neurheinau. **RB** Take minor road to Ellikon and follow surfaced cycleway to Flaach. **T** Take cycleway to Flaach.
31	Flaach (362m)	Follow R2 over a summit (440m), down to Teuffen (421m). Cross the River Töss (346m) and climb on an initially unsurfaced path (1km) to Eglisau (355m). Follow a minor road to Weiach (376m). Pick up local road and follow it to Zurzach (340m). Follow R2 to Koblenz.
66	Koblenz (321m)	

FACILITIES							
	Distance (km)	Camp site	YH/BP	B&B	Hotel	Station	Bike shop
Diessenhofen	1	✓			1	✓	✓
Büsingen	5			✓	1		
Schaffhausen	9	✓	✓	✓	Many	✓	✓
Neuhausen	13			✓	1	✓	✓
Dachsen	15		✓			✓	
Rheinau	20			✓	2		
Flaach	27	✓			1		✓
Eglisau	37				Many	✓	✓
Zurzach	59	✓		✓	Many	✓	✓
Koblenz	66	✓			1	✓	
Waldshut/Tiengen (off route)	68	✓			Many	✓	✓
Ober/Unter-lauchringen (off route)	72			✓	3	✓	✓

TOURIST INFORMATION			
From/to	Name	Address	Telephone/Website
Diessenhofen/ Schaffhausen	Internationale Bodensee Tourismus GmbH	Hafenstr. 6 D-78462 Konstanz	+49 (0)75 31/90 9490 www.bodensee-tourismus.com
Zurzach/ Koblenz	Aargau Tourismus c/o aarau info	Graben 42 Postfach CH 5001 Aarau	+41 (0)62 824 7624 www.aargautourismus.ch/
Waldshut	Tourismus Marketing GmbH Baden-Württemberg	Esslinger Strasse 8 D 70182 Stuttgart	+49 (0)711 238 580 http://www.tourismus-bw.de

Stage 9: Koblenz (Hochrhein) – Basel
71km; 80m; easy

R2 winds its way towards Basel. If you spend a night in Waldshut you can take a ferry to Full. Before WWII the Swiss built a series of blockhouses on the Rhein bank to make sure that the Germans realised that invading Switzerland would not be a pushover. These are no longer in use, but very evident and the villages of Full and Reuenthal have two military museums: a former artillery fort (open on Saturdays) and a military vehicle collection open at weekends.

From Stein, Bad Säckingen is accessible via a roofed wooden bridge. Rheinfelden has a superb old town and a 'quaint' very large brewery. Somewhat later, you come to

Augst and Augusta Raurica, with extensive excavations and recreations of a Roman city. Do not miss the Roman sewers or the arena. The dreaming spires of the Swiss chemical industry welcome you to Basel with its museums, its old town, its cathedral and three railway stations of different nationalities.

In bad weather, take the train to Basel.

ITINERARY

Distance (km)	Location	Directions
0	Koblenz (321m)	**T** RT through Full on R2. Follow track through Bernau to Schwaderloch. R2 climbs through Etzgen then track through forest to Laufenburg (318m). SO through Kaisten to Stein (AG), Mumpf and Wallbach on a tarred cycleway. Take Rhein-side track to Riburg then TR towards Rheinfelden. **RB** Stay on road to Laufenburg and rejoin R2 through Kaisten to Stein (AG), then to Mumpf. Pick up minor road after Mumpf to Möhlin. TR in village towards Riburg. TL towards Rheinfelden.
47	Rheinfelden (268m)	Follow cycleway along the road to Kaiseraugst. In Kaiseraugst TL to follow R2 through the Roman city. Cross under MW then climb through industrial estate to cross railway lines. Follow R2 through Pratteln and Muttenz to Basel. If you are going to climb back to Andermatt on R3 then TL after the level crossing.
71	Basel (260m)	

FACILITIES

	Distance (km)	Camp site	YH/BP	B&B	Hotel	Station	Bike shop
Full – Reuenthal	3					Ferry	✓
Laufenburg (CH,D)	19				Many	✓✓	
Stein (CH) – Bad Säckingen (D)	29				Many	✓✓	✓
Wallbach	33						✓
Möhlin	43	✓		✓			✓
Rheinfelden (CH, D)	47	✓		✓	Many	✓✓	✓
Kaiseraugst/ Augst	56	✓			1	✓	✓
Pratteln	61			✓	2	✓	✓
Muttenz	66			✓	3		
Basel	71	✓	✓	✓	Many	✓	✓

Cyclists are welcome in Zurzach (Rhein valley)

TOURIST INFORMATION

From/to	Name	Address	Telephone/Website
Full/ Rheinfelden (CH)	Aargau Tourismus c/o aarau info	Graben 42 Postfach CH 5001 Aarau	+41 (0)62 824 7624 www.aargautourismus.ch/
Rheinfelden (D)	Tourismus Marketing GmbH Baden-Württemberg	Esslinger Strasse 8 70182 Stuttgart	+49 (0)71 1/2 38 580 www.tourismus-bw.de/
Augst/Basel	Baselland Tourism	Altmarktstrasse 96 CH-4410 Liestal	+41 (0)61 927 6535 www.baselland-tourismus.ch/ fspopenglish.htm
Basel	Basel Tourismus	Aeschenvorstadt 36 CH-4010 Basel	+41 (0)61 268 6868 www.baseltourismus.ch

3 NORTH–SOUTH ROUTE, BASED ON R3

ROUTE SUMMARY			
From/to	Distance (km)	Climb (m)	Grade
Basel/Bellinzona	578 (15)	8090	Strenuous

SUMMARY OF STAGES				
Stage	From/to	Distance (km)	Climb (m)	Grade
1	Basel/Sursee	86	670	Moderate
2	Sursee/Gersau	126	1220	Strenuous
3	Gersau/Linthal	73	1290	Difficult
4	Linthal/Altdorf	46	1300	Difficult
5	Altdorf/Disentis	68	1590	Strenuous
6	Disentis/Bellinzona	84	900	Moderate
7	Bellinzona/Maccagno/ Bellinzona	95	1120	Difficult
Total	**Basel/Bellinzona**	**578**	**8090**	

LOCAL MAPS	
Swisstopo 1:100,000 Composite	
102	Basel–Luzern
103	Zürich–St Gallen
107	Ticino–Tessin
110	Vorderrhein–Hinterrhein

This is a hard but rewarding route giving superb views of the of the Alps. It runs from the northern border of Switzerland to Ticino, the Italian-speaking canton in the south. It can be followed in the other direction but then its grade approaches 'exceedingly strenuous'. The climb up the Alps is much steeper when coming from the south. Obviously the Jura and the Alps stand in the way south meaning there is some climbing to do on your trip between the Black Forest and Italian Lakes.

However, keen cyclists might not find enough meat to chew on if they stick to the classic Veloland Schweiz route. Three variations have been made to the standard R3 route here, to add some spice to the trip and increase the length to over 500km with about 8000m climbing. The possibility that one would want to do this route using public transport has not been considered, although the services are listed for use in case of emergency.

The passes are the reasons for doing this route. The classic R3 is 363km long with a climb of 3180m from north to south from Basel via Sursee, Luzern, Brunnen, Altdorf, Andermatt, the St Gotthard Pass and Bellinzona to Chiasso. Like all Swiss National

Descending Lukmanier on RR36 (Stage 6)

Routes it is well signposted and easy to follow. In addition, routes are suggested back north from Bellinzona.

The official language from the start to the top of the Oberalppass is German. It then switches to Romansh from the Passo del Lucomagno summit to the Ticino border, where Italian is spoken.

LINKS TO OTHER ROUTES		
Location	**Route/s**	**To**
Basel	R7: Jura Route	Vallorbe, Nyon
Pratteln	R2: Rhein Route	Bodensee, Chur, Andermatt
Aarau	R5: Mittelland Route	East: Zürich, Romanshorn (Bodensee)
		West: Biel/Bienne, Lausanne
	R8: Aare Route	North: Koblenz
		South: Bern, Thun, Gletsch
Luzern	R9: Lakes Route	East: Rorschach (Bodensee)
		West: Gstaad, Montreux
Altdorf	R4: Alpine Panorama	East: St Margrethen (Bodensee)
		West: Thun, Aigle
Andermatt	R1: Rhône Route	Gletsch, Martigny, Montreux, Genève
Andermatt/ Disentis	R2: Rhein Route	Chur, Bodensee, Basel
Bellinzona	R6: Graubünden Route	Chur, St Moritz, Inn Valley

Public transport backup
The public transport on this route is superb, although the railway is in tunnels through the Jura and the Alps. The railway on the south bank of Lago Maggiore between Bellinzona and Luino operated by the SBB does not take bicycles at the time of writing.

PUBLIC TRANSPORT BACKUP		
Section	Service	Comment
Basel – Sissach – Aarau	Train	
Aarau – Sursee – Luzern – Zug	Train	
Luzern – Brunnen – Flüelen	Ship	*April to October*
Zug – Oberägeri	Bus	
Sattel – Einsiedeln	Train	
Flüelen – Göschenen – Andermatt	Train	
Andermatt – Disentis	Train	
Disentis – Biasca	Bus	
Biasca – Bellinzona – Locarno	Train	
Luino – Locarno	Ship	*April to October*

Stage 1: Basel – Sursee
86km; 670m; moderate

Outside Basel Bad Bahnhof

There is a tendency to think that an 800m maximum height Jura pass is a mere pimple in comparison to the Alpine passes to the south at over 2000m high. However, on the day, the climb is steep and there is no café at the hilltop for a much-needed Ovomaltine or quick Rivella, and the road the other side is just as steep. The Jura hills demand respect.

After the Jura section our route description follows surfaced roads to bypass a long section of unsurfaced track down to Sursee. If you and your bicycle are happy cycling on unsurfaced track then just follow the R3 signs to Sursee.

In bad weather, take the train.

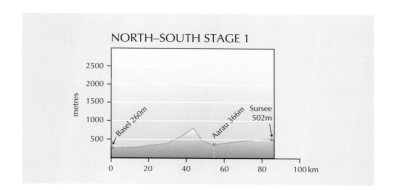

ITINERARY		
Distance Location (km)		**Directions**
0	Basel Swiss Station SBB (260m)	Cross square on north side of station. Follow R3 along Nauenstrasse (cycleway). RT along Münchensteinerstrasse R3, over the rail bridge into Emil Frey Strasse. LF into Schwertrainstrasse. LT into Muttenzerstrasse. SO over motorway.
0	Basel Bad Bahnhof (260m)	Cross Schwarzwaldstrasse to cycleway. TL to cross Rhein. Follow DB Birstrasse, RT into Nasenweg. LT along Lehenmattstrasse to end. LT into Stadionstrasse. RT into Birstrasse. Cross main road by stadium into park/sports complex to Muttenzerstrasse. TL. SO over motorway. Join route from SBB
6	Muttenz (291m)	Follow R3 cycleways and minor roads through Muttenz to Pratteln.

14	Pratteln (289m)	Follow R3 minor road by level crossing and cycleway to Liestal.
19	Liestal	R3 to Gelterkinden via Sissach.
30	Gelterkinden	R3 (road) to Ormalingen.
32	Ormalingen	Follow quiet road or parallel cycleway to Rothenfluh onwards to the summit, via Anwil and Oltingen.
44	Summit (791m)	
45	Rohr (578m)	R3 (road) to Stüsslingen
49	Stüsslingen (473m)	LT to Erlinsbach.
53	Erlinsbach (403m)	RT to Niedererlinsbach and R3 to Aarau
55	Aarau (366m)	R3 to Suhr.
59	Suhr (397m)	R3 goes right across fields SO. LT under railway. Follow Helgenfeldweg to crossroads with Obertelweg. TR. Follow minor road and Wättimattweg via Unter- and Obermuhen, Hirschthal to Schöftland.
70	Schöftland (461m)	RT to Wittwil. SO to Attelwil. Reitnau, Wilihof, Knutwil, St Erhard.
84	St Erhard (526m)	LT to Sursee
86	Sursee (502m)	

FACILITIES							
	Distance (km)	Camp site	YH/BP	B&B	Hotel	Station	Bike shop
Basel	0	✓	✓	✓	Many	✓	✓
Muttenz	6			✓	3		
Pratteln	14			✓	2	✓	✓
Kaiseraugst/Augst (off route)	18	✓			1	✓	✓
Liestal	19				Many	✓	✓
Sissach	27				1	✓	✓
Buckten (off route southsoutheast of Sissach)	39				1	✓	
Gelterkinden	30				2	✓	
Rothenfluh	36				1		
Rohr	44	✓		✓	3		
Stüsslingen	49	✓		✓			
Aarau	55			✓	Many	✓	✓
Sursee	86	✓			Many	✓	✓

TOURIST INFORMATION			
From/to	Name	Address	Telephone/Website
Basel	Basel Tourismus	Aeschenvorstadt 36 CH-4010 Basel	+41 (0)61 268 6868 www.baseltourismus.ch
Basel/ Gelterkinden	Baselland Tourism	Altmarktstrasse 96 CH-4410 Liestal	+41 (0)61 927 6535 www.baselland-tourismus.ch /fspopenglish.htm
Aarau	Aargau Tourismus	Graben 42 Postfach CH-5001 Aarau	+41 (0)62 824 7624 www.aargautourismus.ch
Sursee	Luzern Tourismus AG Tourist Board	Zentralstrasse 5 CH-6002 Luzern	+41 (0)41 227 1717 www.luzern.org/en/

Stage 2: Sursee – Gersau
126km; 1220m; strenuous

Brunnen on Vierwaldstätter See

The route rises to almost 1500m. The climate here can be very raw. Don't worry, the hill climbing will keep you warm, but wrap up well when you descend.

In bad weather, take the train or ship on Vierwaldstätter See from Luzern (or the short cut from Sattel).

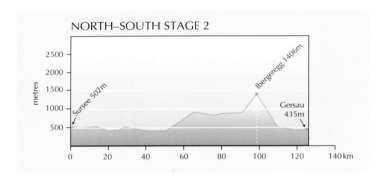

ITINERARY		
Distance (km)	**Location**	**Directions**
0	Sursee (502m)	R3 to Sempach partly on road.
8	Sempach (511m)	TO right after first arch. Follow R3 through second arch. TL. TR into Gotthardstrasse. Follow quiet road over motorway to somewhat busier road. On R3 RT to Rothenburg.
17	Rothenburg (542m)	Over hill in town centre. Descend to cycleway on road. TL to follow quiet road to reach and cross airfield in Emmen. (Beware if it's in use!)
20	Emmen (428m) (R9)	Follow path right along River Reuss. Cross to right bank and stay on this side until directed across a bridge in the *Altstadt* (historic quarter).
26	Luzern (436m)	LT into Krongasse, left on Jesuitenplatz into Bahnhofstrasse. SO to station, landing stages and TO in station. Cross River Reuss away from station following Meggen signs. LF to Meggen on RR38.
29	Top of hill by Meggen (484m)	SO to Küssnacht.
38	Küssnacht	Road to Immensee.
43	Immensee	RT towards Arth along RR77.
51	Arth	RR77 to Sattel.

62	Sattel (750m)*	LT. Climb R9 towards Rothenthurm. Take the military option road rather than R9 unless you value riding on rough tracks through cow pats well away from any traffic. Rejoin R9 by TL in Erste Altmatt on the other side of Rothenthurm. Follow R9 to Biberbrugg and Einsiedeln. Section on road to Einsiedeln.
81	Einsiedeln (905m)	R9 LT through town centre and cross viaduct to Willerzell (889). RT. Follow RR76 to Ibergeregg.
99	Ibergeregg (1406m)	RR76 to Schwyz.
110	Schwyz (516m)	RR76 to Seewen. RR77 to Brunnen. R3/4 to Gersau.
126	Gersau (435m)	

* RT in Sattel for a short cut to Steinen, Seewen and Brunnen.

FACILITIES							
	Distance (km)	Camp site	YH/BP	B&B	Hotel	Station	Bike shop
Sempach	8	✓		On camp site	2	✓	✓
Rothenburg	17				1	✓	✓
Emmen	20			✓		✓	✓
Luzern	26	✓	✓	✓	Many	✓	✓
Meggen	31			✓	4	✓	
Küssnacht	38	✓			Many	✓	
Immensee	43				4	✓	
Arth	51				3	✓	
Sattel	62	✓		✓	4	✓	
Steinen	64			✓			
Rothenthurm	66				Many	✓	
Biberbrugg	76				1	✓	
Einsiedeln	81				Many		
Willerzell	85			✓			
Ibergeregg	99				1		
Schwyz	110		✓	✓	Many	✓	
Brunnen	119	✓		✓	Many	✓	✓
Gersau	126		✓		Many	Ship	

TOURIST INFORMATION			
From/to	Name	Address	Telephone/Website
Sursee/ Küssnach	Luzern Tourismus AG	Tourist Board Zentralstrasse 5 CH-6002 Luzern	+41 (0)41 227 1717 www.luzern.org/en
Arth/Gersau	Schwyz Tourismus	Bahnhofstrasse 4 Postfach 655 CH 6431-Schwyz	+41 (0)41 855 5950 www.schwyz-tourismus.ch

Stage 3: Gersau – Linthal
73km; 1290m; difficult

This is a quiet stage on a very minor road over a little-known pass – the Pragelpass. There are few villages until you reach the Linth Valley so stock up on essentials before leaving Brunnen. Leaving the wonderfully coloured Vierwaldstätter See behind, the route heads right into Muotathal guarded by tooth-like red limestone hills and into a remote world of farm, forest and crags. It is not surprising that few venture

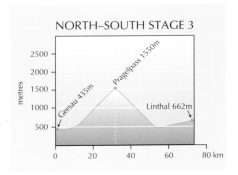

NORTH–SOUTH STAGE 3

Gersau 435m
Pragelpass 1550m
Linthal 662m

In Klöntal

up the Pragelpass but the views are rewarding and the cycling testing as the pass climbs and climbs. Just above the treeline, then into a territory of goats and limestone pavements before a rapid descent on an almost traffic-free road towards dramatic scree-draped slopes above the Klöntalersee. There's another tremendous freewheel down into the wide streets of Glarus, then along the valley, rising gradually to Linthal, formerly a textile centre.

In bad weather or for a day off, you can get there by train, taking a circuitous route.

ITINERARY		
Distance Location (km)		**Directions**
0	Gersau (435m)	R3/4 to Brunnen.
9	Brunnen (435m)	LT in village then RT on minor road to Schonenbuch. Climb through Muotathal (626m) to reach Pragelpass summit.
34	Pragelpass (1550m)	Drop down on RR83 through Richisau, Klöntal and Riedern to Glarus.
55	Glarus (472m)	Follow road to Schwanden.
63	Schwanden (521m)	Follow minor road to east of main road to Betschwanden. Follow R4 to Linthal.
73	Linthal (662m)	

FACILITIES							
	Distance (km)	**Camp site**	**YH/BP**	**B&B**	**Hotel**	**Station**	**Bike shop**
Brunnen	9	✓		✓	Many	✓	✓
Muotathal	18				2		
Richisau	35				1		
Klöntal	40				1		
Riedern	53				2		
Glarus	55			✓	Many	✓	✓
Mitlödi	60			✓	1	✓	
Schwanden	61				3	✓	✓
Rüti	71					✓	✓
Linthal	73				4	✓	✓

TOURIST INFORMATION			
From/to	**Name**	**Address**	**Telephone/Website**
Gersau/ Pragelpass	Schwyz Tourismus	Bahnhofstrasse 4 Postfach 655 CH-6431 Schwyz	+41 (0)41 855 5950 www.schwyz-tourismus.ch
Pragelpass/ Linthal	Touristinfo Glarnerland	Raststätte A3 CH-8867 Niederurnen	+41 (0)55 610 2125 www.glarusnet.ch/tourismus/ htm/to_eng.htm

Stage 4: Linthal – Altdorf
46km; 1300m; difficult

There are not many kilometres today, but a lot of vertical metres. The Klausenpass should be approached with care, as it is quite a climb, but gives great views towards Hausstock and other 3000m mountains to the south. At weekends the road is extremely busy. On the descent take especial care on exposed corners, since uphill motorcyclists use the middle of the road to avoid flimsy barriers.

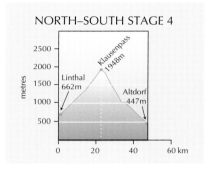

There are magnificent bird's eye views of Unterschächen before a short climb and a final gentle spin into Altdorf. This was, by tradition, Wilhelm Tell's home town, marked by a suitably heroic statue in the market square. If you are feeling full of get up and go you can shorten tomorrow's 1650m climb by continuing to Erstfeld and beyond. You could also cycle down to Flüelen and doze on the beach. There are plenty of hotels in Flüelen and the next three days are fairly tough going.

In bad weather or for a day off, take the Postbus.

ITINERARY		
Distance (km)	**Location**	**Directions**
0	Linthal (662m)	Climb to Urner Boden on R4.
15	Urner Boden (1372m)	Over the Klausenpass (1948m) through Unterschächen and Spiringen to Altdorf.
46	Altdorf (447m)	Pay homage to Wilhelm Tell.

FACILITIES							
	Distance (km)	**Camp site**	**YH/BP**	**B&B**	**Hotel**	**Station**	**Bike shop**
Urner Boden	15				1		
Klausenpass	23				1		
Unterschächen	31				1		
Altdorf	46	✓		✓	Many	✓	✓
Flüelen	49	✓		✓	Many	✓	✓

TOURIST INFORMATION			
From/to	Name	Address	Telephone/Website
Linthal/ Klausenpass	Touristinfo Glarnerland	Raststätte A3 CH-8867 Niederurnen	+41 (0)55 610 2125 www.glarusnet.ch/tourismus/ htm/to_eng.htm
Klausenpass/ Flüelen	Tourist Info Uri	Tellspielhaus Schützengasse 11 Postfach CH-6460 Altdorf	+41 (0)41 872 0450 www.uri.info

Stage 5: Altdorf – Disentis
68km; 1590m; strenuous

A word of warning: after Erstfeld you are committed to cycling as far as Göschenen, which has the next railway station. The road between Göschenen and Andermatt, through the Schollenen Gorge, is to be avoided. It's a steep busy, main road with trucks, caravans and long dark snowsheds. Avoid this by taking the train for 5km to Andermatt.

If you really want to 'do' this part of the route, then book into accommodation in Andermatt, nip back on the train and walk up the path from Göschenen Station. This is

Cheerful, colourful Swiss pensioners in a wet Disentis

less pleasant now since the path on the avalanche gallery roofs is closed, because of rockfall danger. It is a two-hour walk allowing a visit to the Surovrov Monument and the Devil's Bridge. The Russian general Count Surovrov's forces took part in the Napoleonic wars and fought their way through here returning home from Italy. The monument is situated on Russian territory. The

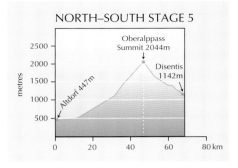

NORTH–SOUTH STAGE 5

Devil's Bridge was built in 1830 replacing an earlier bridge that was supposedly built by the Devil, the price for constructing it being the soul of the first being to cross the bridge. The locals, naturally, sent a goat across.

If you want to make the trip a day shorter, take R3 over the St Gotthard Pass on an easy old road built for horses and drop down into Airolo and Biasca. Otherwise continue to Disentis via the relatively easy Oberalppass from Andermatt.

ITINERARY		
Distance Location (km)		**Directions**
0	Altdorf (447m)	R3 to Erstfeld.
7	Erstfeld (458m)	LT to station and hotels, otherwise SO on R3 to Gurtnellen.
19	Gurtnellen (700m)	RT into village for hotel. Take old Gotthard road uphill on R3 to Wassen.
25	Wassen (916m)	Take old road uphill on R3 to Göschenen.
30	Göschenen (1100m)	Veloland Schweiz recommends taking the train to Andermatt. Take main road to Andermatt on R3 if very brave and well insured. There is a zebra crossing well up the hill, which allows access to a good unsurfaced road on left to the Devil's Bridge, the Surovrov Monument and back to the Andermatt road.
36	Andermatt (1436m)	TO on corner by station with list of B&Bs. Follow R1/R2/R3 then TL to follow R2 on road over Oberalppass. Dark snowshed near summit.
47	Oberalppass (2044m)	Follow R2 on road through Sedrun to Disentis.
68	Disentis (1142m)	

FACILITIES							
	Distance (km)	Camp site	YH/BP	B&B	Hotel	Station	Bike shop
Erstfeld	7				Many	✓	
Gurtnellen Station	19				2		
Wassen	25				Many		
Göschenen	30	✓			Many	✓	
Andermatt	36		✓ (Hospental)	✓	Many	✓	✓
Oberalppass	47				1	1	
Tschamut	54				1	✓	
Rueras	59	✓			2		
Sedrun	61				Many	✓	
Disentis	68	✓			Many	✓	✓

TOURIST INFORMATION			
From/to	Name	Address	Telephone/Website
Flüelen/ Oberalppass	Tourist Info Uri	Tellspielhaus Schützengasse 11 Postfach CH-6460 Altdorf	+41 (0)41 872 0450 www.uri.info
Oberalppass/ Disentis	Graubünden Vacation	Alexanderstrasse 24 CH-7001 Chur	+41 (0)81 254 2424 http://ferien. graubuenden.ch/en

Stage 6: Disentis – Bellinzona
84km; 900m; moderate

This stage is busy at weekends and on public holidays, but during the week the Lukmanierpass/Passo del Lucomagno road is quiet. There are tunnels and snowsheds on both sides. Soon after leaving Disentis the road twists through a short gorge with tunnels then climbs and snakes upwards though delightful green meadows. The Lukmanier summit is only just above the treeline and almost immediately below the summit reservoir and Ospice you enter a landscape of white pines and pastures. Limestone crags make jagged summits contrasting with peat filled moorland hollows, giving a tremendous range of plant and wildlife habitats.

It's almost a wrench to descend a layer but RR36 provides a superb terrace run through romantic villages down to the vineyards and into Biasca. Once in the main valley don't miss the open air stray cats' home on the outskirts of Bellinzona, although there's unlikely to be room in your panniers to take one with you.

In bad weather or for a day off, take the Postbus.

Lukmanierpass summit

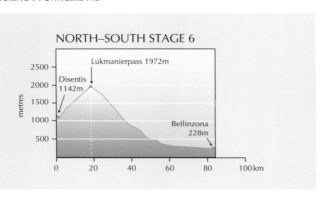

NORTH–SOUTH STAGE 6

ITINERARY		
Distance Location (km)		Directions
0	Disentis (1142m)	Follow RR36 towards the Lukmanier summit.
20	Lukmanierpass summit (1972m) in tunnel	Follow road downhill.
24	Acquacalda (1700m)	Shortly after Acquacalda, **T** take RR36 left **RB** stay on road.
29	Campra (1410m)	Shortly after Campra follow the RR36 signpost (right for **RB**) to follow an almost unused section of old road. Take the signposted very quiet surfaced road off right at the peak of the next left turn hairpin to travel through Largario, Ponto Valentino, Marolta, Prugiasco, Acquarossa, Dongio, Ludiano to Biasca.
61	Biasca (300m)	Follow R3 under motorway and over River Ticino. Left at minor road to Iragna.
64	Iragna (287m)	LT on to R3 surfaced cycleway, later good unsurfaced path to Moleno.
72	Moleno (270m)	R3 through Preonzo. Left over road bridge. Left to surfaced cycleway to Castione.
78	Castione (242m)	R3 (cycleway, quiet road) to Bellinzona.
84	Bellinzona (228m)	Follow *stazione* signs to reach shops and TO.

FACILITIES							
	Distance (km)	Camp site	YH/BP	B&B	Hotel	Station	Bike shop
Curaglia	6				1		
Lukmanierpass summit	20				1		
Acquacalda	24				1		
Biasca	61	✓			Many	✓	
Bellinzona	84	✓	✓	✓	Many	✓	✓

TOURIST INFORMATION			
From/to	Name	Address	Telephone/Website
Oberalppass/ Disentis	Graubünden Vacation	Alexanderstrasse 24 CH-7001 Chur	+41 (0)81 254 2424 http://ferien. graubuenden.ch/en
Passo del Lucomagno (Lukmanierpass)/ Bellinzona	Ticino Tourismo	Casa postale 1441 Via Lugano 12 CH-6501 Bellinzona	+41 (0)91 825 7056 www.ticino-tourism.ch

Stage 7: Bellinzona
95km; 1120m; difficult

Lago Maggiore near Vira with Mt Gambarogno behind

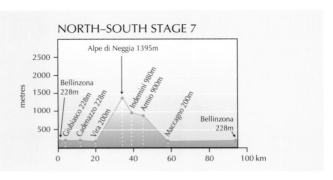

NORTH–SOUTH STAGE 7

Stop two nights in Bellinzona. This means you will have a lighter bike for the trip to Indemini over the Alpe di Neggia. This is a last spin that brings the cyclist high into the hills, a 1200m climb, with superb views of Lago Maggiore and the Alps to the north. **You leave Switzerland today so do not forget your passport.**

The road over the Alpe di Neggia, through mature chestnut woods, is shadier in the mornings. Once back on the Lago Maggiore shoreline it is best to head for Luino, since there are many more ships from Luino to Locarno than from Maccagno. You will need to inform the cashiers at the pier in Luino that you have a bicycle, so they can ask the captain whether he is prepared to take it. They will say yes, but they like to be asked.

In bad weather, stay in bed!

ITINERARY		
Distance Location (km)		Directions
0	Bellinzona (228m)	Follow R3 towards Chiasso and Lago Maggiore to Giubiasco.
4	Giubiasco (228m)	RT over motorway on surfaced farmer's road to R3 left (4km after motorway) to Cadenazzo.
12	Cadenazzo (228m)	RT onto busy road to Magadino and Vira. Take LF to Quartino to avoid traffic.
20	Vira (200m)	LT signposted Indemini, Alpe di Neggia. Minor road.
34	Alpe di Neggia (1395m)	SO to Indemini.
39	Indemini (980m)	SO to Armio (Italy), signposted Italia.
45	Armio (900m)	SO to Maccagno.
58	Maccagno	TR to return to Switzerland. If you wish to use public transport, you should TL to Luino (6km) and take the ship to Locarno.
95	Bellinzona	

You might need it on the way up: the Postbus in Indemini

If you wish to collect more passes then you have at least three options:

- take R6 from Bellinzona to Chur via Thusis (128km, 1881m).
- ride up to Andermatt and follow the Alpine Star Routes.
- take R3 north to Airolo from Bellinzona and follow the road over the Nufenenpass/Passo de Novena from Airolo, following signs to Oberwald (see chapter 1). From Oberwald you can follow R1 over the Furkapass, through Gletsch to Andermatt.

ROUTE SUMMARY		
From/to	Distance (km)	Climb (m)
Bellinzona/Airolo	62	920
Nufenenpass/Gletsch	47	1748
Furkapass: Gletsch/Andermatt	31	672

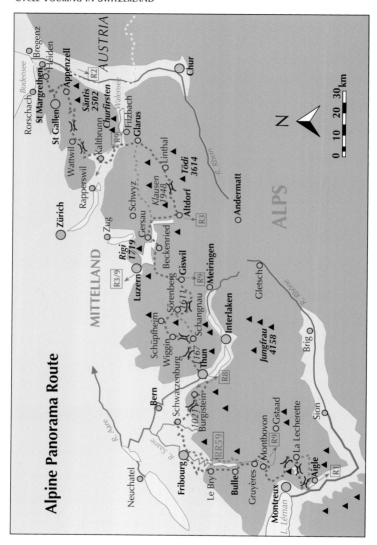

Alpine Panorama Route

4 THE ALPINE PANORAMA ROUTE, R4

ROUTE SUMMARY					
From/to	Distance (km)*	Climb (m) with public transport	Climb (m) without public transport	Grade with public transport	Grade without public transport
St Margrethen/ Aigle	489 (10)	5130	7550	Difficult	Strenuous
Aigle/ St Margrethen	489 (10)	5510	7720	Difficult	Strenuous
* without the prologue and epilogue					

SUMMARY OF STAGES (WITHOUT PUBLIC TRANSPORT)				
Stage	From/to	Distance (km)	Climb (m)	Grade
Prologue	Rorschach	25	0	Easy
	or Bregenz/St Margrethen	17	0	Easy
1	St Margrethen/Heiden	17	500	Moderate
2	Heiden/Kaltbrunn	76	1300/1630	Difficult/Strenuous
3	Kaltbrunn /Gersau	110	1700	Strenuous
4	Gersau/Sörenberg	57	1200	Difficult
5	Sörenberg/Burgistein	RB: 73 T: 55	1100	Difficult
6	Burgistein/Bulle	78	630	Moderate
7	Bulle/Aigle	78	1120	Difficult
Total	**St Margrethen/Aigle**	**489**	**7550**	
Epilogue	Aigle/Montreux	15	0	Easy

LOCAL MAPS	
Swisstopo 1:100,000 Composite	
101	Thunersee–Zentralschweiz
102	Basel–Luzern
103	Zürich–St Gallen
105	Valais–Wallis

This is another route for fit cyclists, with superb views of the Alps, not suitable for families. There is almost no unsurfaced track apart from the additional kilometres suggested at the start, so it is a good route for narrow tyred road bikes and those who ride them. The route climbs and traverses Switzerland from NE to SW through the hills of Appenzell with glimpses of Säntis, over the Klausenpass (1948m), around the Vierwaldstätter See, into the little known hills north of the Brienzer Rothorn. Then it descends into Thun before climbing into the French speaking Suisse Romande near

115

Churfirsten Mountains (Stage 2)

regional route rather than the national route before reaching remote hills and a fabulous long drop into the vineyards of the Rhône Valley. The route can be only cycled between June and October. The pass roads are closed at other times. The stretch between St Margrethen and Fribourg/Freiburg is German speaking. There you cross the Röstigraben (rösti trench – the language border) into French-speaking Switzerland.

One thing clear to us is that hotel prices in Switzerland can be a major problem. This route has been planned to stop in the cheapest accommodation we could find and ignored a couple of hundred additional metres and/or extra kilometres that this entails. This is budget bikers' route planning. Obviously you can stop in more luxurious hotels. If you are in a larger group then you will need alternative accommodation to the B&B, which normally only take one or two couples. The first day is a short one, so as to give time to adjust the bike, loosen up the legs or recover from jet lag.

LINKS TO OTHER ROUTES		
Location	**Route/s**	**To**
St Margrethen	R2: Rhein Route	West: Basel
		South: Chur, Andermatt
	R9: Lakes Route	Luzern, Gstaad, Montreux
Kaltbrunn	R9: Lakes Route	West: Luzern, Gstaad, Montreux
		East: St Margrethen
Altdorf	R3: North–South Route	North: Luzern, Basel
		South: St Gotthard Pass, Lago Maggiore, Chiasso
Stansstad/ Giswil	R9: Lakes Route	East: Rorschach (Bodensee)
		West: Gstaad, Montreux
Thun	R8: Aare Route	North: Bern, Koblenz
		South: Gletsch
Bulle	R9: Lakes Route	West: Montreux
		East: Gstaad, Luzern, Rorschach (Bodensee)
Aigle	R1: Rhône Route	West: Genève
		East: Martigny, Gletsch, Andermatt

PUBLIC TRANSPORT BACKUP		
Section	**Service**	**Comment**
Rorschach – Heiden	Train	
Appenzell – Urnäsch	Train	
Wattwil – Linthal	Train	
Linthal – Altdorf	Postbus	*End June to end September*
Flüelen – Brunnen	Train	
Flüelen – Brunnen or Gersau	Ship	
Gersau – Beckenried	Car ferry	
Stansstad – Giswil	Train	*Luzern to Interlaken*
Giswi – Glaubenbielenpass – Sörenberg	Postbus	*End June to end September*
Sörenberg – Schüpfheim	Postbus	
Schüpfheim – Escholzmatt	Train	
Gruyères – Montbovon – Montreux	Train	

Prologue: Rorschach or Bregenz – St Margrethen
25 or 17km; 0m; easy

Both Rorschach and Bregenz have youth hostels. You can stop in Rorschach and have
an easy day by taking the rack railway to Heiden from Rorschach or you can fight the
crowds cycling along the Bodensee shore to St Margrethen, before the grind up the side
of the Rhein Valley.

ITINERARY		
Distance (km)	Location	Directions
0	Rorschach (398m)	Follow R2 to St Margrethen railway station or bypass the town and then pick up the R4 signs.
0	Bregenz (398m)	Follow Bodensee route to St Margrethen railway station or bypass the town and then pick up the R4 signs.

FACILITIES							
	Distance (km)	Camp site	YH/BP	B&B	Hotel	Station	Bike shop
Rorschach	0		✓		Many	✓	✓
Bregenz	0	✓	✓	✓	Many	✓	✓
St Margrethen	25 (from Rorschach) 17 (from Bregenz)	✓			1	✓	✓

TOURIST INFORMATION			
From/to	Name	Address	Telephone/Website
Rorschach/ St Margrethen	Internationale Bodensee Tourismus GmbH	Hafenstrasse 6 D-78462 Konstanz	+49 (0)75 31/90 9490 www.bodensee-tourismus.com
Bregenz/ St Margrethen	Vorarlberg Tourismus	Bahnhofstrasse 14 A-6901 Bregenz	+43 (0)55 7442 5250 http://www.vorarlberg.travel

Stage 1: St Margrethen – Heiden
17km; 500m; moderate

Church near Heiden

St Margrethen is a good supply stop. The hills start as you leave the built-up area and it's a 500m ascent to Oberegg before dropping into Heiden, where there is at least one budget hotel. Nearby, to the west, there are two B&Bs in the oddly named village of Grub. Henri Dunant, the founder of the Red Cross, lived in Heiden for 23 years and is commemorated by a museum.

In bad weather, take the train from Rorschach.

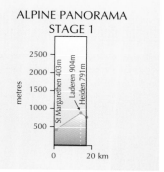

ALPINE PANORAMA STAGE 1

ITINERARY

Distance (km)	Location	Directions
0	St Margrethen (403m)	Leave St Margrethen railway station on R2 and follow R4 through Au and Oberegg to Heiden.
17	Heiden (807m)	

FACILITIES

	Distance (km)	Camp site	YH/BP	B&B	Hotel	Station	Bike shop
Au	6				1	✓	✓
Heiden	17				Many	✓	✓
Grub	19			2			

TOURIST INFORMATION

From/to	Name	Address	Telephone/Website
St Margrethen/ Heiden	Appenzellerland Tourismus AR	Bahnhofstrasse 2 CH-9410 Heiden	+41 (0)71 898 3300 www.appenzell.ch/en

Stage 2: Heiden – Kaltbrunn/Filzbach
76 or 93km; 1300 or 1630m; difficult or strenuous

This ride is marked by short, intense hills rising to 1100m. Canton Appenzell is Switzerland as we all imagine it, with small farms, men and women wearing brightly-coloured *Tracht* (traditional costume), views of the Alps to the south and, in Appenzell, the cantonal capital, a surfeit of souvenir shops selling dolls, penknives and pottery cows but redeemed by a fine market square.

In bad weather, you can get there by train, but you will need to change.

Checking the map in Wattwil

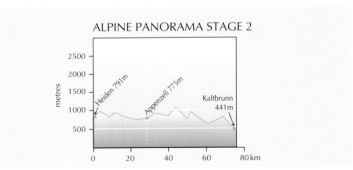

121

ITINERARY

Distance (km)	Location	Directions
0	Heiden (807m)	Follow R4 through Kaien to Trogen.
11	Trogen (903m)	Drop down and then climb to Speicher.
13	Speicher (910m)	Down and then up to Teufen.
16	Teufen (833m)	Follow quiet roads to Appenzell.
29	Appenzell (764m)	Climb out of Appenzell towards Urnäsch.
40	Urnäsch (832m)	On to almost 1100m after Cinchona. A drop of 100m into the valley near Hemberg is followed by a 200m climb into the village. R4 makes a long drop into Wattwil.
61	Wattwil (613m)	Follow R4 over the low pass (805m) after Ricken and drop into Kaltbrunn.
76	Kaltbrunn (441m)	If you wish to stop in the nearby YH in Filzbach follow R4/9 through Schänis and Ziegelbrücke to Niederurnen. Follow R9 to the turnoff to Filzbach and then climb 310m.

FACILITIES

	Distance (km)	Camp site	YH/BP	B&B	Hotel	Station	Bike shop
Trogen	11				3	✓	✓
Speicher	13				4	✓	✓
Teufen	16				Many	✓	✓
Appenzell	29	✓		✓	Many	✓	✓
Urnäsch	40				Many	✓	✓
Hemberg	50	✓		✓	Many		
Wattwil	61				3	✓	✓
Kaltbrunn	76		✓		2	✓	✓
Oberurnen	88						✓
Filzbach (off route)	93		✓		Many		

TOURIST INFORMATION

From/to	Name	Address	Telephone/Website
Heiden/ Filzbach	Ostschweiz Tourismus	Bahnhofplatz 1a CH-9001 St Gallen	+41 (0)71 227 3737 www.ostschweiz.ch

Stage 3: Kaltbrunn – Gersau
over the Klausenpass or through the Klöntal Valley
110 or 100km; 1700m; strenuous

Klausenpass. Take care!

The route crosses a wide plain, meets R9 and then beyond Niederurnen after R9 turns off, enters a narrow valley to reach Glarus, the canton's capital. From there you can swing right on RR83 over a 1550m pass through Riedern and Hinter Klöntal and over the Pragelpass to Schwyz and Brunnen via Muotathal. This is an especially striking but tough route (see chapter 3). The Pragelpass road opens late but is closed near the summit to motorised traffic at weekends in summer.

The direct route heads to Linthal and the Klausenpass (1948m) road. You can take a bus over the pass but only from the end of June to the end of September (to secure bike transport book the trip in advance by telephone: (0)41 870 2136). From Linthal the first few hairpins retain cobbles on the bends and have short tunnels. Enjoy the Alpine views to the south before reaching the open hanging valley, inhabited by many, many cattle. The final ascent is another serious climb taking you where no one would ever think to build a road and to the essential café at the top. **Take great care at weekends on the descent** as there is one narrow stretch with a 400m drop to the left, which has

123

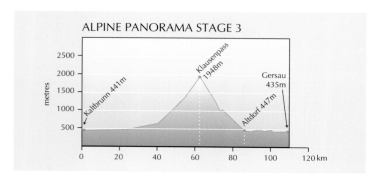

very poor safety barriers. The weekend motorcycling fraternity love to test their skills by staying as close as possible to the middle line, so make sure you keep well over to the right on the bends.

It is a long wonderful freewheel to Altdorf and Flüelen, on the photogenic Vierwaldstätter See. Altdorf was Wilhelm Tell's base, celebrated by a suitably heroic monument. North from Flüelen R4 uses the Axenstrasse, an old military road cut into the cliff sides above the lake. The Swiss cycling authorities recommend you take a ship or a train to Brunnen. The road can be very busy and has tunnels, but has had a makeover with a cycleway, mostly shared with walkers. If you start the Axenstrasse and change your mind halfway along, there is a railway station and harbour in Sisikon.

In bad weather or for a day off, take the train, Postbus or ship.

ITINERARY		
Distance (km)	Location	Directions
0	Kaltbrunn (441m)	Follow R4, then R4/9 to Schänis.
6	Schänis (418m)	R4/9 towards Ziegelbrücke and Oberurnen.
11	Oberurnen (430m)	Follow R4.
15	Näfels (437m)	Follow R4.
20	Netstal (464m)	Follow R4.
24	Glarus (472m)	Follow road to Schwanden.
31	Schwanden (521m)	Follow minor road to east of main road to Betschwanden. Follow R4 to Linthal.
41	Linthal (662m)	Climb to Urner Boden on R4.
55	Urner Boden (1372m)	Over the pass (1948m) through Unterschächen and Spiringen to Altdorf.

87	Altdorf (447m)	Pay homage to Wilhelm Tell and then follow R3/R4 through the fields to Flüelen.
90	Flüelen (438m)	See notes on *Axenstrasse* above. The authorities recommend you take a ship or train to Brunnen.
102	Brunnen (436m)	Follow R3/R4 to Gersau on a minor road.
110	Gersau (435m)	

FACILITIES							
	Distance (km)	Camp site	YH/BP	B&B	Hotel	Station	Bike shop
Schänis	6					✓	✓
Näfels	15		✓		Many	✓	✓
Mollis	16			✓	1	✓	✓
Netstal	20				3	✓	✓
Riedern	22				2		
Glarus	24			✓	Many	✓	✓
Mitlödi	28			✓	1	✓	
Klöntal	37	✓			1		
Schwanden	31				3	✓	✓
Rüti	40					✓	✓
Linthal	41				4	✓	
Urner Boden	55				1		
Unterschächen	71				1		
Altdorf	87	✓		✓	Many (Schattdorf)	✓	✓
Flüelen	90	✓		✓	Many	✓	✓
Brunnen	102				4	✓	✓
Gersau	110		✓		Many		

TOURIST INFORMATION			
From/to	Name	Address	Telephone/Website
Filzbach/ Niederurnen	Ostschweiz Tourismus	Bahnhofplatz 1a CH-9001 St Gallen	+41 (0)71 227 3737 www.ostschweiz.ch
Niederurnen/ Klausenpass	Touristinfo Glarnerland	Raststätte A3 CH-8867 Niederurnen	+41 (0)55 610 2125 www.glarusnet.ch/tourismus/ htm/to_eng.htm
Klausenpass/ Flüelen	Tourist Info Uri	Tellspielhaus Schützengasse 11 Postfach CH-6460 Altdorf	+41 (0)41 872 0450 www.uri.info

Variation via Klöntal

ITINERARY		
Distance (km)	Location	Directions
0	Glarus (472m)	TR in town centre and follow Riedern and Klöntal signs (RR83).
2	Riedern (500m)	Climb towards Hinter Klöntal and on over the Pragelpass.
21	Summit (1550m)	Enjoy the downhill!
29	Muotathal (624m)	Follow Schwyz and Brunnen signposts, then Brunnen.
44	Brunnen (436m)	

Stage 4: Gersau – Sörenberg
57km; 1200m; difficult

It is a bit far to cycle round the lake through Luzern, so take one of the car ferries across to Beckenried or Niederdorf. Then it's a long easy trip through Stans with its elegant market square, Alpnach and Sarnen to Giswil. The climb of about 1200m to the summit of the Glaubenbielenpass (1611m) goes on and on but gives fantastic views over the lakes towards Luzern. You can take a bus, but only from the end of June to the end of September. To be certain of your

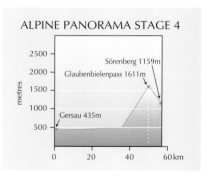

ALPINE PANORAMA STAGE 4

bike transport book the trip in advance by phone: 041 484 15 10. This is not the back of beyond but you can see it from here. There are no towns until Thun, but on the other hand you have good glimpses of the Alps to the south and quiet roads through pasture land and forest, through parts of Switzerland known only to aficionados and local farmers. Stock up on groceries when you get the chance. If you have time and the weather is good, take a cable car up to the summit of the Brienzer Rothorn for magnificent views of even more Alps to the south.

In bad weather or for a day off, take the ferry and then train or Postbus.

Salwedeli signpost in snow

ITINERARY		
Distance (km)	**Location**	**Directions**
0	Gersau (435m)	Take car ferry to Beckenried or cycle 2km towards Vitznau to take the car ferry to Niederdorf.
0 (car ferry)	Beckenried	Follow minor road to Niederdorf and pick up R3/4 to Buochs.
2	Buochs	Cycle through fields to Stans.
8	Stans	Follow R3/4 to Stansstad.
12	Stansstad	LT under motorway to follow R4/9 along lakeside past Alpnachstad, where you can take the steepest rack railway in the world to the summit of Mount Pilatus. Stay on R4 to reach Alpnach.
20	Alpnach	Follow R4 up and down dale to Sarnen, where R9 comes in again.
25	Sarnen	Follow R4/9 along the shore of Sarner See (Lake Sarnen) to Giswil.
35	Giswil	TR along R4 and climb 1125m in 13km to the pass summit on a very narrow minor road. Drop down in to Sörenberg.
57	Sörenberg (1159m)	There is more economical accommodation just beyond Sörenberg in a farmhouse B&B and an inn at Salwideli (follow R4 towards Schüpfheim, TL (signposted) in Südelhöchi, 200m climb).

127

FACILITIES							
	Distance (km)	Camp site	YH/BP	B&B	Hotel	Station	Bike shop
Beckenried	0			✓	Many	✓	
Buochs	2	✓			4		✓
Stans	8				Many	✓	✓
Stansstad	12				2	✓	✓
Alpnach	20	✓			4	✓	✓
Sarnen	25			✓	4	✓	✓
Giswil	35	✓			Many	✓	
Sörenberg	57	✓		✓	Many		
Salwideli (off route)	60			✓	1		

TOURIST INFORMATION			
From/to	Name	Address	Telephone/Website
Sisikon/ Giswil	Luzern Tourismus AG Tourist Board	Zentralstrasse 5 CH-6002 Luzern	+41 (0)41 227 1717 www.luzern.org/en/ welcome.cfm
Sörenberg	Sörenberg Flühli Tourismus	Rothorn-Center 2 CH-6174 Sörenberg	+41 (0)41 488 1185 www.soerenberg.ch

Stage 5: Sörenberg – Burgistein
RB: 73km, T: 55km; 1100m; difficult

Superb farmhouse near Thun

The stage starts with more up and down in the Voralpen, then climbs over the gentle Schallebergpass (a mere 1167m) before a long, intermittent glide into Thun and its interesting double decker old town. You cross the wide Aare Valley then climb into the hills again. Tourists can follow a shorter mountain bike route via Salwideli. It is not technically difficult but you may need to walk the odd stretch.

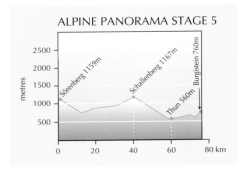

In bad weather or for an easier option, take the train to Thun.

ITINERARY		
Distance (km)	**Location**	**Directions**
0	Sörenberg (1159m)	**T** Follow R4 to Südelhöchi where there is a short cut, a road off left, which leads to Schangnau (17km). It features 1km or so of steep bumpy gravel, but is fine for touring bikes. It saves 24km, but the climb is about the same. **RB** Follow road to Schüpfheim. Insignificant tunnel just before Schüpfheim.
15	Schüpfheim (729m)	TL and follow a rolling R4 to Escholzmatt.
22	Escholzmatt (858m)	R4 towards Wiggen. TL through Marbach to Schangnau.
34	Schangnau (930m)	Towards Steffisburg on R4 over the Schallebergpass (much loved by motorcyclists).
39	Schallebergpass (1167m)	Steep drops and slight rises through Oberlangenegg, RT after Texan block house by Hot Spot Restaurant on very quiet roads through Unterlangenegg and Fahrni to Steffisburg.
56	Steffisburg (566m)	Follow trail alongside railway lines into Thun along R4/8.
58	Thun (560m)	R4 RT through underpass by railway station to Allmendingen.
62	Allmendingen (574m)	R4 TR towards Wahlen and Wattenwil.
71	Wattenwil (595m)	Climb up to Burgistein, just off R4 (B&B).
73	Burgistein (750m)	There is a hotel 330m above Rüti (Hotel Gurnigelbad tel: (0)31 809 0077). If the climb is too much the hotel will pick you up in Rüti.

FACILITIES							
	Distance (km)	Camp site	YH/BP	B&B	Hotel	Station	Bike shop
Kemmeriboden (on short cut)	12				1		
Schüpfheim	15				1	✓	✓
Escholzmatt	22				1	✓	
Schangnau	34	✓			Many		
Fahrni	54			✓			
Steffisburg	56				3	✓	✓
Thun	58			✓	Many	✓	✓
Allmendingen	62			✓			
Wattenwil	71			✓			✓
Burgistein	73	✓		✓			

TOURIST INFORMATION			
From/to	Name	Address	Telephone/Website
Sörenberg/ Marbach	Sörenberg Flühli Tourismus	Rothorn-Center 2 CH-6174 Sörenberg	+41 (0)41 488 1185 www.soerenberg.ch
Steffisburg/ Schwarzen- burg	Destinationen Berner Oberland	Postfach CH-3800 Interlaken	+41 (0)33 821 2870 www.berneroberland.ch

Stage 6: Burgistein – Fribourg/Bulle
78km; 630m; moderate

The route crosses into French-speaking Switzerland today. This is an easier stage, with a number of short but not too steep climbs with good views of the Berner Oberland mountains, verdant countryside, imposing farmhouses and some relaxing descents. On a warm day, you may be glad to call a halt in Fribourg with its dramatic walls and towers – time to explore the steep streets,

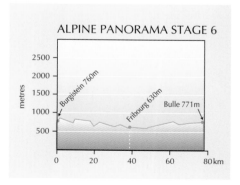

ALPINE PANORAMA STAGE 6

Looking across towards Fribourg near Burgistein

enjoy la vie Suisse and have a coffee or a Rivella in the shade – but be warned that you will need to climb back up that steep descent to continue on.

If you wish to pay the penalty of a longer last day's mileage, you could stay in the youth hostel in Fribourg. You climb back the way you came into town to leave R4 for a hillier variation through quiet roads on RR59 that brings you to Broc and its famous chocolate factory. (That is the white building on your left as you approach the village. If you miss it, follow the Nestlé signs.)

In bad weather or for a day off, take the Postbus.

ITINERARY		
Distance (km)	**Location**	**Directions**
0	Burgistein (750m)	Return to R4. Steep climb to Grundbach.
2	Grundbach (856m)	Follow R4 through Rüti (823m) towards Gräben. RT. Climb towards Mamishaus (796m) and Schwarzenburg.
18	Schwarzenburg (792m)	Drop into river gorge (653m) by Chatzenstig then climb to Heitenried (762m). LT through St Antoni and Tafers to Fribourg. Wonderful descent into city, but you will need to climb back up to the turnoff to RR59 later.
39	Fribourg (581m)	Follow R4 back towards Schwarzenburg. RT on RR59 towards Pierrafortscha, Tentlingen, RT, drop down and climb to Praroman, Treyvaux, Pont-la-Ville and La Roche. Slightly busier road to Corbières, Villavolard, Botterens and Broc.
67	Broc (718m)	RT to Morlon and Bulle.
78	Bulle (771m)	

FACILITIES							
	Distance (km)	Camp site	YH/BP	B&B	Hotel	Station	Bike shop
Schwarzenburg	18			✓	2	✓	✓
Fribourg	39	✓	✓	✓	Many	✓	✓
Pont-la-Ville	52				1		
Broc	67				2		
Morlon	75		✓		1		
Bulle	78			✓	Many	✓	✓

TOURIST INFORMATION			
From/to	Name	Address	Telephone/Website
Schwarzen-burg	Destinationen Berner Oberland	Postfach CH-3800 Interlaken	+41 (0)33 821 2870 www.berneroberland.ch
Fribourg/ Gruyères	Fribourg Region Information	Restoroute de la Gruyère CH-1644 Avry-dt-Pont	+41 (0)26 915 9292 www.fribourgregion.ch
Pont-la-Ville/ Bulle	La Gruyère Tourisme	Place des Alpes 26 CH-1630 Bulle	+41 (0)84 842 4424 www.la-gruyere.ch

Stage 7: Bulle – Aigle
78km; 1120m; difficult

This is heart attack country, not because the hills are frequent and steep but because of the products of the local farmers: cheese and a delicious double cream called Crème de la Gruyères (45 per cent fat!). The only cure is probably to cycle quickly through this area and descend to the Rhône Valley to drink red wine, a well-known way of avoiding heart problems. However the scenery and the views of the Alps will tempt you to linger.

You pass beneath Gruyères. It is a tiny place and has over a million visitors a year, so admire it from afar. From Montbovon, R4 climbs into remote wild valleys and over cols to pumped storage reservoir Lac de l'Hongrin, with more climbing to La Lecherette. This area from Montbovon to La Lecherette has no villages or shops and there were no water points after the washrooms on Montbovon station, so **make sure your waterbottles are well topped up**. The road is tarmac all the way but is not well maintained and road bikers may want to push for 100m or so from time to time. There are few cars, so the short tunnel by the Lac de l'Hongrin, although wet, does not present any problems. There is a general store with an adjacent WC in La Lecherette.

After La Lecherette cyclists follow R4 through a military training area, which is only open on Saturdays and Sundays from June to October, and every day from 1 July to 15 August. However, there is a shorter, less hilly substitute route over the Col des Mosses through Ormont-Dessous with less spectacular views. It is a great descent into Aigle for those with strong nerves, through occasional tunnels.

In bad weather or for an easier option, take the train to Montbovon.

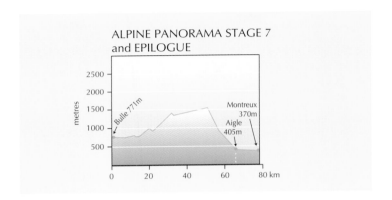

Lac de Hongrin reservoir

ITINERARY		
Distance (km)	Location	Directions
0	Bulle (771m)	Return to R4 on R9. RT and follow R4/9 towards Gruyères.
10	Gruyères (830m)	Cycle round Gruyères. The town lies 80m above you. Cycle on R4/9 through Grandvillard and Lessoc to Montbovon.
25	Montbovon (797m)	RT along R4 toward distant La Lecherette, roughish road in places. Short unlit tunnel near Hongrin. If military zone is open (see dates above), climb gradually to 1558m and then descend to Corbeyrier. Beware unlit tunnel on way down. Otherwise over Col des Mosses and thrilling descent to Aigle.
68	Corbeyrier (920m)	Follow steep road down to Aigle.
78	Aigle (405m)	

FACILITIES							
	Distance (km)	Camp site	YH/BP	B&B	Hotel	Station	Bike shop
Gruyères	10			✓	4	✓	
Enney	17	✓			1		
Grandvillard	17				1		
Montbovon	25			✓	1		
Corbeyrier	68			✓	1		
Aigle	78	✓		✓	3	✓	✓

TOURIST INFORMATION			
From/to	Name	Address	Telephone/Website
Bulle/ Montbovon	La Gruyère Tourisme	Place des Alpes 26 CH-1630 Bulle	+41 (0)84 842 4424 www.la-gruyere.ch/
Aigle	Aigle Tourisme	Rue Colomb 5 CH-1860 Aigle	+41 (0)24 466 3000 www.aigle.ch

Epilogue
15km; 0m; easy

The next youth hostel is in Territet, a Montreux suburb. The Montreux jazz festival takes place during the last two weeks of July. During this period it will be difficult to find accommodation in Montreux.

ITINERARY		
Distance (km)	Location	Directions
0	Aigle (405m)	Take RR to Villeneuve and Montreux.
15	Montreux (396m)	

FACILITIES							
	Distance (km)	Camp site	YH/BP	B&B	Hotel	Station	Bike shop
Villeneuve	11				3	✓	✓
Montreux	15	✓	✓	✓	Many	✓	✓

TOURIST INFORMATION			
From/to	Name	Address	Telephone/Website
Villeneuve/ Genève	Office du Tourisme du Canton de Vaud	Avenue d'Ouchy 60 Case Postale 164 CH-1000 Lausanne 6	+41 (0)21 613 2626 www.lake-geneva-region.ch

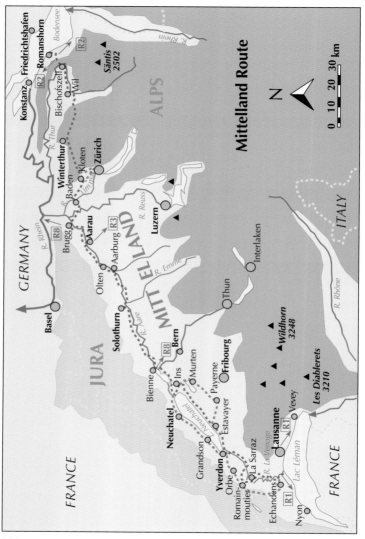

5 THE MITTELLAND ROUTE, R5

ROUTE SUMMARY

From/to	Distance (km)	Climb (m) with public transport	Climb (m) without public transport	Grade with public transport	Grade without public transport
Romanshorn/ Lausanne	374 (85)	1280	1500	Easy	Moderate
Lausanne/ Romanshorn	374 (85)	1280	1490	Easy	Moderate

SUMMARY OF STAGES (WITHOUT PUBLIC TRANSPORT)

Stage	From/to	Distance (km)	Climb (m)	Grade
1	Romanshorn/Winterthur	75	360	Moderate
2	Winterthur/Aarau	79	390	Moderate
3	Aarau/Biel/Bienne	86	290	Easy
4	Biel/Bienne/ Yverdon-les-Bains	81	190	Easy
5	Yverdon-les-Bains/ Lausanne	53	270	Easy
Total	**Romanshorn/Lausanne**	**374**	**1500**	

LOCAL MAPS

Swisstopo 1:100,000 Composite	
102	Basel–Luzern
103	Zürich–St Gallen
104	Lausanne–Bern
111	Ajole–Fribourg

This is a tour for anyone who can ride a bike, as the distance and height variations show. It can be cycled in the opposite direction, but there is a short but steep climb at the start between Lausanne and Yverdon-les-Bains. Riders who enjoy greater challenges could use it as a warm up for Alpine routes, make some diversions or run some stages together.

Our description starts in Romanshorn, on the Bodensee and wends its way through gentle hills with good views of the Alps to the south. After Baden the route runs in tandem with R8 along the Aare valley via delightful towns like Solothurn. This is low land but is certainly not flat as Ice Age deposits provide plenty of short ascents and descents while avoiding the steeper slopes of the Jura to the northwest. Beyond Biel/Bienne R5 and R8 diverge. The Mittelland Route hugs the eastern shores of Lakes Biel and Neuchâtel on the way to Yverdon-les-Bains.

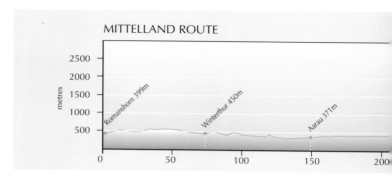

Across the two lakes the slopes of the Jura become closer and closer. The final section cuts through hills using wide and then narrow valleys that run roughly south/north leading to Lausanne and Lac Léman. There are some short steep climbs, through ancient La Sarraz, pinched by the rock outlier of Mormont. Riders seeking more climbing could take hillier routes south of Yverdon, as described later. Biel/Bienne marks the language border between French and German.

Neuchâtel (Stage 4)

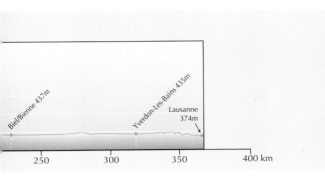

LINKS TO OTHER ROUTES		
Location	**Route/s**	**To**
Romanshorn	R2: Rhein Route	West: Basel
		South: Chur, Andermatt
Brugg	R8: Aare Route	North: Koblenz
		West: Bern, Thun, Gletsch
Aarau	R3: North–South Route	North: Basel
		South: Luzern, St Gotthard Pass,
		Lago Maggiore, Chiasso
Biel/Bienne	R8: Aare Route	East: Koblenz
(Hagneck)		South: Bern, Thun, Gletsch
Lausanne	R1: Rhône Route	East: Martigny, Gletsch, Andermatt
		West: Genève

PUBLIC TRANSPORT BACKUP	
Section	**Service/*Comment***
Romanshorn – Winterthur – Aarau – Biel/Bienne – Yverdon-les-Bains – Lausanne	Train
Romanshorn – Bischofszell – Wil	Train
Biel/Bienne – Yverdon-les-Bains	Lake steamer *June to October*

Stage 1: Romanshorn – Winterthur
75km; 360m; moderate

B&B near Bischofszell

Romanshorn is a transport node linking rail, road and lake systems. The lakeside is pleasant for picnics or even to have a swim. The tourist office is at the railway station with shops nearby. The route leads quickly up into fruit-growing country along the Seerücken, a ridge rising about 150m above the Bodensee. Apples, pears and soft fruit are netted against hailstones, rather than birds. In Hagenwil there is a small moated castle, with a restaurant.

Heading southwest, through small villages, orchards and forests with short steep rises and falls across the Sitter valley, the trail runs into Bischofszell, worth a visit with its ancient churches and merchants' houses. There is a notable change of landscape along the Thur valley to Wil, on gravel, pebbles and mud surfaces after rain, with a very rough slog up to Wil from the valley. (It might be better to walk.) Wil is an interesting mixture of walled town, ancient hostelries glimpsed through archways and a surprising new development next to the station. There are good views of the Alpine outliers to the south from the walls.

Beyond Wil, R5 heads west over low hills and pretty countryside, with farmhouses embellished by colourful gardens into the Toss valley. Remnants of water-powered textile production can be seen in Turbenthal. Winterthur, rather larger than Romanshorn, lies off the route 4km or so to the north. The old town is traffic free and prides itself on being bicycle friendly. The fortunes made by 19th century industrialists are reflected in the imposing buildings. There are several museums and lots of cafés.

In bad weather, take the train to Winterthur.

ITINERARY		
Distance (km)	**Location**	**Directions**
0	Romanshorn (399m)	From railway station by harbour LT towards Arbon, then RT by VSIB onto R5. Follow trail on minor roads over hill and dale to Bischofszell.
16	Bischofszell (506m)	Continue past station, town to right. (**RB** Continue on road along railway to Niederbüren and Oberbüren. Cross river to Sonnental, Züberwangen and Wil, then LT at rail station to rejoin R5.) **T** Zoom down moraines into Thur valley and over poor surfaces via Oberbüren to Wil.
34 (**RB** 40)	Wil (568m)	Through edge of town, over autobahn, through Sirnach, parallel to railway at first, then Balterswil, past Bichelsee on left, then meandering narrow valley route to Turbenthal, Zell and Kollbrunn on dedicated cycleways and quiet roads. **RB** SO in Sennhof to Winterthur on cycleway next to and on road. **T** Follow poor surface section of R5 through forest along river to autobahn underpass and RT into Winterthur to follow cycleway into town.
75 (**RB** 78)	Winterthur (560m)	

FACILITIES							
	Distance (km)	**Camp site**	**YH/BP**	**B&B**	**Hotel**	**Station**	**Bike shop**
Romanshorn	0		✓	✓	3	✓	
Lütschwil		✓					
Bischofszell	16			✓	Many	✓	✓
Wil	34			✓	3	✓	✓
Turbenthal	58				2	✓	✓
Winterthur	75	✓		✓	Many	✓	✓

TOURIST INFORMATION			
From/to	**Name**	**Address**	**Telephone/Website**
Romanshorn/ Wil	Internationale Bodensee Tourismus GmbH	Hafenstrasse 6 D-78462 Konstanz	+49 (0)75 31/90 9490 www.bodensee-tourismus.com
Winterthur	Zürich Tourism	Stampfenbachstrasse 52 Postfach CH-8023 Zürich	+41 (0)44 215 4000 www.zuerich.com

Stage 2: Winterthur – Aarau
79km; 390m; moderate

Little big city – Zürich

Just after Winterthur the route climbs steeply to Winterberg. Shortly beyond the village there is a hummock off to the right surrounded by trees. In clear weather this gives you a good view of the Alps. This stage links together hill crossings and valleys through one of the most densely populated parts of Switzerland close to the financial centre of Zürich and its airport. Inevitably the route approaches autobahns occasionally but it is overwhelmingly rural. Airports have a tendency to expand but, despite new roads, R5 is clearly signposted. Plane spotters can enjoy incoming aircraft.

Suburban train services also run from the airport into Zürich, an interesting highly prosperous little city, set on a lake and with many museums, cultural events and shopping opportunities. Walk down the Bahnhofstrasse and look in the jewellers' windows at watches that cost the price of a small car. You can also take a look down at Zürich from one of the three large church towers – Grossmünster, Frauenmünster or St Peter – and take a break from Swiss cuisine in the numerous 'ethnic' restaurants, tucked away in side streets. Lots of the locals cycle but road traffic is heavy and roadworks are always 'ongoing'.

Beyond Regensdorf, R5 returns to wide valley landscapes, and marshy nature reserves. A few drumlins raise the heartbeat. The walls and towers of Baden, a spa town since before Roman times, rise imposingly from the River Limmat and its wooden covered bridge. The public *Thermalbad* is by the river, before a short steep climb through the town. There is another twisting section through the forest before a lovely downhill ride above the Reuss, which flows into the River Aare downstream of Brugg.

In Windisch, as you approach Brugg, there is a superb set of 11 medieval stained glass windows in the monastery church (now part of a psychiatric hospital). Ancient castle walls and the Black Tower (disappointingly pale grey) go back to Roman times (Fortress Vindonissa). The old town is delightful with towers, churches and old merchants' houses including 'the Englishman's house'. Aarau nestles on the right bank of the river and has many impressive tall wooden buildings with painted overhanging eaves. Summer bathing is possible along the Aare.

In bad weather or for a day off, take the train.

ITINERARY		
Distance Location (km)		**Directions**
0	Winterthur (450m)	South out of town over autobahn on local cycleway to rejoin R5 and very steep climb to Winterberg then onto Lindau (**RB** avoid poor surface (2km) after Lindau by TL to Tagelswangen then TR to Baltenswil, then TR second R to rejoin R5). Continue on to Kloten (Zürich Airport). Route leads to edge of autobahn, along to south, then across bridge and by edge of airport buildings to VSIB in Glattbrugg. Use train or cycle into Zürich (9km) if you wish to visit.
17	Glattbrugg (430m)	TR by VSIB and follow trail among a multitude of airport offshoots – Rümlang, Affoltern and Regensdorf. (**RB** To avoid long poor section from Regensdorf to Hüttikon, TR in Regensdorf on road to Regensberg, then almost immediately TL via Buchs and Otelfingen to rejoin trail close to Wettingen.) **T** Take hard-packed trail along valley floor to Wettingen and nearby thermal resort of Baden.
44	Baden (383m)	R5 twists over low hills and along Reuss into Brugg, with its covered bridge. Leaving town after bridge over autobahn before Birmenstorf (note memorial to Wellington bomber crew right).
57	Brugg (358m)	R5 and R8 run together to the Bielersee/Lac de Biel. **RB** Avoid poor surfaces by using network of quiet roads on west of Aare, linking Villnachern, Veltheim, Auenstein and Biberstein into Aarau. **T** Follow river bank trail into Aarau. (Town is on the right bank.)
79	Aarau (371m)	

FACILITIES							
	Distance (km)	Camp site	YH/BP	B&B	Hotel	Station	Bike shop
Kloten	16			✓	✓	✓	✓
Glattbrugg	17				Many	✓	✓
Zürich	25	✓	✓	✓	Many	✓	✓
Dällikon	34				2		✓
Wettingen	43				4		✓
Baden	44		✓	✓	Many	✓	✓
Brugg	57		✓	✓	3	✓	✓
Aarau	79			✓	Many	✓	✓

TOURIST INFORMATION			
From/to	Name	Address	Telephone/Website
Winterthur/ Zürich	Zürich Tourism	Stampfenbachstrasse 52 Postfach CH-8023 Zürich	+41 (0)44 215 4000 www.zuerich.com
Baden/Aarau	Aargau Tourismus	Graben 42 Postfach CH-5001 Aarau	+41 (0)62 824 7624 www.aargautourismus.ch

Stage 3: Aarau – Biel/Bienne
86km; 290m; easy

This entire section follows the Aare upstream often through wide flat sections where the river meanders through fields and marshes to link Olten, Aarburg and Solothurn. These bridging points all have old town centres with interesting buildings, narrow streets and places to eat and drink. Olten has a covered bridge and the town is best viewed from the right bank of the river. The white painted houses built into the old town wall are crowned by the bell tower of the town church.

Railway enthusiasts will be interested to note that Olten became the first railway junction town in Switzerland in 1856. A dramatic narrow section close to the river bank leads to Aarburg, a rather forlorn little town grouped around a photogenic castle on a huge crag. After a brief section alongside an autobahn, R5 takes to the fields and woods above the Aare. The Aare is dammed for electricity production en route to Wangen, a delightful town with an ancient wooden bridge. In Solothurn the cathedral and old town perch on the left bank of the Aare, well worth a visit. After this you can look forward to the massive backdrop of the Jura from the valley floor (and a stork colony at Altreu).

Biel/Bienne is a Swiss town where both German and French are official languages so the names and signposts are somewhat confusing. The locals flip seamlessly between

Aarau gateway

Swiss German, High German and French. (It's the kind of situation that politicians seem to believe that people cannot cope with, so just enjoy this practical demonstration that it is quite normal.) The old town has an idiosyncratic *Rathaus/Hôtel de Ville* (town hall) and 'wedding cake' villas, but the cobbled streets are hard on the cyclist.

Biel developed quickly after the railway arrived, becoming the centre of industrialised watch-making. Well-known brands are still produced here. The level of Bielersee/Lac Biel was lowered by two metres in 1878 as part of a marshland-draining programme along the Aare, producing good wildlife habitats in shoreline reed beds. On the steep northern shores of the lake vines are grown. The cable car up the prominent

Magglingen hill west of Biel also takes bikes, making an excellent excursion in good weather. You can continue southwards along the western lake side.

In bad weather or for a day off, take the train.

ITINERARY		
Distance Location (km)		Directions
0	Aarau (371m)	Take riverside trail to Olten. (**RB** Avoid poor surface by staying on the north bank in Niedergösgen and taking road to Winznau to rejoin trail.)
14	Olten (419m)	Follow narrow gorge west side of Aare trail to Aarburg.
17	Aarburg (395m)	Short stretch of busy road, then quiet trails beyond Boningen to Fulenbach and Wolfwil. (**RB** Stay on road to Wolfwil.) Riverside route to Berken and Wangen, through river meadows to Solothurn, edged by light industries.
52	Solothurn (432m)	The route continues through a much wider valley, backed by steep Jura slopes to north. (**RB** Take minor roads through villages south of the Aare, such as Lüsslingen to Büren, and then rejoin north bank trail via bridge.) Route runs via Biel port and access to city is via RR64 over bridge by VSIB beyond Aegerten.
86	Biel/Bienne (437m)	

FACILITIES							
	Distance (km)	Camp site	YH/BP	B&B	Hotel	Station	Bike shop
Niedergösgen	4				1		✓
Schönenwerd (off route)	4				3	✓	✓
Olten	14			✓	Many	✓	✓
Aarburg	17	✓			2	✓	✓
Aarwangen	31				2		✓
Wangen-an-Aare	42		✓	✓	2	✓	✓
Solothurn	52	✓	✓	✓	Many	✓	✓
Grenchen (off route)	64			✓	3	✓	✓
Biel/Bienne	86	✓	✓	✓	Many	✓	✓

TOURIST INFORMATION			
From/to	Name	Address	Telephone/Website
Olten/Biel/ Bienne	Schweizer Mittelland Tourismus	c/o Bern Tourismus Amthausgasse 4 Postfach 169 CH-3000 Bern 7	+41 (0)31 328 1212 www.smit.ch

Stage 4: Biel/Bienne – Yverdon-les-Bains
81km; 190m; easy

Sandwiched between the two large lakes of Biel and Neuchâtel and the raised fluvio-glacial deposits bordering the Alpine foothills to the southeast are low elongated hills and large flat fields. These were probably all lakes that became marshes, originally difficult to cultivate and occupied by poor farmers. In modern times giant drainage alterations like that of the Aare into the Bielersee via the canal at Hagneck and drainage ditches have resulted in the peat soils becoming the basis for salad and vegetable-growing on a mighty scale.

At weekends it is great to see the cycleways are crowded with families, with youngsters in trailers or small bikes. R5 runs through flat land, a hive of farming activity during the summer. Fresh fruits and vegetables can be bought from wayside stalls or

'Danger tramlines' sign at the Hagneck Canal

farmhouses in season, including pick your own strawberries. The Jura, with forests above and vines below, provides a contrast across the lakes while each of the small towns on the shores – such as Le Landeron – has its own delights. Along the shoreline are hides for bird watching. Although off route, Neuchâtel is worth a visit, as perhaps the most typically French-feeling large town in Switzerland, spread along the lakeside with its namesake 'New Castle' dating from the 12th century right in the centre. This building is still partly used as cantonal offices. There is much to see in an amble round the old town when the sun lights up the golden sandstone buildings.

Leaving the lowlands, R5 climbs drumlins and twists high above Estavayer-le-Lac before plunging down through the picturesque little town. The low hills crowd closer to the water's edge, obscured by woods, nearing Yverdon-les-Bains, another spa town well-known to the Romans at the southwest end of Lac de Neuchâtel. This town guards the route south to Lac Léman, resulting in many fortresses before the present one built by Peter II of Savoy in 1261. In this castle Heinrich Pestalozzi began his work in 1805 by opening a school for poor boys. His methodology, placing the child's needs foremost is still practised today. The historic town has houses with decorated facades as well as lakeside leisure activities. The hot springs still function at the nearby spa.

In bad weather or an easier option, take the train and/or ship.

ITINERARY		
Distance Location (km)		Directions
0	Biel/Bienne (437m)	Return south across Aare and TR along east shore of Lac Biel/Bielersee, an undulating route, low hills on left. At Aare-Hagneck-Kanal junction TR over lock (R8 turns left away from lake). (**RB** Avoid next rough section by TL to Hagneck then TR over canal and along road to Lüscherz village.) Continue along lakeshore to Erlach and along canal across to Thielle between Lakes Biel and Neuchâtel. (**RB** Use road between Erlach and Ins.) Shortly after Thielle beside a VSIB those wanting to visit Neuchâtel should TR onto RR50/94 (+10km) on surfaced cycleways and minor roads.*
25	Thielle (440m)	At a VSIB, TL to Ins then TR across drained bog, now farmed, then TR along base of Mont Vully and climb southwest to Champmartin. TL and cross a road to follow a tarmac cycleway then TR at the next junction. (It may not be signposted.) The route goes close to lake shore via Portalban, Estavayer-le-Lac and Yvonand to Yverdon-les-Bains. (**RB** Avoid short poor section beyond Font by using road into Yvonand.)
81	Yverdon-les-Bains (435m)	

* Regional 50/94 continues from Neuchâtel along western shore of lake to join R5 in Yverdon.

FACILITIES							
	Distance (km)	Camp site	YH/BP	B&B	Hotel	Station	Bike shop
Ipsach	1				2		✓
Erlach	17	✓			4		
Le Landeron (off route)	22					✓	✓
Neuchâtel (off route)	36			✓	Many	✓	✓
Ins	30			✓	2	✓	✓
Avenches (off route)	52		✓		4	✓	
Estavayer-le-Lac	60	✓		✓	Many	✓	✓
Yvonand	72	✓		✓	1	✓	✓
Yverdon-les-Bains	81	✓	✓	✓	3	✓	✓

TOURIST INFORMATION			
From/to	Name	Address	Telephone/Website
Ipsach/Erlach	Schweizer Mittelland Tourismus	c/o Bern Tourismus Amthausgasse 4 Postfach 169 CH-3000 Bern 7	+41 (0)31 328 1212 www.smit.ch
Estavayer-le-Lac	Fribourg Region Information	Restoroute de la Gruyère CH-1644 Avry-dt-Pont	+41 (0)26 915 9292 www.fribourgregion.ch
Yverdon-les-Bains	Office du Tourisme du Canton de Vaud	Avenue d'Ouchy 60 Case Postale 164 CH-1000 Lausanne 6	+41 (0)21 613 2626 www.lake-geneva-region.ch

Alternatives
*   Along the northwestern edge of the Bielersee, to Twann, La Neuveville to Le Landeron and back to R5 or on to Neuchâtel and southwards to Yverdon-les-Bains. This uses RR50/94, a wonderfully varied route on surfaced, good unsurfaced cycleways and minor roads through Neuchâtel resort and gives a balcony panoramic view of the Alps.
*   From Ins south on R5, then turning left around the northern end of Mont Vully, famed for glacial erratics, into Bas-Vully and across the end of Lac de Morat then turning right into ancient Murten. Its walls conceal a small baroque pearl of a town, scene of a historic victory in 1476 when Swiss federal forces vanquished the Burgundian king, Charles the Bold. This route continues via Avenches, capital of Roman Switzerland where a sensational bust of Marcus Aurelius was found in 1939 (original now in Lausanne). Further south, Payerne is dominated by its massive Gothic abbey church. Cross over the old lake bed and continue via Bussy to Estavayer-le-Lac to rejoin R5.

Stage 5: Yverdon-les-Bains – Lausanne
53km; 270m; easy

Cumulus clouds over the Jura

The final section of R5 follows an ancient route on foot, horseback, along canals and rivers and more recently by rail and modern autobahn. Those with a historical interest should make a pilgrimage to Bosceaz, 2km north of Orbe, to visit extensive Roman mosaic remains on the site of a villa. South of Yverdon the wide Orbe valley is blocked by Mormont, a great chunk of limestone, rising to 600m. Clearly this was a good place to build a castle and walled town – La Sarraz –guarding the rich farmlands and forests and resulting in a steep climb for cyclists. Mormont defeated plans to build a canal to connect Lakes Léman and Neuchâtel, although there was a canal waterway between Yverdon and Cossonay up until 1829. At Mormont traces of workings can be seen in flooded ditches east of the SBB station at Eclépens. Plans for locks and a canal tunnel through Mormont were finally abandoned around 1980.

The trail continues southwards over spurs in the narrow La Venoge valley where beavers have made a comeback since 1950 after being hunted to extinction for their fur and meat. (Beavers could be eaten in Lent.) Beaver dams can sometimes be found near the Venoge inflow into Lake Léman.

Some say Lausanne is the prettiest city in Switzerland. Cyclists will find the somewhat vertical streets a challenge, but wonderful to ride down from the centre to the lakeshore. Snow-capped Alps rise around the lake and, in sunshine, Lac Léman's water sparkles blue and white. After days deprived of urban sights, or shops more exciting than a small supermarket, Lausanne deserves to be lingered over and enjoyed. Both guidebook information and on-the-spot tourist facilities are excellent. In the old town, Notre Dame cathedral, founded in 1245, is an elegant Gothic building despite several renovations. In Place de la Palud there are umpteen pavement cafés where you can indulge in people-watching.

Swiss cities are fascinating places because of the sheer variety of the people encountered. Lausanne has been a meeting point of religions, cultures, ideas, artists and politicians for many hundreds of years. Forget French and German and just try to guess the language being spoken or marvel at the dress (punk, exotic or fashionable) of the passers-by. Then there's window-shopping, perhaps a trip on a lake boat to arrange or a dip in the lake after a wander through the gardens. As you would expect, all this and more can be arranged at the tourist office at the station or in the Hôtel de Ville in the old town.

In bad weather, take the train.

ITINERARY		
Distance (km)	Location	Directions
0	Yverdon (435m)	Return to R5/RR22. Head southwest to autobahn, use underpass and continue on one or other side of the autobahn until the route takes to the valley proper south of Chavornay. (**RB** Avoid very rough surface beyond Bavois by taking local road over rail line to junction with track at tunnel.) Trail swings out into valley to avoid rock outlier of Mormont. At Orny, TL onto busy road for short distance into La Sarraz.
22	La Sarraz (490m)	Route from here is exciting with several steep ups and downs. Follow busy road to Eclépens then TR along track to Lussery, steep climb to cross railway then TR sharply into Cossonay.
32	Cossonay (434m)	Head south in narrow defile beside railway, then swing R to Gollion, then TL to return to valley and Moulin du Choc. (From here **RB** should TL across La Venoge river and take minor road parallel to railway, then rejoin route in Echandens.) The route has poor surface on west bank of river.
45	Echandens (432m)	Take busy road over autobahn south into Denges then continue to junction with R1 and TL to follow R1/5 to Lausanne.
53	Lausanne (374m)	YH in Vidy. TL at roundabout by camp site.

Eclépens with Mormont behind

FACILITIES							
	Distance (km)	Camp site	YH/BP	B&B	Hotel	Station	Bike shop
Orbe (off route)	12	✓			2	✓	
Chavornay	14	✓			1		
La Sarraz	22	✓		✓	2	✓	
Lausanne	53	✓	✓	✓	Many	✓	✓

TOURIST INFORMATION			
From/to	Name	Address	Telephone/Website
Yverdon-les-Bains/ Lausanne	Office du Tourisme du Canton de Vaud	Avenue d'Ouchy 60 Case Postale 164 CH-1000 Lausanne 6	+41 (0)21 613 2626 www.lake-geneva-region.ch

Alternative route from Yverdon to Lausanne

Distance: c50km; climb: c400m

Take R5 out of town south. By autobahn underpass TR onto RR50, along west edge of valley to Orbe, Romainmôtier-Envy, Moiry, Cuarnens, Chavannes le Veyron, Vullierens and Aclens then on to rejoin R5 at Echandens via Romenel and Bremblens. The autoroute around Lac Léman is a barrier to cyclists in places.

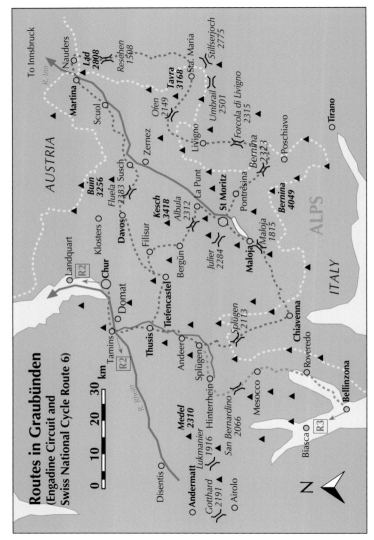

Routes in Graubünden
(Engadine Circuit and
Swiss National Cycle Route 6)

To Innsbruck

R. Inn

Nauders

Lad
2808

Resehen
1508

Std. Maria

Stilfserjoch
2775

Martina

Scuol

Tavra
3168

Ofen
2149

Umbrail
2501

Forcola di Livigno
2315

Livigno

Tirano

AUSTRIA

Zernez

Bernina
2323

Poschiavo

Susch

Buin
3256

Fluela

Susch
2383

La Punt

St Moritz

Bernina
4049

Klosters

Davos

Kesch
3418

Albula
2312

Pontresina

Filisur

Landquart

R2

Chur

Domat

Bergün

Julier
2284

Maloja
1815

Maloja

ALPS

Tamins

Tiefencastel

R2

Thusis

Andeer

Splügen
2113

Chiavenna

ITALY

Splügen

Roveredo

km

Mesocco

Bellinzona

R. Rhein

Medel
2310

Hinterrhein

San Bernardino
2066

R3

Lukmanier
1916

Biasca

0 10 20 30 km

Disentis

Andermatt

Gotthard
2191

Airolo

N

6 AN ENGADINE CIRCUIT, AND BEYOND
(BASED ON R6)

ROUTE SUMMARY					
From/to	Distance (km)*	Climb (m) with public transport	Climb (m) without public transport	Grade with public transport	Grade without public transport
Round trip from Chur	531	4180	7840	Strenuous	Strenuous

SUMMARY OF STAGES (WITHOUT PUBLIC TRANSPORT)					
Stage	From/to	Pass	Distance (km)	Climb (m)	Grade
1	Chur/Chiavenna	Splügenpass/ Passo dello Spluga	91	1540	Strenuous
2	Chiavenna/St Moritz	Majolapass	50	1490	Strenuous
3	St Moritz/Davos	Albulapass	79	1290	Difficult
4	Davos/Nauders	Flüelapass	83	1740	Strenuous
5	Nauders/Santa Maria	Reschenpass/ Passo di Résia	64	970	Difficult
6	Santa Maria/ Pontresina	Ofenpass/ Pass dal Fuorn, Forcola di Livigno, Passo del Bernina	78	1630	Strenuous
7	Pontresina/Chur	Albulapass	86	810	Difficult
Total	**Round trip**		**531**	**7840**	
Southern leg	Splügen/Bellinoza	San Bernadino	78	760	Moderate

* RB are directed away from the unsurfaced sections as far as possible.
There is one short (2km) unsurfaced but smooth section

LOCAL MAPS	
Swisstopo 1:100,000 Composite	
107	Ticino–Tessin
109	Basel–Luzern
110	Vorderrhein–Hinterrhein
Kompass 1:50,000	
WK 52 Vinschgau–Val Venosta	

Above Ardez in the Inn Valley (Stage 4)

R6 is the odd one out among Swiss National Cycle Routes because it consists of two legs, which divide or connect at Thusis in the Hinterrhein Valley. The eastern leg continues over the Albulapass to the Inn Valley (Engadine) then northeast to Martina on the Austrian border, with a short diversion to St Moritz. The southern leg continues up a Rhein tributary to the San Bernardino Pass and beyond to Bellinzona, almost on the Italian border. Both routes lie mostly within Graubünden, although the descent from the San Bernardino Pass leads into Italian-speaking Ticino.

Graubünden combines all the properties of wildness and romance that delighted so many early travellers to Switzerland, although it has become increasingly accessible. There's a wonderful mixture of 'Ruritanian' elements because of the Romansh language with dialects that change almost from village to village, the distinctive local architecture and characteristic Swiss efficiency in the transport links and tourism. Passes loop between many mountains over 3000m, raw peaks devoid of plants and between which considerable glaciers like those on Piz Bernina (4049m) glitter against clear blue skies. In Switzerland's only national park, bordered by the Inn Valley, not only do an amazing variety of plants, smaller animals and birds of prey including the bearded vulture find a home, but even lynx and the occasional bear have been spotted. The National Park Centre in Zernez is off the route but worth a detour for a wonderful introduction to the park.

Both Chur and Bellinzona are accessible by mainline SBB trains, and St Moritz and Scuol (close to Martina) by the little red trains of the Rhätische Bahn. It would be a pity to miss cycling at least part of these routes which are set among magnificent scenery and because the Engadine is culturally very different from better-known parts of Switzerland. The Thusis–Bellinzona segment, although not nearly as remote, is a superb ride.

Clearly the R6 would be enjoyed most by fit and experienced riders but some sections, such as the Albulapass northwards from La Punt to Alvaneu, are within most active cyclists' capability. Families with children between 11 to 15 have been known to complete this stage with enjoyment (tinged with wonder) after a few training days along the Inn.

Eastern Graubünden also contains fantastic possibilities. The Engadine Circuit, therefore, is a suggested route that follows sections of both branches of R6 but also includes excursions into Austria and Italy. It gives energetic cyclists the chance to ride high passes to their heart's content. The circuit starts and finishes in Chur, a thriving ancient city just downstream of Reichenau, at the confluence of two main Rhein tributaries. Chur has been a trading post (and talking shop) for travellers over the Alps for centuries. It is a good place to start or complete a bike trip, with rail connections, shopping facilities and a friendly tourist office. It has a truly Alpine feel. The mountains are already rather large and very close.

As a postscript, a description of the southern leg of Route 6, which goes from Splügen to Bellinzona, is also provided and this 78km stretch could be added on to your circuit for a slightly longer expedition.

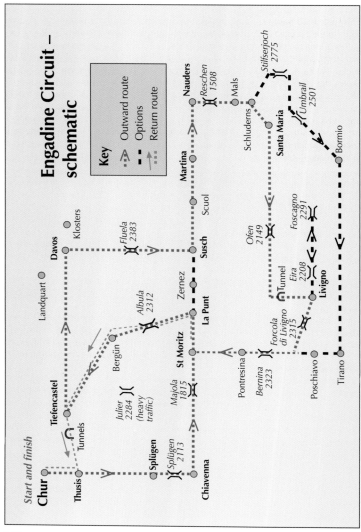

Engadine Circuit – schematic

Key

Outward route

Options

Return route

Start and finish

Chur

Thusis

Splügen 2113

Chiavenna

Tiefencastel

Tunnels

Julier 2284 (heavy traffic)

Majola 1815

Bergün

Albula 2312

Landquart

Davos

Klosters

Fluela 2383

St Moritz

La Punt

Zernez

Susch

Scuol

Martina

Nauders

Reschen 1508

Mals

Schluderns

Stilfserjoch 2775

Umbrail 2501

Santa Maria

Bormio

Ofen 2149

Foscagno 2291

Tunnel

Eira 2208

Livigno

Forcola di Livigno 2315

Poschiavo

Tirano

Pontresina

Bernina 2323

Note on the languages

This route is a linguistic dream or nightmare depending on your point of view. From Chur to the Splügen Pass summit the official languages are German and Romansh. Italian is then the official language until the Swiss border at Castasegna where the official language becomes Romansh, although German is spoken extensively. Not until the cyclist reaches Davos does the official language switch back to German. Shortly after Davos the official language reverts to Romansh until the Austrian border where it changes to German. At the next border crossing with the semi-autonomous Italian province of Südtirol it switches to German and Italian. This is followed by Romansh at the Swiss border. Once over the Pass del Fuorn/Ofenpass and through the tunnel, it becomes Italian once again. Shortly afterwards, in Switzerland, the official language becomes Romansh and remains so until Tiefencastel where the official languages are German and Romansh.

LINKS TO OTHER ROUTES		
Location	**Route/s**	**To**
Chur	R2: Rhein Route	North: Bodensee, Basel
		West: Andermatt
Bellinzona	R3: North–South	North: St Gotthard Pass, Andermatt, Luzern, Basel
		South: Lago Maggiore, Chiasso
Martina	The Inn Valley Cycleway	Landeck, Innsbruck, Passau

PUBLIC TRANSPORT BACKUP	
Section	**Service/Comment**
Chur – Thusis	Train
Thusis – Splügen	Bus
Thusis – Chiavenna	Train to St Moritz, bus to Chiavenna
	The Italian subcontractor to the Swiss Post will not take bicycles – not even folded Bromptons!
Chiavenna – St Moritz	Bus
St Moritz – Davos – Scuol	Train
	The Bernina and Glacier Expresses will not take bicycles, but local trains will.
Scuol – Nauders – Santa Maria	Bus
Santa Maria – Pontresina	Bus to Zernez, train to Pontresina
Livigno – Pontresina	Bus: Livigno – Bormio – Tirano.
	Train: Tirano – Pontresina – Chur
	It is up to individual bus drivers whether they take bicycles.
Pontresina – Chur	Train

Stage 1: Chur – Chiavenna
91km; 1540m; strenuous

After exploring the quaint alleys of Chur and stocking up on supplies of food, fluids and energy bars, it is time to head upstream into the mountains proper. Chur has a large Swiss army training area so do not worry if you hear gunfire or the occasional blast from heavy weapons as you ride south. The major chemical complex nearby may be considered a blot on the landscape, but the Swiss realised long ago that they couldn't eat the scenery. Jobs and exports matter too.

R6 out of Chur is unsurfaced and leads into the Hinterrhein valley below an unstable rock wall. Our advice is to take R2 from Chur, through Tamins, across the Vorderrhein confluence by Reichenau and into Bonaduz on the road. Then rejoin the signed route in Rothenbrunnen and continue to Thusis with its white church outlined against the dark trees. Beyond Thusis, the southern leg of R6 climbs steeply up several rock steps where the Rhein has cut a deep gorge, called the Via Mala. There are three noisy short tunnels – take your sunglasses off, put your lights on and keep pedalling. After the tourist stop where the Rhein is accessible down steep steps the road is quiet, though motorbikes make their presence felt at the weekends. Coaches travelling to the Via Mala viewpoint travel one way in the tunnel, towards you, which is not too bad.

The valley opens out pleasantly by Zillis, famed for its church of St Martin with painted ceiling lozenges dating from 1160. Another steep narrow climb brings you to

Intestinal curves on the Swiss side of the Splügenpass

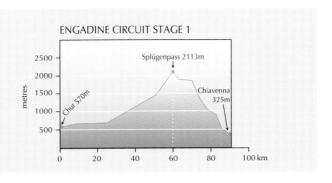

ENGADINE CIRCUIT STAGE 1

the amazing turquoise dammed lake near Sufers. 'Chocolate box' pictures may be taken on sunny days. From here it is a short stretch along this upland valley to the unspoiled compact village of Splügen. It has been cited many times as 'best kept' and 'best cared for' and the old wooden houses clustered by the stream make an appealing picture. Here the horses pulling coaches over the San Bernardino and Splügen passes were stabled and changed, travellers rested overnight and stories of derring do, encounters with robbers and bears no doubt exchanged. One of the old inns is still there – a comfortable place, although bears and footpads are fortunately rare.

In Splügen you leave R6. Our route takes the Splügenpass to Chiavenna. The downhill section is dramatic and technically difficult. From Splügen a ramp climbs to the first curves, taking you quickly up from village height. It flattens off, teetering along the edge of a wooded gorge before a gentler section through meadows. An impressive series of tight curves lies in wait before the ancient Splügen Berghaus is reached, a café with excellent views down valley. After a few more turns you reach Italy at the Splügenpass summit. Have your passport handy as the guards can be keen.

The descent to Montespluga and its reservoir is but a foretaste of things to come on a quiet, but spectacular road with occasional cattle to circumnavigate. (They seem to respond best to shouting and arm waving.) The real excitement begins through stacked galleries and tight hairpins down towards Chiavenna. Some of these can be avoided by turning right towards Isola, still providing plenty of thrills, although the exciting route goes left via Pianazzo. This is a wild route, through villages that look like film sets, houses huddled amid huge rockfalls, pitch black snowsheds, tunnels and local drivers ignoring the basic laws of physics. You can breathe again in historic Chiavenna, which is a delight – a wonderful mixture of ancient buildings, churches and the most elegant of shops or market stalls right next to each other. Hemmed in by steep mountain walls and terraced vineyards defying gravity, it is bliss to linger in the narrow streets and savour a home-made ice cream.

NB: In bad weather, the only way to Chiavenna with a bike is to take a train to St Moritz from Thusis and then a Postbus to Chiavenna. There is a Postbus from Chur to Splügen, but no link to carry bicycles over the Splügenpass to Chiavenna because the Italian bus subcontractor does not carry them.

ITINERARY		
Distance (km)	Location	Directions
0	Chur (570m)	From SBB station TR following R2/6 signs, over railway lines and beneath autobahn bridge. Soon R6 TL to follow Autobahn. **T** Stay on R2 through Tamins and Bonaduz (climbing). **RB** Follow R2 to Felsberg, TL to cross autobahn and then TR along road through Reichenau to Bonaduz.
12	Bonaduz (655m)	SO at junction on road to Rhäzüns and Rothenbrunnen. TL over autobahn and rejoin R6 by TR on far side of bridge. Continue into Thusis village.
25	Thusis (683m)	Avoid R6 branch to Tiefencastel. Check lights for tunnel sections and busy road stretch past Via Mala.
36	Zillis (945m)	Back to quiet roads with short steeper climbs through Andeer to Sufner See (**RB** on road along north side of lake to avoid rough track) then into Splügen.
51	Splügen (1457m)	LT for the Splügenpass.
60	Splügenpass (2113m)	Check lights/reflectors and be on your guard...
63	Montespluga (1908m)	Follow the pass road to the T-junction with the Madésimo road. RT, then LT to Pianazzo shortly. Follow R36 through Campodolcino and San Giácomo-Filippo to Chiavenna.
91	Chiavenna (325m)	

FACILITIES						
	Distance (km)	Camp site	YH/BP	B&B	Hotel	Station	Bike shop
Chur	0	✓		✓	Many	✓	✓
Thusis	25	✓			3	✓	✓
Andeer	37	✓			2		
Sufers	47			✓	1		
Splügen	51	✓			Many		
Montespluga	63				2		
Chiavenna	91			✓	Many	✓	

TOURIST INFORMATION			
From/to	Name	Address	Telephone/Website
Chur/Splügen	Graubünden Vacation	Alexanderstrasse 24 CH-7001 Chur	+41 (0)81 254 2424 http://ferien. graubuenden.ch/en
Monte Spluga/ Chiavenna	Consorzio per la promozione Turistica della Valchiavenna	Via Consoli C 11 I-23022 Chiavenna	+39 (0)34 337 485 www.valchiavenna.com

Stage 2: Chiavenna – St Moritz
50km; 1490m; strenuous

This stage is primarily on surfaced roads. It falls into two parts: a long climb from Chiavenna, testing towards the end, hemmed in by vineyards on steep slopes to Maloja, then a long winding section past the lakes into St Moritz. Everyone has heard of St Moritz, winter sport paradise for the rich and famous, but in summer it is not very attractive, although the Engiadinais Museum (local history and culture) and some collections by local painters are notable.

Top of the Majolapass

However, the scenery is fantastic – the reason the place developed, first as a summer spa and second as a winter playground. Neither St Moritz nor Pontresina are noted for budget accommodation, so you may want to consider the youth hostels in Maloja, Pontresina and St Moritz. There is a friendly international atmosphere at the one in St Moritz. Alternatives are La Punt-Chamues-ch or Celerina (home of the Cresta Run).

In bad weather or for a day off, take the Postbus.

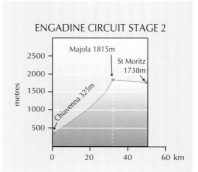

ITINERARY		
Distance Location **(km)**		**Directions**
0	Chiavenna (325m)	Take road to Maloja signposted St Moritz.
		Cross border into Switzerland by Castasegna (696m).
32	Maloja (1815m)	RR65 on road to Sils.
39	Sils (1797m)	Tourists switch to track on south side of the Silvaplaner See.
		RB stay on road to Silvaplana.
46	Silvaplana (1816m)	RR65 on road to St Moritz.
50	St Moritz (1738m)	

FACILITIES							
	Distance (km)	**Camp site**	**YH/BP**	**B&B**	**Hotel**	**Station**	**Bike shop**
Maloja	32	✓	✓		Many		✓
Silvaplana	46	✓		✓	Many		✓
St Moritz	50	✓	✓		Many	✓	✓
Pontresina	60	✓	✓		Many	✓	✓

TOURIST INFORMATION			
From/to	**Name**	**Address**	**Telephone/Website**
Maloja/ St Moritz	Graubünden Vacation	Alexanderstrasse 24 CH-7001 Chur	+41 (0)81 254 2424 http://ferien. graubuenden.ch/en

Stage 3: St Moritz – Davos
79km; 1290m; difficult

Enjoy the *sgraffiti* – curly scrollwork and symbols scratched into the pale stucco of the massive houses, more fortresses than farmhouses – and the village store in La Punt-Chamues-ch before leaving the Inn valley to climb the Albulapass, back on R6 again. The road is quiet, except at weekends, rising quickly above the treeline through scenery that resembles Scotland. Once at the top you can stop at the Ospiz for an Ovomaltine, change your sweaty garments for something drier and put on windproofs for the fast descent to Tiefencastel. However a word of warning: inside the Ospiz, a notice in German requests cyclists to change their clothes in the toilets rather than in the middle of the café, so have something to drink and get the key from the bar for the toilets. The folks are friendly, the food good and reasonably priced.

It is a long fast drop to Filisur and can be cold enough to warrant skull caps under helmets, winter tights, jackets and full gloves. Your hands may be aching by Preda, the junction with the railway which descends 700m in 13km by coiling around the road in tunnels and on bridges. The village museum in Bergün has an excellent model of the railway and scenes showing the simplicity and the hardship of local rural life. The road drops through a spectacular gorge beyond Filisur crossing the River Landwasser. Below Filisur, accessed by a side road just after a bridge, is the Landwasser Viaduct where the railway swings round a curved bridge to disappear into the Landwasser Tunnel.

At Surava our route turns east to head for Davos, rising rapidly to give grandiose views of valley and mountain. Closer to Davos by Bärentritt there is a 3km road tunnel, which may be bypassed on a gravel track. This ride is rather like canyoning on a bike

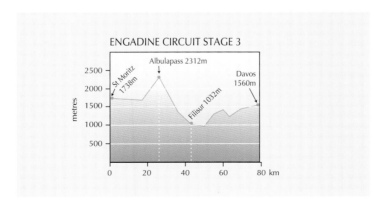

165

and you may prefer to risk the fume-filled, car-packed tunnel. Davos is set amongst dramatic mountains and the youth hostel is splendid, but the town itself is undistinguished. The Winter Sport Museum may be of special interest to Britons.

In bad weather or for a day off, take the train.

On the old post road to Davos deep in the gorge

ITINERARY		
Distance (km)	Location	Directions
0	St Moritz (1738m)	RR65 (not always surfaced, but adequate) through Samedan to La Punt/Chamues-ch.
18	La Punt/ Chamues-ch	R6 over Albulapass to Filisur on a quiet road. In Bellaluna, below Bergün: **T** follow a forest track; **RB** stay on the road.
48	Filisur (1032m)	Landwasser railway viaduct accessible from car park on right after the road bridge, via gravel footpath leading along cul de sac (20min walk). RT to Alvaneu. Climb to Wiesen on minor road. About 180m before the tunnel (2km after Wiesen) take mountain bike track left to drop down to gravelled tunnel bypass. RT to climb to Davos.
79	Davos (1560m)	The main TO is on the promenade near Davos Platz station.

FACILITIES							
	Distance (km)	Camp site	YH/BP	B&B	Hotel	Station	Bike shop
Celerina	7	✓			Many	✓	✓
Samedan	10	✓			Many	✓	✓
La Punt/ Chamues-ch	18	✓			Many	✓	✓
Preda	34				2	✓	
Bergün	41	✓			Many	✓	✓
Filisur	48	✓			4	✓	
Surava (off route)	54				1		
Alvaneu	55				2		
Wiesen	61				2		
Glaris	68				1		
Frauenkirch	73				2		
Davos	79		✓	✓	Many	✓	✓

TOURIST INFORMATION			
From/to	Name	Address	Telephone/Website
St Moritz/ Davos	Graubünden Vacation	Alexanderstrasse 24 CH-7001 Chur	+41 (0)81 254 2424 http://ferien. graubuenden.ch/en

Stage 4: Davos – Nauders
83km; 1740m; strenuous

The River Inn below Scuol church

Both road bikes and tourists need to head towards the Flüelapass, a road that begins with disarming gentleness and culminates in a lunar landscape of giant rockfalls and glacier-scraped outcrops some lung-testing kilometres later. It's a relief to speed down to the Inn Valley in Susch/Süs with its enormous Engadine sgraffiti houses.

Downstream from Zernez the Inn has cut narrow gorges into the local slates. The villages all lie on the south-facing slopes to catch the midwinter sun. In summer they make the idea of living close to nature seem very romantic but all suffer from economic pressures that make upland farming difficult, just as in Scotland or the Appalachians. Tourists are both a lifeline and a curse, since they bring money but may destroy the beauty and peace. R6 follows very rough tracks parallel to Road 27 from Susch/Süs, not recommended for road bikes. Road 27 is quiet during the week, but there are occasional trucks.

R6 branches off up quiet steep roads, mostly well-surfaced, en route to Ftan. The views of 3000m mountains and the Inn Valley are tremendous in clear weather, but in poor visibility the main road would be better. From impressive Guarda village, there is a rapid plunge downhill to Ardez, then another steep climb into Ftan. From here there's a 400m freewheel to Scuol, the biggest town for miles and a well-known spa, which modestly calls itself the 'Queen of the Alpine Spa Towns'. The thermal baths here are something else, with the Roman-Irish Bath offering all combinations of wet and dry possibilities, perhaps a bonus for weary cyclists.

Back in the shady woods along the Inn, the route is enlivened by sculptures, because this area is a centre of artists in wood and marble. However, between Scuol and St Nicla, R6 follows really rough trails, over rockfalls and so road bikers should use the hilly main road. Beyond St Nicla, little more than an ancient church tower joined onto a barn, it is a delightful tarmac ride to Martina, another picturesque village, almost at the edge of Switzerland, with access to Austria, over the Alpine Inn. (The Inn here resembles a doubtful-looking, milky blue energy drink.) R6 ends here, although the Inn Valley Cycleway continues to Innsbruck.

This is probably one of the finest mountain areas in the world for cyclists. From the Austrian border post, the shortcut to Nauders ascends 300m over 7km, followed by a short descent into the town. This is a good centre for those wanting more challenges, so contact the

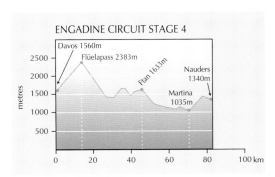

ENGADINE CIRCUIT STAGE 4

Davos 1560m
Flüelapass 2383m
Ftan 1633m
Nauders 1340m
Martina 1035m

metres

tourist office in Nauders for alternative routes. Every summer in June up to 3500 cyclists take part in the Dreiländergiro – a 165.8km, 3379m cycle event on public roads over the Reschenpass, Stilfserjoch, Umbrailpass and Ofenpass.

In bad weather or for a day off, take the train or Postbus.

ITINERARY		
Distance Location (km)		Directions
0	Davos (1560m)	Take Flüelapass road.
14	Flüelapass summit (2383m)	Drop down to Susch.
28	Susch (1426m)	**T** cross Road 27 to follow R6 on unsurfaced tracks through Lavin (1412m) to Guarda (1653m). Then on tarmac to Ardez (1464m) and climb through Ftan (1633) to Scuol. **RB** LT to follow Road 27 until Giarsun and then climb off left to Guarda to follow tourist route.
53	Scuol (1423m)	**T** follow R6 across to the other side of the valley. Follow surfaced and unsurfaced tracks to Martina. **RB** stay on Road 27.
72	Martina (1035m)	TR into Austria. Climb the B185 over Norbertshöhe (1468m) to Nauders.
83	Nauders (1340m)	

FACILITIES							
	Distance (km)	Camp site	YH/BP	B&B	Hotel	Station	Bike shop
Susch	28	✓			Many	✓	✓
Ardez	40			✓			
Scuol	53	✓	✓	✓	Many	✓	✓
Sur En	60	✓					
St Nicla	68			✓			
Strada	70	✓		✓			
Martina	72	✓			1		
Nauders	83				Many		✓

TOURIST INFORMATION			
From/to	Name	Address	Telephone/Website
Davos/ Martina	Scuol Tourismus AG	CH-7550 Scuol	+41 (0)81 861 2222 www.engadin.com
Nauders	Tourismusverband Nauders	Dr Tschiggfrey Strasse 66 A-6543 Nauders	+43 (0)54 738 7220 www.nauders.info

Stage 5: Nauders – Santa Maria
64km; 970m; difficult

The church tower of the old village of Graun submerged beneath the Reschensee

This is regarded locally as a nice gentle trip from Austria into Italy and Switzerland. You could if you wanted get to Santa Maria via the Stilfserjoch/Passo dello Stélvio (2775m) with its 48 hairpins and the Umbrailpass, but our route gives good views of the glaciers, mountains and the scenery of the Vinschgau for less effort. The route leads over the Reschenpass into the Südtirol, alongside the Reschensee where probably the most photographed church tower anywhere in the Alps sticks up out of the lake. There is an out-and-back from Graun up to the Endstation Bar in Melag where one can sip an espresso while gazing at the peaks and glacier remnants.

Another option is a right turn in Reschen along a minor road and then a tarmac cycleway along the west bank to reach St Valentin. This probably rules out the climb to Melag and a close-up of the drowned church tower. However, after several dry winters the lake level has dropped and the tower view is rather disappointing. The route slips away from the busy pass road after St Valentin to climb and fall to Mals with its Romanesque churches and towers. Then you take another quiet road to Laatsch, meeting the main road at Calvabrücke and via Taufers to the Swiss border at Müstair. This village has the oldest church in Switzerland, part of a Benedictine convent and a Unesco World Heritage Site – very large and impressive. Santa Maria lies 3km farther and 140m higher.

In bad weather, take buses and miss the excursion to Mals.

171

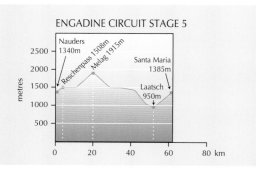

ENGADINE CIRCUIT STAGE 5

ITINERARY		
Distance (km)	**Location**	**Directions**
0	Nauders (1340m)	Stand with your back to the TO and go right to the Hotel Tia Monte, across the mini-roundabout to pass the Hotel Maultasche and swing round towards the castle. TL to follow the Via Claudia Augusta signs climbing to the Italian border on a minor road under the cable car. Follow the cycleway behind the Italian customs office, cross the main road after the border and climb on a well-signposted cycleway to Reschen. (Did you see the mistake on the height diagram at the border?)
6	Reschen (1500m)	In Reschen, **T** TL and TR to follow a cycleway between the road and the lake to Graun; **RB** TL, climb to the road and TR to Graun and a short, lit tunnel just before the village. In Graun, TL to Pedross and Melag (1915m).
20	Melag (1915m)	Return to Graun. TL and take the surfaced/unsurfaced cycleway by the lake to St Valentin-auf-der-Haide. Lots of snowsheds to be avoided by using surfaced track to right.
35	St Valentin auf der Haide	FL by the church, climb to Dörfl on a quiet road. On to Ulten and Mals.
48	Mals (1050m)	RT at junction with R40. TL along minor road to Laatsch (signposted Schweiz).
52	Laatsch (950m)	SO through village under the church on a minor road to Calvabrücke to climb to Taufers on R41, the Swiss border, Müstair and Santa Maria.
64	Santa Maria (1385m)	

FACILITIES							
	Distance (km)	Camp site	YH/BP	B&B	Hotel	Station	Bike shop
Reschen	9		✓		Many		✓
Graun	12				2		✓
St Valentin-auf-der-Haide	35				Many		✓
Mals	48				Many	✓	✓
Laatsch	52				3		
Taufers	54				1		
Müstair	59	✓			Many		
Santa Maria	64			✓	✓	Many	

TOURIST INFORMATION			
From/to	Name	Address	Telephone/Website
Reschen/ Taufers	Tourisverband Vinschgau	Kapuzinerstr 10 I-39028 Schlanders	+39 (0)47 373 7000 www.vinschgau.it
Santa Maria	Scuol Tourismus AG	CH-7550 Scuol	+41 (0)81 861 2222 www.engadin.com

Stage 6: Santa Maria – Pontresina
78km; 1630m; strenuous

There is an alternative to today's route – cycling over the Umbrailpass, the highest border crossing in Switzerland at 2501m, and onwards via Bormio, Tirano and the Forcola di Livigno to enjoy 123km and a 2991m climb – but our route is much shorter and involves less climbing. The route follows the Val Müstair over the dramatic, eroded Ofenpass/Pass dal Fuorn. There's a gripping descent into the Parc Naziunal Svizzer (Swiss National Park).

You then turn left through a well-lit 3km tunnel to Livigno, which is free for cyclists. Traffic is one way for half hour periods, controlled by traffic lights with border formalities after the tunnel. Cycle around the Lago di Livigno on a lightly rolling road with snowsheds to Livigno, a duty-free area in Italy. This has spawned both traffic and new buildings but a glance at the older farms shows just how poor the people were before. You have the option of buying VAT-free perfume, spirits and sugar.

The next pass – Forcola di Livigno – involves climbing 500m, but fairly gently on a narrow road. You descend past crumbling pink slopes to reach the Swiss customs office on the Bernina road. TR to climb 275m steeply, but with fantastic glaciers on your left. Replenish calories with pasta or Ovomaltine at the Bernina summit café, then it is 17km downhill, mostly in long visible curves to Pontresina. (A left turn at the junction

Three jolly Dutchmen in Mstair

with the Bernina road would bring you to Tirano (436m). This is a superb ride, but you would then probably need to stop overnight and return over the pass next day or take a train back up the hill.)

In bad weather or for a day off, take the bus to Zernez and train to Pontresina.

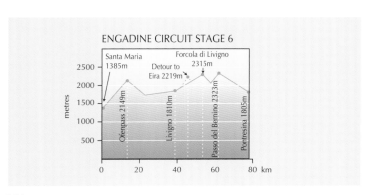

ENGADINE CIRCUIT STAGE 6

ITINERARY

Distance (km)	Location	Directions
0	Santa Maria (1385m)	Follow the road towards Zernez to reach the Ofenpass summit (2149m) and drop down to Punt la Drossa.
24	Punt la Drossa	Follow tunnel and lakeside road to Livigno.
39	Livigno (1810m)	Follow Forcola di Livigno road over the pass.
53	Forcola di Livigno (2315m)	Descend to Tirano–Pontresina road. TR to ascend Passo del Bernina towards Pontresina.
62	Bernina summit (2323m)	Downhill all the way to Pontresina.
78	Pontresina (1805m)	

FACILITIES

	Distance (km)	Camp site	YH/BP	B&B	Hotel	Station	Bike shop
Il Fuorn Ofenpass	15				1		
Livigno	39	✓		✓	Many		
Bernina summit	62				1	✓	
Pontresina	78	✓	✓		Many	✓	✓

TOURIST INFORMATION

From/to	Name	Address	Telephone/Website
Santa Maria/ Punt la Drossa	Scuol Tourismus AG	CH-7550 Scuol	+41 (0)81 861 2222 www.engadin.com
Livigno	Azienda Promozione Turistica	via Saroch 1098a c/o Plaza Plachéda I-23030 Livigno	+39 (0)34 205 2200 www.livigno.it
Bernina summit/ Pontresina	Graubünden Vacation	Alexanderstrasse 24 CH-7001 Chur	+41 (0)81 254 2424 http://ferien. graubuenden.ch/en

Stage 7: Pontresina – Chur
86km; 810m; difficult

This stage brings you back into the Inn Valley and the starting point. It involves climbing over the Albulapass again, but the alternatives are either longer, higher or cycling over busier passes: Via Susch and the Flüelapass (2383m) to Davos or over the truckladen Julierpass (2284m) from Silvaplana.

From La Punt you need to climb the familiar 625m hill to the Albulapass Ospiz. The 31km descent starts between boulder fields but leads down into green meadows by Tiefencastel. Unfortunately the Julierpass traffic filters in at Tiefencastel, just as the road rises 100m. There is a long steep drop to Thusis, involving two tunnels 500m and 1190m in length. Veloland Schweiz considers these tunnels dangerous and recommends taking the train to bypass them. However, the tunnels are safe as long as you have adequate lighting. (With children or anyone who feels unsafe under these circumstances, consider taking the train to Thusis.)

After Tiefencastel, the road descends into a hanging valley giving superb views into the Hinterrhein valley embellished by castle ruins. If you are hungry for more passes then a left turn in Thusis will bring you onto the R6 southern leg through Splügen to the San Bernardino Pass. Similarly a left turn later in Bonaduz allows access to the Oberalppass and Andermatt.

In bad weather, take the bus (Livigno–Bormio–Tirano) and train (Pontresina–Chur).

Back over the Albula to Bergün

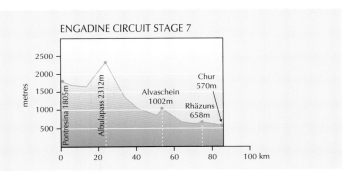

ITINERARY		
Distance (km)	Location	Directions
0	Pontresina	RR65 to La Punt.
14	La Punt/ Chamues-ch (1687m)	R6 over Albulapass (2312m) to Filisur on a quiet road. In Bellaluna, below Bergün: **T** follow a forest track, **RB** stay on the road.
41	Filisur (1032m)	R6 or road through Surava to Tiefencastel.
51	Tiefencastel (851m)	R6 on road to Thusis and watch out for tunnels! Route avoids the first by climbing to Mistail, near Alvaschein.
64	Thusis (723m)	R6 to Rothenbrunnen. TL, cross over motorway and follow minor road to Bonaduz. **T** Follow R2 to Chur via Felsberg. **RB** Follow road through Domat/Ems to Chur
86	Chur (570m)	

FACILITIES							
	Distance (km)	Camp site	YH/BP	B&B	Hotel	Station	Bike shop
Pontresina	0	✓	✓		Many	✓	✓
Samedan	6	✓			Many	✓	✓
La Punt/ Chamues-ch	14	✓			Many	✓	✓
Albulapass summit	22				1		
Preda	27				2	✓	
Bergün	34	✓			Many	✓	✓
Filisur	41	✓			4	✓	
Tiefencastel	51				1		
Thusis	64	✓			3	✓	✓
Chur	86	✓		✓	Many	✓	✓

177

TOURIST INFORMATION			
From/to	Name	Address	Telephone/Website
Pontresina/ Chur	Graubünden Vacation	Alexanderstrasse 24 CH-7001 Chur	+41 (0)81 254 2424 http://ferien. graubuenden.ch/en

The southern leg of Route 6:
Splügen – Bellinzona
78km; 760m; moderate

Between Splügen and Hinterrhein is a wide U-shaped upland valley with sharp rocky peaks on the skyline. The autobahn disappears into a tunnel and the cyclist can enjoy the well-graded turns, grinning at motorists from Europe's flatter bits who seem to come here for a rite of passage. The trees disappear and the slope slackens with roches moutonées emerging from grassy clumps as 2000m is reached. Shortly afterwards the welcome roof of the Ospizio appears with its less desirable hordes of motorised pass-grabbers. Take a break, eat an energy bar and then dress up for the descent.

After the lake there's a great feeling of exposure. Once down the first few hairpins there are magnificent long runs that traverse the hillside. Many additional roller coasters follow, through villages bypassed by the main road and apparently in a time warp with their massive timber houses and few services. Down, down and down until it is hard to imagine that further descent is possible past Roveredo and into Castione where the main Gotthard route joins, shortly before reaching Bellinzona. Suddenly there is a Mediterranean feel with the scent of fruit trees and grapes strung on poles.

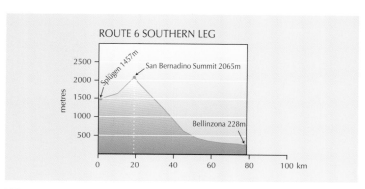

ROUTE 6 SOUTHERN LEG

Bellinzona's very name explains why the town has three castles, all needed for defence at different times from warring armies and groups. Today they make good viewpoints for anyone with energy to spare. The squares of the bustling little town are interesting places to relax over coffee or a glass of wine after the exertions of the ride. The official language is German to Hinterrhein and Italian thereafter. (See chapter 3 for description of a possible excursion from Bellinzona.)

In bad weather, take the Postbus.

ITINERARY		
Distance (km)	Location	Directions
0	Splügen (1457m)	Follow trail to Medels, then continue on road to Nufenen and Hinterrhein. Then climb to top of San Bernardino Pass.
19	San Bernardino Pass (2065m)	Descend with care to Castione. (**RB** Take road beyond San Vittore into Castione.)
74	Castione (300m)	TL at junction with R3, pinched between road, railway and motorway, left at VSIB in Bellinzona to station.
78	Bellinzona (228m)	

FACILITIES							
	Distance (km)	Camp site	YH/BP	B&B	Hotel	Station	Bike shop
Medels	4			✓			
Nufenen	7			✓			
Hinterrhein	10			✓			
San Bernardino	27				Many		
Soazza	45				1		
Cabbiolo	51		✓				
Bellinzona	78	✓	✓	✓	Many	✓	✓

TOURIST INFORMATION			
From/to	Name	Address	Telephone/Website
Splügen/ Cabbiolo	Graubünden Vacation	Alexanderstrasse 24 CH-7001 Chur	+41 (0)81 254 2424 http://ferien. graubuenden.ch/en
Belllinzona	Ticino Tourismo	Casa postale 1441 Via Lugano 12 CH-6501 Bellinzona	+41 (0)91 825 7056 www.ticino-tourism.ch

Jura Route

FRANCE

R. Doubs

R. Rhein

R2

Basel

R3

JURA

MITTELLAND

Porrentruy ○   Lucelle

Courgenay ○   *Col 780*   Kleinlutzel ○ Ettingen

Col de la Croix 789   ○ St Ursanne

Col 1008

Les Enfers ○   ○ St Brais

Saignelégier   *Col 1016*

○ Les Breuleux

Mont Soleil 1248

La Chaux-de-Fonds ○   *R. Aare*

Col 1156   L. Biel

○ Le Crêt

Cret Pelaton 1082

Pontarlier ○   Travers   L. Neuchâtel   Bern ○

Buttes ○   *R. Aare*

○ Bullet

Bolles de Vent 1075   St Croix

Col de l'Aiguillon 1320   ○ Baulmes

○ Vallorbe

Col 1050   Le Pont   R5

Le Brassus ○   Lausanne   R9

Col 1339   ○ Montreux

Bassins ○

St Cergue ○ Nyon   *Lac Léman*

R1

FRANCE

N

○ Genève

0   10   20   30 km

7 THE JURA ROUTE, R7

ROUTE SUMMARY					
From/to	Distance (km) surfaced/ unsurfaced	Climb (m) with public transport	Climb (m) without public transport	Grade with public transport	Grade without public transport
Basel/Nyon	282/20	2590	4260	Moderate	Strenuous
Nyon/Basel		2200	4300	Moderate	Strenuous

SUMMARY OF STAGES (WITHOUT PUBLIC TRANSPORT)				
Stage	From/to	Distance (km)	Climb (m)	Grade
1	Basel/Courgenay	58	780	Moderate
2	Courgenay/ La Chaux-de-Fonds	74	1430	Strenuous
3	La Chaux-de-Fonds/ Baulmes	72	1030	Difficult
4	Baulmes/Nyon	78	1020	Difficult
Total	**Basel/Nyon**	**282**	**4260**	

LOCAL MAPS	
Swisstopo 1:100,000 Composite	
104	Lausanne–Bern
108	Gruyère–Le Léman
111	Ajole–Fribourg

Our route description runs from Basel to Nyon. There is less climbing in the other direction but from the north there's a glorious 40km final drop into Nyon with Alpine views. Starting in Nyon with a long climb is less appealing. At the start, the hills to the north are in France and on one day the route crisscrosses the border with France, although there are no border posts. The route starts in German-speaking Basel, but after 40km enters the French-speaking part of Switzerland.

Although this route is short, it is wonderfully varied and offers many testing climbs for the purist, which lesser mortals can avoid by judicious use of Postbus/train connections. In early October, the mixed woods are at their most colourful. Late spring and early summer would also be ideal, as long as the highest regions near Nyon are snow and ice free, although you are likely to get mists and fogs. A great benefit of the sparse population of this region is that autobahns are rare, as is the rumble of traffic, but you would be wise to buy provisions before leaving your overnight stop as many villages are too small to support a shop.

The route leaves Basel and heads with short climbs into the first of the parallel ridges of the Jura. Woods cloak the steep hillsides and cereals grow on the gentler

French-style flair in Porrentruy (Stage 2)

slopes. There are old villages and small towns, often with remnants of walls and fortresses as at Porrentruy, just off your route. As you wind southwestwards across the Jura, the route crosses several of the lines of folds, sometimes in a river gorge, like that of the Doubs in St Ursanne, and sometimes by a pass, like the Col de l'Aiguillon (1320m) near St Croix. Along the way you can appreciate all the features of limestone scenery – cliffs, coombes, dry valleys, swallow holes and springs. The tops of the folds have often been eroded away. As you progress, the hill climbs increase in scale and challenge interspersed by long descents. There are wide upland valleys, as between Le Crêt and Les Ponts-de-Martel, where the farms cling to the valley sides away from the once-marshy floor. There is much excellent pasture so milk from goats, sheep and cows is made into renowned cheeses. Saignelégier is a major horse breeding region.

There are beautiful lakes, like Lac du Joux, where a bathe might be refreshing before tackling the climb to 1390m beyond Le Brassus and the remote National Park of the High Jura with its karst landscape. Finally the route begins a long, beautifully graded descent with a vast Alpine panorama, backing the waters of Lac Léman, as you freewheel and curve down into a semi-tropical landscape of vines and small villages. This an inspired bit of route-making, twisting through the fields, vine groves and rural landscapes right into Nyon itself with only a few kilometres along roads with traffic. After quiet days only meeting the occasional tractor, it is a gentle reintroduction to the real world.

LINKS TO OTHER ROUTES		
Location	**Route/s**	**To**
Basel	R2: Rhein Route	Bodensee, Chur, Andermatt
	R3: North–South	Luzern, Andermatt, St Gotthard Pass, Lago Maggiore, Chiasso
Nyon	R1: Rhône Route	West: Genève
		East: Montreux, Martigny, Gletsch, Andermatt

Public transport backup

Because this is such a thinly populated area, direct rail links between many of the towns visited are either poor or non-existent. In some cases it is possible to reach your destination by train, but only by making long detours and possibly several changes. Some towns like Vallorbe and Fleurier are linked to the SNCF via Pontarlier and so accessible in a somewhat tortuous manner. Some settlements at heads of valleys are railheads, for example Buttes and St Croix. However, there are Postbus services, linking these railheads, over many of the cols. Information about both rail and Postbus connections is usually displayed outside Swiss railway stations but the traveller can sometimes fall foul of the cantonal organisation. In Fleurier, for example, there are timetables for trains to Neuchâtel (away from the route) but little about St Croix (further along the route). In Buttes there is both information and a Postbus.

PUBLIC TRANSPORT BACKUP		
Stage	**Route**	**Service/*Comment***
2	Courgenay – St Ursanne – Saignelégier	Rail
4	Le Brassus – Col du Marchairuz	Bus
		Saturdays & Sundays, June to September, reservations necessary

Stage 1: Basel – Courgenay
58km; 780m; moderate

The character of the whole Jura route is summed up in this first stage: up and down over limestone ridges and valleys, small towns and villages, farms and forests, few people, the cries of hawks and the wind whistling through your clothes on fast downhills. Despite being Switzerland's second biggest city, Basel is tiny by international standards, with about 200,000 inhabitants, and full of fellow cyclists. **Remember that trams always have priority.** Basel has many museums, a wonderful historic centre with magnificent *Rathaus* (town hall) and ancient *Münster* (cathedral), together with elegant houses originally built by the rich (merchants) and the great (nobility). Check out www.baseltourismus.ch before you leave home.

Bronze Helvetia takes a break in Basel

Cycle out of Basel through garden suburbs, gently uphill then out into the fields with the first tree-clad Jura ridges on your left. The first pass is easy up to Bättwil, then Mariastein, in front of the next limestone ridge. Mariastein's 14th century church is still a pilgrimage centre with useful cafés. In spring there's cherry and apple blossom on wayside trees and thirst-quenching cherries in summer. France lies to the northwest. There is a youth hostel nearby at Rotberg.

From Metzerlen you climb again to a col, then a forest track on the spine of the ridge. In autumn the beeches glow orange against the icy valley mist dropping down into the Lützel Valley and on into France. After World War I this road was designated as an International Road, with free passage for locals on either side of the border and those who have right of entry into both countries. The wooded valley is overhung by limestone bluffs. The road climbs gently to frontier town Lucelle, with its relics of a great Benedictine Abbey and a modern conference centre.

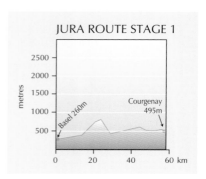

JURA ROUTE STAGE 1

More climbing follows past remnants of abbey farms and an unlikely pink *mairie* (town hall). Then the landscape changes as you go downhill away from France and into a broad basin where, in late summer, recently harvested cereal fields shine gold in the afternoon sun. Despite the siren call of the lowlands, the route bucks and turns uphill then down again and over the top of a main road tunnel into the hills beneath. The farming village of Courgenay, lies downhill just off the route. This is famed for its *pierre percée*, a giant stone-with-a-hole from the Stone Age, which may be a burial chamber entrance, through which bones of the departed were passed. Nearby Porrentruy, the main town of the Ajoie region with its chateau, water bubbling up from underground springs and typical French architecture, is worth a detour. (It also boasts a large supermarket with a café.)

In bad weather, take a train from Basel via Delémont.

ITINERARY		
Distance (km)	Location	Directions
0	Basel Bad Station	Follow R7 signs to TR, then across road by traffic lights, LT then through Messe (exhibition grounds). Follow signs LT, RT, LT and RT (note pensive 'Helvetia' bronze on right overlooking Rhein). Cross Rhein bridge with traffic, RT then LT through University Quarter (lots of bikes and graffiti) up slight rise SO to join R7.
0	Basel SBB (Rhein 260m, SBB 300m)	TL following R7 signs, then via Binningen, Oberwil and Therwil to edge of Ettingen.
10	Ettingen (330m)	RT along road to Bättwil, then climb through gorge, RT to visit Mariastein village and church (off route). LT to reach mock castle YH at Rotberg.
14	Mariastein/Rotberg (510m)	Return to road, up and down to Metzerlen then climb to col at 747m. Views into Laufental. **RB** continue down hill on road to Röschenz, RT to Kleinlützel then rejoin R7. **T** RT at col along forest track (pines and beeches) on ridge edge, superb descent to Kleinlützel village.
26	Kleinlützel (420m)	Rejoin road along French/Swiss border, Painted flags on bridge abutments indicate country. Slow pleasant climb to Lucelle through almost uninhabited valley.
41	Lucelle (604m)	Sharp RT almost at border post then stiff climb past pink mairie (town hall) on right. Sharp LT down narrow road into Charmoille.
46	Charmoille (515m)	Through village, LT at T-junction then via Fregiécourt, Cornol, twisting up and down, over major road by tunnel entrance to T-junction at church. RT to descend to Courgenay or Porrentruy.
58	Courgenay (495m)	

FACILITIES							
	Distance (km)	Camp site	YH/BP	B&B	Hotel	Station	Bike shop
Basel	0	✓	✓	✓	Many	✓	✓
Ettingen	10	✓					✓
Mariastein	14		✓	✓	3		
Lucelle	41	✓			1		
Courgenay (off route)	58	✓			2	✓	
Porrentruy (further off route)	61	✓			Many	✓	✓

TOURIST INFORMATION			
From/to	Name	Address	Telephone/Website
Basel	Basel Tourismus	Aeschenvorstadt 36 CH-4010 Basel	+41 (0)61 268 6868 www.baseltourismus.ch
Battwil/ Roggenburg	Kanton Solothurn Tourismus	Grabackerstrasse 6 CH-4500 Solothurn	+41 (0)32 622 5131 www.mysolothurn.com
Porentruy	Watch Valley Coordination	Route de Sorvilier 21 CH-2735 Bévilard	+41 (0)32 492 7132 www.watchvalley.ch/e

Stage 2: Courgenay – La Chaux-de-Fonds
74km; 1430m; strenuous

Another stage of pure Jura – deep valleys and white rock, market towns and remote farmsteads. (Perhaps a bonus on this stretch is the wide variety and ingenuity of cattle grid construction. You have been warned!)

The route makes a long climb from Courgenay to the Col sur la Croix on quiet wooded roads. R7 branches off down a tiny lane across a side valley. (Beware small

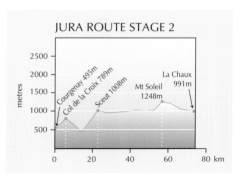

limestone fragments on road.) Below lies the River Doubs, fresh from its deep gorge upstream. St Ursanne is a delightful collection of religious buildings, hotels with faded

Pierre percée *in Courgenay*

paintwork and houses built higgledy-piggledy into, and probably out of, the stonework of the town wall. It owes its origin (AD620) to Irish monk Ursicinus. Perhaps he enjoyed fishing? High limestone cliffs and pinnacles tower above the river, making it a good place for rest or refreshment. Look out for kingfishers, as well as moorhens, kestrels and sparrowhawks.

Climb up beneath the high span of the railway, then again to Montmelon before an undulating stretch to St Brais past some excellent examples of swallow holes. Those on touring bikes should enjoy the panoramic 'parklands' of meadows and coniferous specimen trees around Les Enfers. Saignelégier seems prosperous from its success in breeding horses, seen everywhere in fields and paddocks. Between here and St Imier lies more delightful country before more parkland and a stiff ascent over the shoulder of Mont Solei – visible for miles by virtue of the wind turbines on its summit. St Imier itself lies on the valley floor but the route contours round, falling in short bursts with brief ascents until the final run through outlying farms to the edge of La Chaux-de-Fonds.

The town itself is more populous than better-known Neuchâtel, but with none of the charm of most Swiss cities. Once a small farming village, it was destroyed by fire in 1794 and finally rebuilt nearly 50 years later as an imposing series of wide boulevards and tall, barrack-like blocks set on a gridiron plan. Le Corbusier was born here in 1887, when the town was a wealthy watch and clock-making place. He left his birthplace after a big row when the building costs of the Villa Turque violently overran his estimates but returned to complete his work and the villa is now open to the public. Despite, or perhaps because of, its strange appearance La Chaux-de-Fonds is a good place to visit, especially for its clock museum and Musée des Beaux Arts.

Nearby Le Locle (off route) is where Swiss watch-making actually began after Daniel Jeanrichard moved there in 1705. It, too, has a Musée d'Horlogie (clock and watch museum) in a chateau (on a hilltop, naturally), workshops making magnificent timepieces and fine villas of the watch-making families.

In bad weather or for a day off, take the train (a tortuous route).

ITINERARY		
Distance Location (km)		Directions
0	Courgenay (495m)	Cycle uphill to rejoin R7, then climb to St Croix (789m), RT behind farm, then long descent via Seleute (narrow road, small stones from bank) to T-junction in Doubs valley. LT into St Ursanne village.
14	St Ursanne (438m)	Leave village over old bridge, LT to rejoin road, LT under railway viaduct for 100m then RT onto minor road for climb to Montmelon (594m) and along ridge to Sceut (1008m), another horse-breeding village. **RB** Take LT onto road through Sceut and onto St Brais. **T** Take rough track along exciting route to St Brais. Watch out for cattle grids (bovi stop).
26	St Brais (967m)	Through village, up steep hill to track on left. **RB** Stay on road via Montfaucon to Saignelégier. **T** LT onto track past swallow holes, then RT on underpass beneath road, steep climb to rolling parkland ride with interesting cattle grids. **NB** signs: 'Beware cows will protect calves if you get too close!' Good YH in Le Bémont.
38	Saignelégier (978m)	LT along road then LT onto hilly, horsey section, before back to road and RT. Otherwise onwards up and down, via Les Breuleux and busy road section for 5km. Then LT and steep climb to Mt Soleil with Solar and Wind Power Visitors' Centre near summit.
57	Mt Soleil (1248m)	Rapid short downhill section, then RT along contours with views of St Imier (793m) and its valley far below. Then more switchbacks through empty landscapes, descending in a series of swooping falls to edge of La Chaux-de-Fonds. Great ride!
74	La Chaux-de-Fonds	

Alternative route
St Ursanne (483m) to Les Enfers (952m)

It is reported that there is a route through the Doubs gorge upstream of St Ursanne, using fourth class roads, possibly gravel, on the south bank of the River Doubs to La Charbonnière, then on via Les Moulins to the junction with the road from Soubey (476m). From this T-junction take a hairpin route to Les Enfers. This should cut about 200m off the day's total climbing, but may be hazardous if flooded.

FACILITIES							
	Distance (km)	Camp site	YH/BP	B&B	Hotel	Station	Bike shop
St Ursanne	14	✓		✓	Many	✓	
Saignelégier	38	✓	✓	✓	4	✓	✓
Mt Soleil	57				3		
St Imier (off route)	58					✓	✓
La Chaux-de-Fonds	74	✓		✓	Many	✓	✓

TOURIST INFORMATION			
From/to	Name	Address	Telephone/Website
Porentruy/ La Chaux- de-Fonds	Watch Valley Coordination	Route de Sorvilier 21 CH-2735 Bévilard	+41 (0)32 492 7132 www.watchvalley.ch/e

Autumn tints above the Doubs Valley

Stage 3: La Chaux-de-Fonds – Baulmes
72km; 1030m; difficult

Still typically Jura in feel, the route leaves the bustle of the massive blocks of La Chaux-de-Fonds behind, back into the high meadows and forests and then makes a wonderful curving descent into one-street Le Crêt. Ahead stretches the Vallée des Ponts, an expanse of marsh and peat, formerly a real hazard to travellers. The name 'Valley of Bridges' referred to floating log paths used on the marshes rather than real bridges. All the farms occupy break-of-slope sites, on a dry foothold where springwater was available. Today there are still many rare plants, insects and other creatures as well as thousands of cows. (Watch out for manure on roads!) The valley narrows southwestwards. The tall old buildings of Pont de Martel rise in steps up the steep slopes. Beyond, past numerous swallow holes, the country becomes wilder and rougher and somehow belongs to a previous century, and a passing car comes as a surprise. This is milk for cheese country, however, and Gruyère cheese is now produced here in cooperatives and modern factories.

A surprisingly gentle pass leads from this high valley into the Val de Travers ending in a long scenic drop through beech woods. Here asphalt was mined just south of Travers until 1986 – a rare example of the mineral being found in limestone. Formerly Val de Travers asphalt was used in road-making all over the world. (The mining museum is interesting if you can cope with spoken French or understand Swiss German.) Travers itself is a faded place, without mining jobs and income, and absinthe production has returned to the valley.

Approaching Fleurier the valley is sandwiched dramatically between great limestone cliffs, which the route bypasses into a higher valley running into Buttes, one of the railheads. From here steep scenic passes climb over the Côte-aux-Fées then down into L'Auberson, with its museum of mechanical toys, for which the whole area was once famed. The town of St Croix itself lies slightly off route to the east. The most testing climb to the Col de l'Aiguillon follows. From the col there is an exhilarating plunge along the flanks of the Aiguilles de Baulmes before the hairpin loops into Baulmes itself. Baulmes is an ancient village clustered at the foot of one of the straightest steepest sections of the Jura.

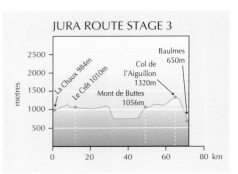

JURA ROUTE STAGE 3

ITINERARY		
Distance (km)	Location	Directions
0	La Chaux-de-Fonds (984m)	Return to R7, on road under rail bridge, then RT beyond roundabout onto minor road, then long gradual climb to road junction, RT to Le Locle, RT over col at 1156, then rapid smooth descent into Le Crêt.
13	Le Crêt (1010m)	RT for short distance on main road through village, then LT onto track along east side of valley (beware excessive cattle manure on road) until Les Ponts-de-Martel. **RB** Stay on main road on west side of valley. **T** RT at Les Petit Ponts road junction into Martel.
21	Les Ponts-de-Martel	**T** LT at lights then quiet road along narrowing valley, past swallow holes and finally swing left with road up short steep section to col (1082m) and lovely flowing descent into Travers.
28	Travers (735m)	RT at major road junction then LT onto track along river bank (Asphalt Museum lies to left after about 1km). Track muddy after rain, so **RB** stay on road to Couvet and Fleurier. Only lower station in Couvet is active.
37	Fleurier (741m)	LT on road through town then swing up along quiet road hugging rail track and climb gently into Buttes, descending to join road. RT uphill after short distance to hairpin steeply to La Côte-aux-Fées (1041m) followed by a rollicking up and down section hugging the 1100m contour, before reaching L'Auberson.
55	L'Auberson (1100m)	RT to begin the 5km climb to Col de l'Aiguillon (1320m), then the traverse below the limestone crags of Mont de Baulmes and its outlying ridges. Wrap up for the final steep descent into Baulmes village.
72	Baulmes (650m)	

Alternatives

- From Buttes, directly opposite the T-junction from Fleurier is a strenuous 12km route directly into St Croix. The first 400m of ascent can be avoided by using a chairlift that also transports bicycles. Otherwise there is a 600m climb to Le Chasseron then mostly downhill to Bullet and St Croix. From here it is a 100m climb to rejoin route at L'Auberson or the alternative route below.
- From L'Auberson, turn left and then follow a 4km undulating route into St Croix, then cycle the numerous hairpins downhill and turn right along base of hill into Baulmes. This route cuts out the Col de l'Aiguillon section.

FACILITIES							
	Distance (km)	Camp site	YH/BP	B&B	Hotel	Station	Bike shop
Le Crêt	13				1	✓	
Les Ponts-de-Martel	21					✓	
Travers	28			✓	2		
Couvet	33				2	✓	
Fleurier	37	✓			1	✓	✓
Buttes	41					✓	
L'Auberson	55	✓		✓			
St Croix (off route)	59		✓	✓	1	✓	✓
Baulmes	72				1	✓	

TOURIST INFORMATION			
From/to	Name	Address	Telephone/Website
La Chaux--de-Fonds/ Baulmes	Watch Valley Coordination	Route de Sorvilier 21 CH-2735 Bévilard	+41 (0)32 492 7132 www.watchvalley.ch/e

Stage 4: Baulmes – Nyon
78km; 1020m; difficult

This is another varied section with a traverse high along the Orbe valley before descending steeply into Vallorbe. Here there is a museum with great train models and layouts. Nearby is a cave system, the Grottes de Vallorbe, where research still continues into the underground drainage of the Jura and its lakes. Across the Orbe valley with some industry harking back to the old iron and wood-working here, R7 climbs steeply again past the prominent Dent de Vaulion cliffs then offers a freewheeling section into Le Pont on Lac du Joux.

This is a small popular ski and summer resort, mostly visited by the Swiss. R7 winds along the lake's north bank, through tiny villages where a few watchmakers still work. Another pretty ride along the lake edge follows, where swimming is possible on hot days if you're happy to brave the mosquitos. In summer, beware of cars towing caravans or boats using the road. There are more watch-making activities in Le Sentier (Musée l'Espace Horloger). As well as the expected lake fish delicacies on offer, mushroom-gathering and eating is a great local sport and locally produced bison is a healthy alternative to beef.

From Le Brassus the next climb begins. If you are struggling, stop frequently and enjoy the lake views and the still-close Dent de Vaulion before reaching the col. Here

Lac de Joux, Dent de Vaulion

R7 leads into the truly remote heart of the Parc Jurassien Vaudois along high valleys, devoid of drainage. A few dry stone walls and lonely barns are the only signs of human incursion, apart from the road itself. Invisible sheep and cattle, bells clanging, lurk in the pines dotting the limestone outcrops. There are magnificent Alpine panoramas on the descent towards Lac Léman.

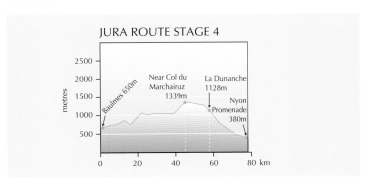

193

Here the landscape changes from something akin to tundra, through coniferous woods to massed vines on the final slopes to the lake. Don't miss the old Swiss army fort and its attendant concrete dragon's teeth or 'Toblerone' fortifications in the woods, with a good viewpoint (signposted La Dunanche Ouvrage Militaire 200m). From here Lac Léman looks close but, even at speed, there's a long way to ride, through Bassins, across a side valley to Genolier and finally into the vines. Approaching Coinsins, you can hear the noise of rumbling tyres on the Lausanne to Genève autoroute. Duillier is the remaining village before R7 slips into Nyon and ends by the railway station, where you can join R1.

Nyon was a settlement even before Julius Caesar in 58BC established a fortress and town there for his veteran soldiers. There's an excellent Musée Romain, an old town, complete with chateau, and displays of fine porcelain among other artefacts in the Musée Historique. Otherwise the lakeside with its promenade and park are pleasant (and you can bathe). Lake boats ply the shore between the harbour and other towns including Genève and Lausanne. Lake fish can be found on the menus displayed in the restaurants and cafés along the promenade, at a price. If you prefer to see the underwater inhabitants of the lake alive and well then visit the aquarium in the Musée du Léman.

ITINERARY		
Distance (km)	**Location**	**Directions**
0	Baulmes (650m)	At foot of hill RT along track to Six Fontaines and over railway lines on rough tracks clinging to hillside to Le Vailloud and climb to Lignerolle village. **RB** Take quiet road to Lignerolle out of Baulmes to avoid mud on track.
9	Lignerolle (760m)	Route parallels major road and climbs steadily on edge of Orbe valley to Ballaigues (861), then drop down, climb and drop into Vallorbe.
16	Vallorbe (749m)	Plunge down through town to valley floor, crossing River Orbe then climbing very steeply on poor rough track in cleft (1060m) below the Dent de Vaulion, then continue with care into Le Pont. **RB** Take road from Vallorbe to Le Pont.
25	Le Pont (1008m)	Head out between small Lac Brenet and larger Lac de Joux, via tiny Les Charbonnières, then undulating route via Le Lien, downhill through the trees for long lakeshore section before Joux delta and small town of Le Sentier. Straight ahead on west of valley before swinging east to Le Brassus.
39	Le Brassus (1036m)	At end of village LT up road to Col du Marchairuz and change into low gear. (Beware motor traffic at weekends!) Up, up and away from the gentle contours of the Joux

		valley into the karst of the High Jura, to T-junction at base of 2km straight section.
45	T junction (1339m)	RT with R7 signs (prohibited to cars). Cruise and climb alternately through the Parc Jurassien Vaudois, a wilderness despite the odd barn and wall. Eventually drop and twist back into forest (**NB** old fort on right) and to Les Platets and Bassins.
64	Bassins (753m)	Route descends sharply then RT and across road then more descents through small villages, using trails through the vines, then along streams via Grenolier into Coinsins and climb over bridge across autobahn. Follow signs, eventually to minor roads into Nyon.
78	Nyon (380m)	

Alternative route

Unsignposted route on road from Le Brassus via Bois d'Amont, Le Rousses (France), La Cure and St Cergue to Arzier on R7 (220m climb).

FACILITIES							
	Distance (km)	Camp site	YH/BP	B&B	Hotel	Station	Bike shop
Ballaigues	13				1		
Vallorbe	16	✓			1	✓	
Le Pont	25			✓	1	✓	
Les Charbonnières	26				1		
Le Sentier	38	✓		✓	1	✓	
Le Brassus	39				3		
Bassins	64				1		
Nyon	78	✓		✓	Many	✓	✓

TOURIST INFORMATION			
From/to	Name	Address	Telephone/Website
Baulmes/ Nyon	Watch Valley Coordination	Route de Sorvilier 21 CH-2735 Bévilard	+41 (0)32 492 7132 www.watchvalley.ch/e/

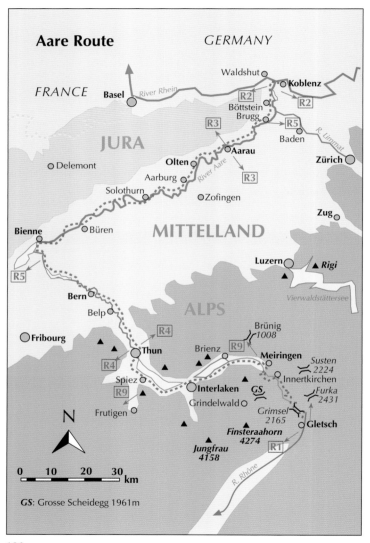

Aare Route

GERMANY

FRANCE

Waldshut

Koblenz

River Rhein

Basel

R2

Böttstein
Brugg

R2

JURA

R3

R5

Aarau

Baden

R. Limmat

O Delemont

Olten

River Aare

Zürich

Aarburg

R3

Solothurn

O Zofingen

MITTELLAND

Bienne

O Büren

Zug o

Luzern

▲ *Rigi*

R5

▲

Bern

Vierwaldstättersee

Belp

ALPS

Fribourg

▲

Brünig
1008

▲ ▲

Brienz

R9

Meiringen

Thun

▲

*Susten
2224*

R4

Innertkirchen

Spiez O

R4

GS

*Furka
2431*

R9

Interlaken

▲

Frutigen O

Grindelwald O

*Grimsel
2165*

Gletsch

*Finsteraahorn
4274*

R1

*Jungfrau
4158*

R. Rhône

N

0   10   20   30
━━━━━━━━━━━ km

GS: Grosse Scheidegg 1961m

8 THE AARE ROUTE, BASED ON R8

ROUTE SUMMARY					
From/to	Distance (km)	Climb (m) with public transport	Climb (m) without public transport	Grade with public transport	Grade without public transport
Koblenz/ Meiringen	281 (70)	790	1310	Easy	Moderate
Meiringen/ Koblenz	281 (70)	530	780	Easy	Easy

SUMMARY OF STAGES (WITHOUT PUBLIC TRANSPORT)				
Stage	From/to	Distance (km)	Climb (m)	Grade
1	Koblenz (Hochrhein)/ Brugg	20	150	Easy
2	Brugg/Zofingen	48	130	Easy
3	Zofingen/Solothurn	44	120	Easy
4	Solothurn/Bern	77	380	Moderate
5	Bern/Interlaken	64	200	Easy
6	Interlaken/(Brienz) Meiringen	(19) 28	330	Easy
Total	**Koblenz (Hochrhein)/ (Brienz) Meiringen**	**(272) 281**	**1310**	

LOCAL MAPS	
Swisstopo 1:100,000 Composite	
101	Thuner See–Zentralschweiz
102	Basel–Luzern
103	Zürich–St Gallen
104	Lausanne–Bern
108	Gruyère–Le Léman
111	Ajole–Fribourg

This route has two very different parts. The first starts in Gletsch and climbs the Grimselpass to Meiringen high in Alpine country. The other follows the Aare Valley meandering over mainly gentle pimples. The Grimselpass section from either the north (very hard work) or south is serious top-grade cycling. The Aare Valley is a great route for a family holiday, especially with trip to nearby Luzern to visit the Verkehrshaus (transport museum), take a steamer on the Vierwaldstätter See, a mountain railway to Rigi or the rack railway up Mount Pilatus.

Oberland, with good connections to Luzern and a better finishing point than Koblenz. Routes 8 and Route 5 run together for about 100km. Because this is the Aare route, what follows focuses on the Aare river and its sights. The lower Aare towns like Brugg and Solothurn are mentioned in more detail in chapter 5 (The Mittelland Route). The Grimselpass ascent is also covered in chapter 11 (The Alpine Star). The route is signposted in both directions and is easy cycling. This is the only Swiss National Cycle Route that only has one official language: German.

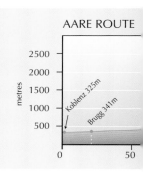

AARE ROUTE

LINKS TO OTHER ROUTES		
Location	**Route/s**	**To**
Koblenz (Hochrhein)	R2: Rhein Route	West: Basel East: Bodensee, Chur, Andermatt
Brugg	R5: Mittelland Route	East: Zürich, Romanshorn (Bodensee) West: Biel/Bienne, Lausanne
Aarau	R3: North–South Route	North: Basel South: Luzern, Andermatt, St Gotthard Pass, Lago Maggiore, Chiasso
Near Aarberg	R5: Mittelland Route	West: Lausanne East: Zürich, Romanshorn (Bodensee)
Thun	R4: Alpine Panorama Route	East: Luzern, St Margrethen (Bodensee) West: Aigle
Spiez	R9: Lakes Route	West: Montreux East: Gstaad, Luzern, Rorschach (Bodensee)
Meiringen	R9: Lakes Route	East: Luzern, Rorschach (Bodensee) West: Gstaad, Montreux

PUBLIC TRANSPORT BACKUP	
Section	**Service/*Comment***
Koblenz – Brugg – Aarau – Olten – Solothurn – Biel – Bern – Thun –Interlaken	Train
Interlaken – Brienz	Train, Ship *Summer only*
Brienz – Meiringen	Train

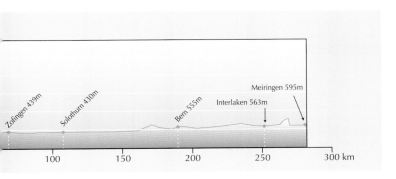

Meiringen 595m
Interlaken 563m
Bern 555m
Solothurn 430m
Zofingen 439m

100   150   200   250   300 km

In the Aareschlucht (gorge) (Stage 6)

Stage 1: Koblenz – Brugg
20km; 150m; easy

The Aare is larger than the Rhein at their confluence. Both the river and its valley show all the features of a mature fluvial landscape, such as a wide valley, terraces and meanders. Shortly after leaving Koblenz you pass the first sign of man-made interference with the Aare, the Klingnauer Stausee, which provides hydro-electric power and is also a bird watcher's paradise. Time permitting, stop, ascend an observation tower and talk to an enthusiast. They are pleased to share their hobby and telescopes and the problem will be getting away!

Beyond Böttingen the modern buildings of the research campus of the Paul Scherrer Institute come in view. The valley widens approaching Brugg, whose old town perched steeply above the Aare is interesting to explore.

In bad weather, take the train.

ITINERARY		
Distance (km)	Location	Directions
0	Koblenz (325m)	Follow track past lake to Kleindöttingen.
5	Kleindöttingen (328m)	Follow R8 along Aare bank, up and down spurs to reach R8.
20	Brugg (341m)	

FACILITIES							
	Distance (km)	Camp site	YH/BP	B&B	Hotel	Station	Bike shop
Koblenz	0				1	✓	
Klingnau	5					✓	✓
Kleindöttingen	5				1		
Brugg	20		✓	✓	3	✓	✓

TOURIST INFORMATION			
From/to	Name	Address	Telephone/Website
Koblenz/ Brugg	Aargau Tourismus	Graben 42 Postfach CH-5001 Aarau	+41 (0)62 824 7624 www.aargautourismus.ch

The start near Koblenz

Stage 2: Brugg – Zofingen
48km; 130m; easy

Along the Aare valley into Aarau the hills of the Jura first become a distinct entity to the right. The valley widens and narrows through farms, woods and nature reserves. Aarau town centre is slightly off route but well worth the climb through the old gatehouse. It was the capital of the Napoleonic Helvetian Republic for six months in 1798 and is now capital of Canton Aargau. It's lovely to sit in the sun drinking an Ovomaltine, gazing at the painted gables.

From here on, the waters of the Aare are used to generate electricity at numerous points. Weirs and dams attempt to protect settlements from floods. In good weather there are many river bathing places but sometimes the Aare is too high as it storms along. Olten's old town features a traditional wooden-covered bridge (and a feisty town cat!).

In bad weather or for a day off, take the train.

ITINERARY		
Distance (km)	**Location**	**Directions**
0	Brugg (341m)	Follow R5/8 into Aarau. To visit Aarau follow R3.
22	Aarau (371m)	Follow R5/8 to Niedergösgen, and Olten to Aarburg.
40	Aarburg (395m)	Take RR74 to Zofingen.
48	Zofingen (439m)	

FACILITIES							
	Distance (km)	**Camp site**	**YH/BP**	**B&B**	**Hotel**	**Station**	**Bike shop**
Aarau	22			✓	Many	✓	✓
Niedergösgen	26				1		✓
Olten	32				4	✓	✓
Zofingen	48		✓		Many	✓	✓

TOURIST INFORMATION			
From/to	**Name**	**Address**	**Telephone/Website**
Olten/ Zofingen	Schweizer Mittelland Tourismus	c/o Bern Tourismus Amthausgasse 4 Postfach 169 CH-3000 Bern 7	+41 (0)31 328 1212 www.smit.ch

Stage 3: Zofingen – Solothurn
44km; 120m; easy

Brown foaming Aare near Solothurn

This is a sleepy stage with a wide, slow-moving river as your constant companion. Handsome villages were built with the proceeds of trade as in earlier times raftsmen moved downstream, carrying goods. Prosperous farm buildings are frequent but there are no major settlements until Solothurn. Solothurn's well-preserved baroque old town features an impressive cathedral, a military museum (Altes Zeughaus), an art gallery (Kunstmuseum), a personal computer museum (only open on Sunday afternoons) and a natural history museum with a whole floor dedicated to Switzerland's geology.

In bad weather or for a day off, take the train.

ITINERARY		
Distance (km)	Location	Directions
0	Zofingen (439m)	Follow R74 to Aarburg.
8	Aarburg	Cross bridge to R5/8 towards Murgenthal and Aarwangen through woods.
22	Aarwangen	Folllow special route for cyclists through the old town. R5/8 to Wangen.

203

33	Wangen	Follow paths and quiet roads to Deitingen.
38	Deitingen	Follow R5/8 on cycleway on road, later on cyclepath. Turn up into centre of Solothurn. TO by cathedral.
44	Solothurn (430m)	

FACILITIES							
	Distance (km)	Camp site	YH/BP	B&B	Hotel	Station	Bike shop
Aarburg	8	✓			2	✓	✓
Murgenthal	15				1		✓
Aarwangen	22				2		✓
Wangen-an-Aare	33		✓		2	✓	✓
Lautenbach	37				2		✓
Solothurn	44	✓	✓	✓	Many	✓	✓

TOURIST INFORMATION			
From/to	Name	Address	Telephone/Website
Zofingen/ Solothurn	Schweizer Mittelland Tourismus	c/o Bern Tourismus Amthausgasse 4 Postfach 169 CH-3000 Bern 7	+41 (0)31 328 1212 www.smit.ch

Stage 4: Solothurn – Bern
77km; 380m; moderate

R8 near Bern offers steep, little hills. The route continues towards Biel/Bienne along the Aare on a mixture of surfaced and unsurfaced tracks. There is a monument to a World War II internment camp on the right after Büren, which is difficult to find but has lots of information about the camp, for those who can read German. Biel/Bienne is bilingual and thus has two names. It is an attractive enough old town and seems a pleasant place to live. R5/8 continues to Nidau along a canalised Aare with houseboats moored, to a rolling route alongside the Bieler See/Lac de Bienne. R8 then leaves R5 where the Aare is corralled via a sluice into the Bieler See. Turning east you ride across steep wooded country beside the Wohlensee, a long hydroelectric reservoir to the edge of Bern, and climb into the city.

Bern is a small capital city, making up in interest what it lacks in size. The old town, with its narrow streets and alleys, is a Unesco World Heritage site, perched on an incised Aare meander. There are museums galore including: the Alpine Museum, the Historical Museum (with frequent special exhibitions), three major art galleries, the Swiss Rifle Museum, the Swiss Salvation Army Museum, museums of communication,

Surprise steps by Wohlersee

psychiatry and natural history. There is a bear garden, in a riverside park and the *Münster* (cathedral) with its tower and *Zytglogge* (astronomical clock), high above.

In bad weather or for a day off, take the train.

ITINERARY		
Distance (km)	Location	Directions
0	Solothurn (430m)	Follow surfaced and unsurfaced tracks and minor roads to Büren.
19	Büren (437m)	Follow canal towards Nidau. Cross river to reach Biel/Bienne.
31	Nidau (440m)	Follow R5/8 up and down along lake towards Hagneck. LT to follow R8.
40	Hagneck (450m)	Good view of the Alps. RT for short section on road. LT to follow unsurfaced/surfaced track along canal to Bargen.
49	Bargen (449m)	Following R8 climb on quiet roads to reach a reservoir dammed to produce hydroelectricity. Alongside the lake tracks are unsurfaced. In Steinisroeg you need to walk the bikes down a steep, and, in rain, slippery wooden ramp.
71	Hinterkappelen (507m)	TR to cross the Aare. TL to climb on a surfaced forest road into Bern, then follow R8 through the university quarter to the Hauptbahnhof and TL to reach Casinoplatz.
77	Bern (555m)	

FACILITIES							
	Distance (km)	Camp site	YH/BP	B&B	Hotel	Station	Bike shop
Grenchen (off route)	12			✓	3		✓
Biel/Bienne (off route)	31	✓	✓	✓	Many	✓	✓
Nidau	31		✓	✓			✓
Ipsach	32				1		✓
Bargen	48			✓			
Aarberg (off route)	49				2		✓
Kappelen (off route)	50			✓			
Bern	77	✓	✓	✓	Many	✓	✓

TOURIST INFORMATION			
From/to	Name	Address	Telephone/Website
Solothurn/ Bern	Schweizer Mittelland Tourismus	c/o Bern Tourismus Amthausgasse 4 Postfach 169 CH-3000 Bern 7	+41 (0)31 328 1212 www.smit.ch

Stage 5: Bern – Interlaken
64km; 200m; easy

Today's route leads towards the Berner Oberland, so there's almost always a view of the Alps, making an excellent excuse to stop.

The route leaves Bern past the heavily guarded US Embassy. The guards are used to the cycling fraternity and ignore them but do not start taking photographs. R8 drops to cross the Aare with a resultant steep climb up the other side. The route leaves the suburbs of Bern running into a series of villages, on river terraces. Amid open farmland, R8 almost traverses the runways of the vanishingly small Bern Airport. Onwards along the Aare, now often glacial blue in colour, you travel through farmland and forest on minor roads and sometimes unsurfaced tracks to Thun. On arrival Thun's old town and castle is above to the left. Downtown Thun has a fascinating 'double decker' street with two layers of shops with pavements along the roofs of the lower shops.

After Thun it is back into woods again, running alongside the autobahn and into Spiez. There is a wonderful view past the castle across the Thunersee to the northern hills from the station above the town. The old town is down the hill by the lake but R8 drops rapidly to the lakeshore beyond Spiez and meanders with fine views to reach Interlaken.

Interlaken is a tourist highpoint, largely because of its mountain views especially of the Jungfrau. Interlaken has two youth hostels in Bönigen and Leissigen, at least one

Paddle ship on Thunersee

delightful B&B in Matten and several backpacker hostels. The latter also offer good value internet cafés. The SBB museum near Interlaken West and the Tourist Museum in Untersee are enjoyable.

Interlaken is an excellent excursion centre: see chapter 10 (The Berner Oberland) and chapter 9 (The Lakes Route) for descriptions.

In bad weather or for a day off, take the train.

ITINERARY		
Distance Location (km)		Directions
0	Bern	From Casinoplatz cross over the Aare on the Kirchenfeld Bridge towards the museum quarter. Follow R8 roughly half right and then SO past the US Embassy through the guarded gates across the street. Drop down to cross the Aare and climb. TL following R8 through Wabern and Belp (Bern Airport). Cycle through fields on tarmac and on unsurfaced tracks to Heimberg. Follow R8 along railway lines to Steffisburg where R4 joins the route into Thun. R4/8 avoids the Old Town by looping southwards along the river.
30	Thun	TO next to railway station. TR just before station to follow R4/8 under railway to Allmendingen.
34	Allmendingen	TL towards to Spiez on R8 following surfaced and unsurfaced tracks.
45	Spiez (628m)	From railway station, go downhill leaving town on busy road to Faulensee, then take a death-defying LT across traffic (use traffic island) and along quieter lakeside roads parallel to railway and main road. In Leissigen the main road goes right and you carry SO. Make sure motorists realise that you are not going to TR. Good views of Thunersee follow into genteel Därligen. Keep your eyes open for racing types approaching all along this stretch. This route is popular with the Lycra-clad and they don't hang about.
59	Därligen (562m)	Follow cycleway perched over lake, finally underneath major highway. About 3km on wide hard shoulder before exit, signposted up exit road to traffic lights. Cross with lights to a cycleway and descend towards the peaceful delta farms. Continue into Unterseen, take care on narrow roads into Interlaken.
64	Interlaken (563m)	

FACILITIES							
	Distance (km)	Camp site	YH/BP	B&B	Hotel	Station	Bike shop
Thun	30	✓		✓	Many	✓	✓
Allmendingen	34			✓			
Spiez	45			✓	Many	✓	✓
Leissigen	55		✓	✓	2	✓	
Interlaken	64	✓	✓ (Bönigen)	✓	Many	✓	✓

TOURIST INFORMATION			
From/to	Name	Address	Telephone/Website
Bern	Schweizer Mittelland Tourismus	c/o Bern Tourismus Amthausgasse 4 Postfach 169 CH-3000 Bern 7	+41 (0)31 328 1212 www.smit.ch
Thun/ Interlaken	Destinationen Berner Oberland	Postfach CH-3800 Interlaken	+41 (0)33 821 2870 www.berneroberland.ch

Stage 6: Interlaken – Meiringen/Brienz
28km; 330m; easy

It may be hard to leave the flat lands of Interlaken, but those seeking an exhilarating finish to their ride should complete the slightly challenging section along the Brienzersee trail. Brienz is a little lakeside resort with many wood carving shops and a steam rack railway up the Brienzer Rothorn.

Nearby is Meiringen and Conan Doyle's famous Reichenbach Falls, the setting for Sherlock Holmes' demise (although five years later popular demand resulted in his reappearance). Rather than climbing the 400m up the road towards Grosse Scheidegg, you can choose to take a rack railway to see the falls.

Say farewell to the Aare in the Aareschlucht between Innertkirchen and Meiringen, a very narrow gorge carved out by the Aare grumbling below. Park your bike at one end or the other, walk through and either take the tram or walk back. It is not far.

From here you can cycle over the Brünigpass on R9 towards Luzern or take the train.

In bad weather, take the train or ship.

Sherlock Holmes memorial near Reichenbach Falls

ITINERARY

Distance (km)	Location	Directions
0	Interlaken	Leave Interlaken with the Interlaken Ost station on your left and follow R8/9 to Bönigen.
2	Bönigen	Follow R8/9 along lakeside.
9	Iseltwald (566m)	There is a section of rough track after Iseltwald. Please walk near the Giessbach Hotel.
17	Stägmatten (577m)	LT to Brienz or RT to Meiringen past the airfield. Your progress may be blocked by the Swiss Air Force rolling out Mirage jets.
28	Meiringen (595m)	

FACILITIES

	Distance (km)	Camp site	YH/BP	B&B	Hotel	Station	Bike shop
Bönigen	2	✓	✓	✓	Many		
Iseltwald	9	✓			Many	✓	
Brienz (off route)	16	✓	✓	✓	Many	✓	✓
Meiringen	28	✓		✓	Many	✓	✓

TOURIST INFORMATION

From/to	Name	Address	Telephone/Website
Interlaken/ Meiringen	Destinationen Berner Oberland	Postfach CH-3800 Interlaken	+41 (0)33 821 2870 www.berneroberland.ch

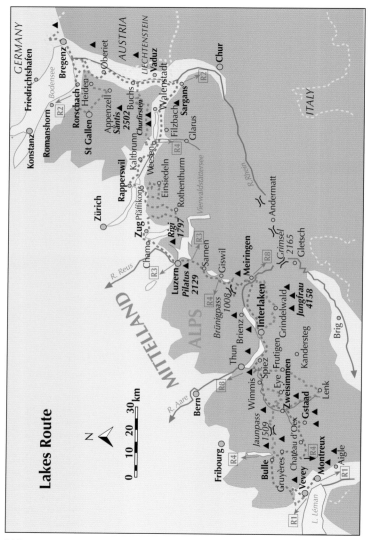

Lakes Route

9 THE LAKES ROUTE, R9

ROUTE SUMMARY					
From/to	Distance (km)	Climb (m) with public transport	Climb (m) without public transport	Grade with public transport	Grade without public transport
Montreux/ Rorschach	483 (50)	1770	3890	Easy	Moderate
Rorschach/ Montreux	483 (50)	2000	3890	Easy	Moderate

SUMMARY OF STAGES (WITHOUT PUBLIC TRANSPORT)				
Stage	From/to	Distance (km)	Climb (m)	Grade
1	Montreux/Bulle	42	500	Moderate
2	Bulle/Gstaad	50	730	Moderate
3	Gstaad/Interlaken	69	510	Moderate
4	Interlaken/Giswil	51	860	Moderate
5	Giswil/Zug	69	200	Easy
6	Zug/Filzbach	89	850	Moderate
7	Filzbach/Buchs	45	150	Easy
8	Buchs/Rorschach	68	90	Easy
Total	**Montreux/Rorschach**	**483**	**3890**	

LOCAL MAPS	
Swisstopo 1:100,000 Composite	
101	Thuner See–Zentralschweiz
103	Zürich–St Gallen
104	Lausanne–Bern
111	Ajole–Fribourg

R9 connects Montreux on Lac Léman with Rorschach on the Bodensee and runs through some of the most dramatic scenery in Switzerland often along the shores of lakes. The towns encountered sound like a wish list of desirable places from Montreux, Vevey, or Gstaad, holiday home to the stars, Luzern where Wagner wrote the 'Meistersinger' and Zug, Switzerland's richest city. The route is challenging, with a number of interesting climbs but public transport backup is excellent, so the less energetic can cherry pick the easier sections. Purists can revel in the glory of ascents and thrilling descents and wave at less energetic rail travellers. The language border between the French and German speaking areas of Switzerland is near Saanen.

The route offers picture-book Switzerland via Bulle, Gruyères and friendly Château d'Oex then Gstaad. After a climb to Zweizimmen the route descends to Spiez

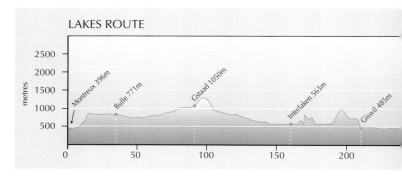

LAKES ROUTE

on the Brienzersee, Interlaken and Meiringen, associated with Sherlock Holmes. R9 is sporting and occasionally uses roads with truck traffic through narrow sections. After Meiringen R9 turns northwards over the low Brünigpass before plunging downhill into Giswil. Pretty Sarnen is followed by nature reserves and lagoons towards Alpnach and Luzern on the Vierwaldstätter See. Luzern is one of our favourite cities and well worth visiting.

Devotees of hill climbs will not be disappointed between Zug and Rapperswil, another foray into rural Switzerland, full of ups and downs with delightful villages. In

Spiez and the Thunersee (Stage 3)

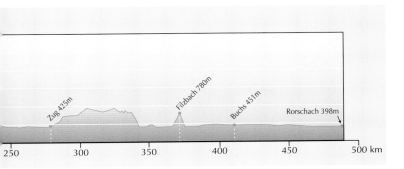

clear weather the view over the Zürichsee above Pfäffikon makes all the sweat worthwhile, especially knowing that there is a gentle but scenic section to come. Soon the Churfirsten mountains appear, great cliffs of folds along the northern Walensee shore. Former road tunnels converted for cyclists make the first part even more interesting. As ever, even riding along a lakeside offers some climbing before the Rhein valley is reached by Sargans.

Along the Rhein flood embankment to the Bodensee, it can be relaxing to bowl northwards with a following wind, some 10m above the river with sharp peaks all around. The mountains continue almost into the Bodensee, hawks using the thermals over the fields as tractors buzz about. The huge delta out into the lake makes an interesting landscape of farms, flowers and birds of all descriptions. Back on the main route terminus of R9, Rorschach is soon reached. R2 continues to Basel, the Bodensee offers bathing and high life so it is decision time again.

LINKS TO OTHER ROUTES		
Location	**Route/s**	**To**
Montreux	R1: Rhône Route	West: Genève
		East: Martigny, Gletsch, Andermatt
Bulle	R4: Alpine Panorama Route	North: Thun, Luzern, St Margrethen (Bodensee)
Montbovon	R4: Alpine Panorama Route	South: Aigle
Spiez	R8: Aare Route	North: Koblenz
Meiringen	R8: Aare Route	South: Gletsch
Giswil	R4: Alpine Panorama Route	West: Thun, Aigle
Stansstad	R3: North–South Route	South: Andermatt, St Gotthard Pass, Lago Maggiore, Chiasso

Luzern (Emmen)	R3: North–South Route	North: Basel
Kaltbrunn	R4: Alpine Panorama Route	East: St Margrethen (Bodensee)
Niederurnen	R4: Alpine Panorama Route	West: Thun, Aigle
Sargans	R2: Rhein Route	South: Chur, Andermatt
Rorschach	R2: Rhein Route	North: Basel

PUBLIC TRANSPORT BACKUP	
Section	**Service/Comment**
Montreux – Vevey	Train, Steamer *Golden Pass Line, steamer, April to October.*
Vevey – Mont Pèlerin	Funicular *Avoids part of climb.*
Vevey – Zweisimmen – Interlaken – Luzern	Train *Golden Pass Line*
Luzern – Zug	Train
Zug – Oberägeri	Bus
Sattel – Rapperswil	Train
Biberbrugg – Einsiedeln	Train
Rapperswil – Sargans – St Margrethen – Rorschach	Train

Stage 1: Montreux – Bulle
42km; 500m; moderate

The route begins at the railway station in Montreux with magnificent mountains to the northeast and the lake in front. Montreux began long ago to cater for travellers over the Great St Bernard Pass, but really blossomed when the railways and lake steamers arrived in the 19th century. It was favoured by wealthy British travellers, early clients of the enormous hotels dating from this period, and no doubt there are still some such around today. In July, during the jazz festival, accommodation is booked up early.

Cycle quickly west along a busy lakeside road to Vevey, former home of Charlie Chaplin, with less razzmatazz than Montreux. The old alleyways, churches and grand squares are full of locals and visitors. Use the cable car up Mont Pèlerin from the Vevey funi station to avoid climbing 400m and freewheel to rejoin the route. Otherwise R9 heads north-northeast along the edge of Mont Pèlerin along the valley cut by the River Veveyse.

Prepare your thigh muscles for the climb to Châtel St Denis, following an ancient cheese trade route. It's not as romantic as the Silk Road but Switzerland and cheese have a long, profitable association. The route uses minor roads with pleasant ups and downs into Bulle, the principle cheese-making town. Despite a fire in 1805, Bulle is worth a visit, especially on market days when many cheeses can be seen, tried and purchased.

In bad weather or for an easy option, take the funicular from Vevey to Mont Pélerin (400m).

ITINERARY		
Distance (km)	Location	Directions
0	Montreux CFF (400m)	Take R9 from station to lake side, RT west to Vevey. RT by VSIB on R9 steeply through town, under autobahn and climb hairpins through woods to Châtel St Denis.
18	Châtel St Denis (809m)	Follow undulating route to La Rogivue, La Verrerie and Vaulruz then criss cross autobahn route into Bulle.
42	Bulle (771m)	

FACILITIES							
	Distance (km)	Camp site	YH/BP	B&B	Hotel	Station	Bike shop
Montreux	0	✓	✓	✓	Many	✓	✓
Vevey	7				Many	✓	✓
Bulle	42	✓		✓	Many	✓	✓

TOURIST INFORMATION			
From/to	Name	Address	Telephone/Website
Montreux/ Vevy	Office du Tourisme du Canton de Vaud	Avenue d'Ouchy 60 Case Postale 164 CH-1000 Lausanne 6	+41 (0)21 613 2626 www.lake-geneva-region.ch
Bulle	La Gruyère Tourisme	Place des Alpes 26 CH-1630 Bulle	+41 (0)84 842 4424 www.la-gruyere.ch

Stage 2: Bulle – Gstaad
50km; 730m; moderate

Quiet trails lead to Broc where the Nestlé/Caillier chocolate factory is open to visitors and Gruyères, a picturesque village, its walls and towers high above the valley. The latter is overrun by tourists. You can buy the famous cheese at various stages of ripeness, without visiting the village, at the show dairy at the bottom of the hill.

R9 runs southwards through superb valley landscapes of green fields and imposing farmhouses, with rocky snow clad mountains above. This is a route to be savoured and admired, rather than rushed through. However the Sarine valley is narrow, especially between Lessoc and Les Moulins so the bike route shares the road with trucks and buses. The chalet-style villages are charming and the Grand-Chalet in Rossinière is amazing. Get some idea of the wealth of a 1754 cheese merchant from the 113 windows of this enormous 'chalet'. The cellars stored 600 cheeses.

Family resort Château d'Oex is famous for ballooning events. Rougemont dates back to a Cluniac monastery founded in 1080 to cultivate the wild landscape, clearly to great effect. Another gorge leads to Saanen and more farmhouses, noted for producing intricate paper-cut pictures, popular with visitors.

In bad weather or for an easy option, take the train from Montbovon to Saanen (585m).

Picnic near Gruyères

ITINERARY		
Distance Location (km)		**Directions**
0	Bulle (771m)	Leave town on R9 up and over to Morlon and junction with R4 at VSIB. RT then LT into Broc. Continue to Gruyères.

10	Gruyères (830m)	LT into town itself or climb gently to station then downhill to road RT for 500m then LT across river bridge, steep climb, along valley to Grandvillard, more climbing beyond to Lessoc.
22	Lessoc (812m)	Sharp RT to rejoin road to Montbovon, continue on R9 (R4 turns right), through pass parallel to railway on track, bypassing La Tine and Rossinière.
31	Rossinière (920m)	Rejoin road beyond Rossinière, LT by VSIB in Les Moulins for **RB** and those visiting Chateaux d'Oex. **T** Continue on track on valley side bypassing town. Reunite at VSIB in Gerignox. Continue to Rougemont.
42	Rougemont (1007m)	Continue through town, rejoin road into Saanen and Gstaad.
50	Gstaad (1050m)	

Alternatives for the energetic
- Bulle (771m) to Boltigen (883m) over the Jaunpass (1509m) and through some tunnels – about 36km. Great scenery but strenuous.
- Take local cycle signposted trip from Gstaad to Lauenensee, a steep climb out of town to southwest.

FACILITIES							
	Distance (km)	Camp site	YH/BP	B&B	Hotel	Station	Bike shop
Gruyères	10	✓		✓	4	✓	
Montbovon	25				1	✓	
Rossinière (off route)	30			✓	Many		
Château d'Oex	37		✓	✓	Many	✓	✓
Rougemont	42			✓	1		
Saanen	47	✓	✓	✓	Many		✓
Gstaad	50			✓	Many	✓	✓

TOURIST INFORMATION			
From/to	Name	Address	Telephone/Website
Bulle/ Montbovon	La Gruyère Tourisme	Place des Alpes 26 CH-1630 Bulle	+41 (0)84 842 4424 www.la-gruyere.ch
Rossinière/ Rougement	Office du Tourisme du Canton de Vaud	Avenue d'Ouchy 60 Case Postale 164 CH-1000 Lausanne 6	+41 (0)21 613 2626 www.lake-geneva-region.ch
Gstaad	Gstaad Saanenland Tourismus	CH-3780 Gstaad	+41 (0)33 748 8181 www.gstaad.ch

Stage 3: Gstaad – Interlaken
69km; 510m; moderate

R9 runs into car-free Gstaad, inevitably associated with the rich, noble or would-be famous. It is a village, rather than a town, with beautifully kept weathered chalets and rather expensive cups of coffee. (The Swiss Open tennis championships are held here in July and the Menuhin Festival in July and August.) If you get tired of star-spotting or window shopping for high class accessoires then head south to Lauenensee for a bit of peace, broken by cattle bells and bees.

Part of the next section to Schönried lies uphill along a busy road with numerous level crossings to slow down speeding traffic. Then, after Saanenmöser, the route sets off alongside the railway line, dropping from around 1100m into Zweisimmen, at the confluence of two Simmen tributaries. The next section descends along the river, although narrows necessitate occasional steep climbs. There are more large farm-houses, some dating from 1500 or later, built by carpenters whose artistic trail can still be followed. Fortunately woodcraft is still alive in Switzerland with new chalets under construction and a cyclist's bridge below Garstatt, financed by local communities.

You will see many fine Simmentaler Fleck dairy cows, supporting cheese produc-tion, and also horses and goats on your travels. River rafting is possible from Oberwil. The notable Stockhorn peak (2190m) rises on left, as the valley widens beyond

Electric fence below Zweisimmen

Wimmis with its little white church, and you carry on over a river gorge and into Spiez on Lake Thun. Across the lake serried ranks of ridges add to the magnificent setting of sloping vineyards and the decorative castle. The mix of colours, the greens of woods and pastures, blue or green lakes and the white boats are a delight. Despite more people and traffic, especially on the busy highway towards Interlaken, it is a great area for cycling. Leave the buses, caravans and cars to stream into the city, turn off and saunter through the lanes and farms of the delta, quietly entering Interlaken via old Unterseen village.

The centre of Interlaken is inevitably given over to the trappings of tourism but enjoy the view of the Jungfrau, visit the railway museum and stock up on necessities. Despite being in the middle of 'tourist' Switzerland, the cyclist can enjoy the high points quietly from the saddle, often seeing more than the madding crowd as it flocks from ferry to train, from bus to hotel. Unterseen offers an impression of Swiss farming villages in pre-tourism times and Bönigen on the Brienzersee glimpses of the genteel hotel life of early railway tourists. (See chapter 10 for excursions from Interlaken.)

In bad weather or for a day off, take the train.

ITINERARY		
Distance Location (km)		Directions
0	Gstaad (1050m)	Leave town on R9 and climb steeply to Schönried to join road through town and on to Saanenmöser.
6	Saanenmöser (1269m)	On outskirts of village TR by station and ride parallel to railway down, up, then a steep descent into Zweisimmen.
14	Zweisimmen (941m)	Cross railway line out into valley then along rough track to rejoin road en route to Garstatt. **RB** Take road out of Zweisimmen to Oberwil. **T** Use signposted rough track parallel with road towards Oberwil. R9 continues on good surface on right bank of river, then two bridges to cross down to Erlenbach.
39	Erlenbach (707m)	Continue down to Oey. TR to Wimmis after level crossing. After Wimmis up and over a series of spurs followed by a short stretch on busy road then interesting cycleway, under autobahn and over metal bridge across river gorge into Spiezmoos, alongside autobahn and uphill into Spiez by railway station.
51	Spiez (628m)	From railway station downhill out of town on busy road to Faulensee, then death-defying LT across traffic (use traffic island) and along quieter lakeside roads parallel to railway and main road. In Leissigen the main road goes right and you carry SO. Make sure other road users realise this. Good views of Thunersee follow on the way into Därligen.

		Keep your eyes open for other cyclists hereabouts because this is a popular training stretch for road bike users and they don't like being delayed.
64	Därligen (562m)	Follow cycleway perched over lake, finally underneath major highway. About 3km on wide hard shoulder before exit signposted up exit road to traffic lights. Cross with lights to security of cycleway and descend into the quiet of the delta farms. Follow route into Unterseen, taking care on narrow roads into Interlaken.
69	Interlaken (563m)	

Alternatives for the energetic (partly unsurfaced)

- Mountain bike route (57km): Zweisimmen (941m) via Lenk (1068m, c13km), then over the Hahnenmoos Pass (1968m) to Adelboden (1300m) and along road to Frutigen (803m) and thence to Spiez (57km).
- Road bike route (30km): near Grübenwald (900m), down valley from Zweisimmen local route via Meienberg (1851m), ridge below the Niderhorn to Eye (1041m) and up to Entschwil (1100m) then down to Erlenbach (707m).

FACILITIES							
	Distance (km)	Camp site	YH/BP	B&B	Hotel	Station	Bike shop
Schönried	3				Many	✓	
Saanenmöser	6				Many	✓	
Zweisimmen	14	✓		✓	Many	✓	✓
Weissenburg	32				1		
Erlenbach	39	✓		✓	1		✓
Oey	40				1		✓
Wimmis	45			✓	1		✓
Spiez	51	✓		✓	Many	✓	✓
Krattigen	57	✓					
Leissigen	60		✓	✓	2	✓	
Interlaken and district	69	✓	✓ (Bönigen)	✓	Many	✓	✓

TOURIST INFORMATION			
From/to	Name	Address	Telephone/Website
Gstaad	Gstaad Saanenland Tourismus	CH-3780 Gstaad	+41 (0)33 748 8181 www.gstaad.ch
Boltigen/ Interlaken	Destinationen Berner Oberland	Postfach CH-3800 Interlaken	+41 (0)33 821 2870 www.berneroberland.ch

Stage 4: Interlaken – Giswil
51km; 860m; moderate

The rough route along the edge of the Brienzersee is superb on a touring bike, with views north along the mountain wall, culminating in the Brienzer Rothorn and over the strikingly deep turquoise lake. Lest you relax too much bowling along the flat valley floor to Meiringen, a close encounter with the Swiss air force is possible, fighter jets roaring up from the airfield out over Lake Brienz. In Meiringen, you have the choice between researching meringues, supposedly invented here, or researching Sherlock Holmes. The fictitious detective died at nearby Reichenbach Falls, but was later revived due to popular demand. It is probably best to visit the Falls on the southern valley side or the Aare Gorge before you reach Meiringen. The Aare has cut and dissolved its way through a massive rockfall, accessible by seemingly precarious walkways pegged above the river. A few meringues in a patisserie in Meiringen while toasting Holmes and Watson with a cup of coffee should calm your nerves.

Swiss route planners do not like cyclists to lose muscle tone, so the next stage heads over the moderate Brünigpass as R9 turns northwards. The official route uses a steep rough track but there is a quiet road via Brünigen village. There are great views

Cowbell ringers in Iseltwald, Brienzersee

towards the Wetterhorn, as well as other 3000m peaks, and the Aare Valley on the hairpins out of Meiringen. After the junction with the road from Brienz, traffic increases. It is busy and rather narrow, but only about a kilometre to the pass top (and endless souvenirs).

The official north side R9 route is extremely rough but goes through delightful woods. Many people choose the road route downhill past a great landslide. The countryside reminded us of the limestone North Pennines of England, dotted with isolated farms, overhanging grey rocks and information about rare plants. In tiny Lungern station an old notice forbids smoking and fires during Föhn winds. These hot dry winds often used to cause whole towns to burn down. Along the rustic tracks on the west shore of the Lungerer See, there is a gentle undulating ride before another thrilling descent into Giswil. This is another place where decorated cows processing through the villages munch the flowers from people's gardens.

For an easy option, take the railway between Meiringen and Brünigpass summit (447m).

ITINERARY		
Distance (km)	Location	Directions
0	Interlaken (563m)	**RB** Either take bridge over the Aare to Goldswil and along road north of the Brienzer See to Brienz and RT onto R9 at end of Lake, or follow the Grossescheidegg route described in chapter 10 (The Berner Oberland). **T** Pick up R9 by station and ride out, passing under autobahn, to Bönigen, then along quiet lakeside road. Then steep, rough, dramatic unfenced section to road junction at Giessbach (smart hotel, waterfalls).
15	Giessbach (758m)	Take downhill plunge on road to delta flats at Stägmatten. Continue to Meiringen on rural roads, across military airfield (controlled when planes cross, very noisy). Follow signs eastwards to Reichenbach Falls access and Aare Gorge (Schlucht) (off route).
28	Meiringen (595m)	**RB** Use road to Brünigen and continue on road over pass and down to Lungern. **T** Either use the road to the summit or follow the R9 rough route through woods above road. R9 trail beyond pass is almost unrideable at first, later very pleasant.
41	Lungern (752m)	**RB** Continue on road to Giswil. Tourists follow R9 along rough track on west of Lungerer See, then back to tarmac and rejoin road for magnificent swoop into Giswil.
51	Giswil (485m)	

Alternatives for the energetic
- Tourist bike route: From Interlaken via Matten on cycleway to Zweilütschinen (652m), turn left to climb to Grindelwald (1034m) and Grosse Scheidegg (1962m) and take the road downhill to a left turn to reach Meiringen on a short cycleway, rough in places.
- Road bike route: Follow the road from Matten to Zweilütschinen, then take road to Grindelwald over Grosse Scheidegg but stay on the road down to the junction with the road from Innertkirchen and then turn left to reach Meiringen.

FACILITIES							
	Distance (km)	Camp site	YH/BP	B&B	Hotel	Station	Bike shop
Iseltwald	11	✓			4	Ship	
Brienz (off route)	20	✓	✓	✓	Many	✓	
Meiringen	28	✓		✓	Many	✓	✓
Hasliberg	33	✓		✓	Many		
Brünig	36				1	✓	
Lungern	41				Many	✓	
Giswil	51	✓			Many	✓	✓

TOURIST INFORMATION			
From/to	Name	Address	Telephone/Website
Interlaken/ Hasliberg	Destinationen Berner Oberland	Postfach CH-3800 Interlaken	+41 (0)33 821 2870 www.berneroberland.ch
Giswil/ Emmen	Luzern Tourismus AG Tourist Board	Zentralstrasse 5 CH-6002 Luzern	+41 (0)41 227 1717 www.luzern.org/en/welcome.cfm

Stage 5: Giswil – Zug
69km; 200m; easy

The main road and railway follow the Sarnersee's east bank, leaving us free to enjoy the switchback west shore and a freewheel into pretty Sarnen, the half-Canton capital. Another drained lakebed with lagoons occupied by aquatic plants and creatures leads to Alpnach on the Alpnacher See, part of the Vierwaldstätter See. Above towers Pilatus (2200m), Luzern's local mountain and viewpoint, accessible by the steepest rack railway in Switzerland from Alpnach. Steep rock walls bound both edges of this lake.

In many countries road and railway needs would probably have ousted walkers and cyclists completely. However, this is Switzerland so, although the cycling may be a

Yet more flags in Zug

bit noisy and shared with walkers, it is possible. Things improve in Stansstad, even though the trail lies partly beneath the autobahn. Beyond Horw a delightful lakeside route wends through fields, past bijou residences into Luzern itself. Rigi Kulm rises steeply across the lake from Pilatus and on clear days a rack railway trip gives fantastic views. You can take a ship to Vitznau from Luzern and explore Luzern's old town and the River Reuss flowing out of the lake with its bridges and fish traps. Above all, don't miss the superb Transport Museum on the lake towards Seeburg, where a magnificent collection of boats, railway engines, cars and many hands-on models bring out the small boy in all of us.

By Luzern, R9 reaches the edge of more densely populated Switzerland. However the route along the River Reuss, turning northeast parallel to the mountains, is quiet, a chance to enjoy a rolling ride and lakeside run into Cham. Lake Zug, protected since 1946, maintains an important fishery and wildlife. Zug is reportedly the richest city in Switzerland because of tax concessions for individuals and companies, so the ancient alleyways are ringed by glass and steel finance houses, containing closely guarded secrets. The open expanse of the Zuger See and the steep bordering mountains may have caused two violent storms fuelled by Föhn winds rocketing down from the Alps. In 1435, 26 houses and their inhabitants were washed away by the waves and in 1887 another 16 houses and 11 people fell victim to the same fate. In the albeit unlikely event that there is a 100-year storm forecast then cycle away uphill on R9 rather than hanging about to eat saibling, the delicious local lake fish.

ITINERARY		
Distance Location (km)		Directions
0	Giswil (485m)	Take R4/9 signs along west side of lake to Sarnen, pleasantly up and down.
10	Sarnen (471m)	**RB** Stay on R4 to Stansstad, avoiding rough trail. **T** RT onto R9 by VSIB out of town, some rough trails through the woods. Use road to Stansstad with care. Pilatus railway from Alpnachstad, ship to Luzern from pier.
23	Stansstad (435m)	LT onto R9 then interesting narrow section under autobahn and along through Hergiswil and climb to Horw. RT on R9 along lake edge, through villages to outskirts of Luzern. Follow R9 to station. Beware trams and other cyclists.
39	Luzern (436m)	**T** Follow R9 alongside the Reuss river, banking quarter on left, past bridges and fish traps, along quiet road towards Emmen, soon surprisingly rustic.
		RB Follow R38 through Meggen and Küssnacht and then on to Immensee. TR to reach Zug from the south via Arth (c30km).
45	Emmen (428m)	**T** Enjoy pleasant ride along the willows and meadows by the Reuss to Cham and Zug on lakeside.
69	Zug (425m)	

FACILITIES							
	Distance (km)	Camp site	YH/BP	B&B	Hotel	Station	Bike shop
Sarnen	10	✓		✓	Many		✓
Alpnach	19	✓		✓	4		✓
Stans (off route)	27				Many	✓	✓
Hergiswil	26	✓		✓	Many		✓
Luzern	39	✓	✓	✓	Many	✓	✓
Emmen	45			✓	Many		
Gisikon	54	✓			2		✓
Cham	64				4		✓
Zug	69	✓	✓	✓	3	✓	✓

TOURIST INFORMATION			
From/to	Name	Address	Telephone/Website
Sarnen/ Emmen	Luzern Tourismus AG Tourist Board	Zentralstrasse 5 CH-6002 Luzern	+41 (0)41 227 1717 www.luzern.org/en/ welcome.cfm
Rotkreuz/Zug	Zug Tourismus	Reisezentrum Zug Bahnhofplatz CH-6304 Zug	+41 (0)41 723 6800 www.zug-tourismus.ch

Stage 6: Zug – Filzbach
89km; 850m; difficult

Out of Zug there is a short, severe road climb, then you get into the farms and villages on the flanks of the Zugerberg, with views back towards the lake. Unterägeri has interesting chalets and fretwork house decorations. The Ägerisee is followed by Sattel village and another hefty climb into Rothenthurm at the start of a stretch of high moorland and old lake beds. (Pollen analysis of peat here has provided information about plant succession since the last Ice Age.) More climbing to leave this basin, then you join a busy route into Einsiedeln.

The massive pilgrim church attracts pilgrims of every persuasion, especially at the weekends, so beware buses and crowds. Legend has it that in 861, two tramps murdered a monk from Reichenau monastery (Bodensee). Harry Potter-style, two observant ravens followed the murderers to Zürich and indicated them to a judge, after which retribution followed. Two ravens still feature in the town coat of arms and in 934 Monk Eberhard, from Strasbourg, founded a monastery here. Einsiedeln became a centre of tourism even in the middle ages. Despite the throngs and tourist kitsch, both the town, with its very ancient hostelries and the giant cathedral, deserve a visit. It is even better to roll along the hilltop and plunge down across the causeway over the remote-seeming Sihlsee, while the tour buses take the main route towards Rapperswil or Zürich.

After more climbs into a lost world of woods and high farmsteads, with luck and clear weather, a panoramic map of Lake Zürich and Rapperswil eventually opens out far below, followed by equally wonderful downhill wheeling, over the autobahn and into rather dreary Pfäffikon. Step on it and reach the causeway cycle route to picturesque Rapperswil, its old harbour and enormous church on the hilltop above.

The route continues along the Obersee with gentle undulations to Schmerikon and then across an old delta, drained by the Linth Canal to reduce annual floods following spring snowmelt. Storks and herons love the feeding opportunities offered by these low-lying fields. Road, railway and cycle route are pinched together by the narrows at Niederurnen, the entrance to the Walensee basin. The cycleway uses the abandoned (but lit) road tunnel under the autobahn with interesting views and surreal sound effects before reaching Filzbach. Here there is a *Rodelbahn* (summer sledge run), 3.5km long, running down the Kerenzer Berg and enjoyed by all ages.

In bad weather or for an easy option, take the bus between Zug and Unterägeri (310m) and train from Sattel to Einsiedeln.

ITINERARY		
Distance (km)	**Location**	**Directions**
0	Zug (425m)	Climb out of Zug by busy road towards Arbach, RT onto steep quiet road to Allenwinden, then back to traffic into Unterägeri. Along lake to the resort of Hauptsee.
19	Hauptsee (726m)	Climb steadily to Sattel, LT and continue to climb and climb towards Rothenthurm, then along border of marshland, climbing and falling to busy little Biberbrugg.
35	Biberbrugg (830m)	Double back and onto busy road to Einsiedeln, view cathedral, eat cake, then rise over flank of hill and descend across causeway over Sihlsee to Willerzell.
44	Willerzell (890m)	LT then continue with sharp ups and downs across a series of hills to viewpoint above Zürichsee and lowlands to north. Great downhill run over autobahn into Pfäffikon.
60	Pfäffikon (420m)	LT onto cycleway over causeway (changes sides midway at lights) and into Rapperswil. **RB** Take road into town and follow to Schmerikon to avoid gravel. **T** RT along on lakeside of station parallel to railway to Schmerikon.
72	Schmerikon (408m)	**RB** Rejoin R9 and cycle over drained marshes to R4 junction, RT to Bilten and Niederurnen. (R4 continues south.) R9 LT by VSIB towards Walensee. Shortly afterwards reach tunnels beneath autobahn by Filzbach.
89	Filzbach (706m)	YH and Filzbach town perch above cycleway. Access either from Mühlehorn or from R4 by Näfels using a minor road along flanks of Kerenzer Berg. A climb is unavoidable but the views of the Churfirsten and Walensee are great.

FACILITIES							
	Distance (km)	Camp site	YH/BP	B&B	Hotel	Station	Bike shop
Unterägeri	10	✓		✓	4		✓
Oberägeri	12				Many		✓
Sattel	19	✓		✓	2		
Einsiedeln	40				Many	✓	✓
Willerzell	44			✓			
Pfäffikon	60	✓			1	✓	✓
Rapperswil	65	✓	✓		Many	✓	✓
Schmerikon	75						✓
Benken (off route)	72				1		✓
Weesen	86				Many		
Filzbach	89		✓		Many		

TOURIST INFORMATION			
From/to	Name	Address	Telephone/Website
Rotkreuz/ Hauptsee	Zug Tourismus	Reisezentrum Zug Bahnhofplatz CH-6304 Zug	+41 (0)41 723 6800 www.zug-tourismus.ch
Sattel/ Pfäffikon	Schwyz Tourismus	Bahnhofstrasse 4 Postfach 655 CH-6431 Schwyz	+41 (0)41 855 5950 www.schwyz-tourismus.ch
Rapperswil/ Filzbach	Ostschweiz Tourismus	Bahnhofplatz 1a CH-9001 St Gallen	+41 (0)71 227 3737 www.ostschweiz.ch

Stage 7: Filzbach – Buchs
45km; 150m; easy

The stars here are the limestone cliffs and green terraces of the Churfirsten wall hanging over the turquoise waters of the glacial lake. There are one or two short thigh-busting ascents and equally breath-snatching descents. There are no roads along the north shore so reach Quinton by boat if you wish to visit it. The south-facing slopes produce excellent wines and figs, kiwi fruit and even bananas grow outside. The lake water is very clean with safe bathing at Walenstadt and Weesen. Walenstadt, an interesting former textile centre, as you can tell from some of the buildings, is now a resort.

The valley route continues to Sargans through fields filled with goats and geese as well as the ubiquitous cattle. Impressive mountains rise on either side approaching the stone tower of Sargans, poking out of the valley floor on a crag. Here R9 and R2 join on the Rhein flood embankment and continue northwards ever so gently downstream. During Föhn conditions, the hot dry winds may fairly whistle down the valley giving

By the Walensee

you a speedy run downhill. Later in the day the wind may reverse, with hefty upvalley winds making northward progress tiring. Despite being close to an autobahn this route never fails to delight, the surface being wonderfully smooth and the mountain slopes uplifting with their green fields, almost white rock outcrops and Heidi associations.

Vaduz, Liechtenstein's capital city, is a very unromantic place full of banks, although the *Kunstmuseum* (art gallery) is excellent. The castle is impressive viewed from the Rhein towpath and the youth hostel at Schaan is comfortable, with restaurant-standard meals. Schaan railway station is also quaint, unstaffed now and served by Austrian railways commuter trains, but one can imagine pre-World War I minor royalty getting down from their Pullmans here to visit the 'Serene Highness of the Principality' in the castle just up the road.

ITINERARY		
Distance Location (km)		Directions
0	Filzbach (706m)	Take minor road to Mühlehorn or continue along R9. Short steep climbs and descents, route sometimes on trail hanging out over lake on run into Walenstadt.
14	Walenstadt (427m)	Follow R9 through town and out along valley. Only climbs over bridges crossing autobahn and into Sargans.

| 26 | Sargans (483m) | Follow twists and turns signposted past castle and station and out across Rhein plain to pass beneath autobahn and onto Rhein embankment. LT by VSIB. Follow into Buchs. |
| 45 | Buchs (451m) | To reach Schaan YH take bike underpass slightly upstream of station and continue to Rhein bridge. Risky section where autobahn exit roads feed traffic into Buchs and Schaan – take care! Then into Schaan on cycleway and RT following YH signs to reach hostel, about 2km from turnoff. |

Alternative for the energetic

Tour of the Churfirsten from Weesen to Buchs with about 700m of climbing. See chapter 2 (The Rhein Route).

FACILITIES							
	Distance (km)	Camp site	YH/BP	B&B	Hotel	Station	Bike shop
Mols	12				1		
Walenstadt	14	✓			3	✓	✓
Sargans	26				1	✓	✓
Buchs	45	✓			Many	✓	✓
Vaduz–Schaan	47	✓	✓		3		

TOURIST INFORMATION			
From/to	Name	Address	Telephone/Website
Filzbach/ Buchs	Ostschweiz Tourismus	Bahnhofplatz 1a CH-9001 St Gallen	+41 (0)71 227 3737 www.ostschweiz.ch

Stage 8: Buchs – Rorschach
68km; 90m; easy

From here to the Bodensee there is a stronghold of Swiss farms offering 'sleeping in the hayloft' accommodation, so, with a sleeping bag and a torch and instead of camping, you might like to try these at Grabser Berg, Gams, Montlingen, Balgach, Eichberg or Thal (see www.abenteuer-stroh.ch). Close to Buchs lies the 'tiniest city in Switzerland', Werdenberg, a row of superb houses crowned by a castle dating from 1230. Enjoy, especially the Doctor's House (a museum) with carvings of snakes under the eaves.

Views along the river change frequently as the valley widens into basins or is restricted by spurs. Formerly the Alpine Rhein caused devastating floods so its course has been controlled. There is a current programme to soften these engineering effects by reintroducing basins and meanders to regenerate local flora and fauna.

Simultaneously flood embankments are being strengthened as a defence against climatic change. Many people paddle and bathe in the river pools but the currents can be strong so take care. Visits to Appenzell from pleasant market town Altstätten, can be made by bike (500m climb) or by taking the rack railway part of the way to Gais. To the Swiss flat land is an infrequent bonus so building levels increase approaching the Bodensee, although the route follows quiet roads through housing areas. Here the Swiss love for gnomes and amazing garden decorations reaches an art form not to be missed.

Beyond St Margrethen the route leads onto the Rhein lake delta. Wild marsh flowers, birds large and small, as well as the evidence of land under construction make this an interesting ride, although you may suffer from windblown sand. By continuing into Bregenz in Austria you can ascend Pfänder mountain (with or without your bike) to view the delta from above, and then make the thrilling ride back to Bregenz. Turning the other way leads to Rorschach, with its historic red *Rathaus* (town hall) and the end of R9 by the station. It is a pleasant little town landward of the busy road along the lakeside, with good excursions possible inland or on the Bodensee. From here you can also take a train up to Heiden (807m), the retirement home of Henri Dumont (founder of the Red Cross) with its Red Cross museum.

The best cycle route to Heiden is from St Margrethen (R4). R2 continues to Basel, or up the Rhein valley to Andermatt. Local routes lead to nearby St Gallen whilst a network of cycleways covers Canton Thurgau.

Dirty weather, crossing the Rhein towards Schaan

ITINERARY		
Distance (km)	Location	Directions
0	Buchs (451m)	Through town towards Werdenberg and on to Grabs, Gams and Augstisried. **RB** Take road through Lienz and rejoin R9 in Rüthi (RT towards Rhein). **T** Continue on gravel over flood plain to reach Blatten by Oberriet.
21	Blatten (425m)	The Rhein embankment route continues from here to St Margrethen. Keep on left (west) bank of river. Otherwise, stay on R9 through busy Oberriet to Altstätten.
29	Altstätten (455m)	**RB** Take the road through town and via Marbach, Rebstein and Balgach to St Margrethen. **T** Stay on R9, descending to plain through industrial estate then on rough track through Widnau and into St Margrethen.
43	St Margrethen (403m)	Stay on Rhein embankment out to Fussach, then LT out onto delta dunes and flats to bridge over old Rhein by Buriet. **RB** Continue along Alter Rhein embankment into Buriet, avoiding rough delta trails. Continue along R9 into Rorschach.
68	Rorschach (398m)	

Woodworking and chalet building live on (Stage 3)

Lungerersee: Landscape with train (Route 9, Stage 4)

FACILITIES							
	Distance (km)	Camp site	YH/BP	B&B	Hotel	Station	Bike shop
Frümsen	14				1		
Oberriet	22	✓		✓	3	✓	✓
Altstätten	29			✓	Many	✓	✓
St Margrethen	43	✓ (Höchst)			1	✓	✓
Thal	58	✓		✓	Many		✓
Rorschach	68		✓	✓	Many	✓	✓

TOURIST INFORMATION			
From/to	Name	Address	Telephone/Website
Buchs/ Rorschach	Ostschweiz Tourismus	Bahnhofplatz 1a CH-9001 St Gallen	+41 (0)71 227 3737 www.ostschweiz.ch

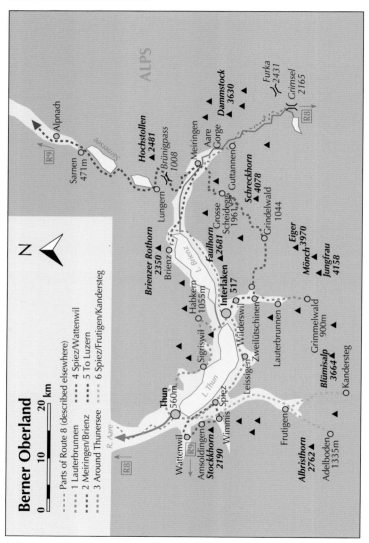

Berner Oberland

N

- - - Parts of Route 8 (described elsewhere)
····· 1 Lauterbrunnen
····· 4 Spiez/Wattenwil
····· 2 Meiringen/Brienz
····· 5 To Luzern
····· 3 Around Thunersee
····· 6 Spiez/Frutigen/Kandersteg

0   10   20 km

ALPS

Alpnach

Sarnen
471m

Sarnersee

R9

Hochstollen
▲ 2481

Brünigpass
1008

Lungern

Meiringen

Aare
Gorge

Dammstock
3630

Furka
2431

Grimsel
2165

R8

Schreckhorn
4078

Guttannen

Brienzer Rothorn
2350 ▲

Brienz

L. Brienz

Faulhorn
▲ 2681

Grosse
Scheidegg
1961

Grindelwald
1044

Eiger
3970

Habkern
1055m

Interlaken
517

Wilderswil

Zweilütschinen

Lauterbrunnen

Grimmelwald
900m

Mönch
4158

Jungfrau
4158

Sigriswil

L. Thun

Leissigen

Blümisalp
3664

Kandersteg

Thun
560m

Spiez

Wimmis

Frutigen

Albristhorn
2762 ▲

Adelboden
1335m

Amsoldingen

Stockhorn
2190 ▲

Wattenwil

R9

R8

R. Aare

236

Crossing the Aare Canal Bridge during an Interlaken town tour (Route 1)

You can easily spend over a week in Interlaken, renting an apartment for greater flexibility and affordability. A plethora of circular routes surround Interlaken and if, as the afternoon wears on, the spirit is willing, but the legs have got weaker, there are trains or ships to bring you back. The tourist office has information about most of these routes and also its four signposted cycle routes (between 8km and 21km long) around Interlaken itself. Since Interlaken has an open air swimming pool, a minor railway museum, a good tourism museum, rail and cable excursions into the mountains and elegant shops – as well as places to hire bikes – it is a good base for a family holiday.

Some of the routes that follow are suitable for families and others can be made so by judicious use of bus, ship or train. The whole area is officially German-speaking, but English is also widely spoken.

LOCAL MAPS
Swisstopo 1:100,000 Composite
101   Thuner See–Zentralschweiz

TOURIST INFORMATION		
Name	**Address**	**Telephone/Website**
Interlaken Tourismus	Höheweg 37	+41 (0)33 826 5300
	CH-3800 Interlaken	www.interlaken.ch

Downhill after the Grosse Scheidegg (Route 3)

Route 1: Lauterbrunnen Valley
33km; 340m; moderate

In Lauterbrunnen

This is a short trip, but clear air makes the views of the mountains breathtaking so keep your camera handy. The Lauterbrunnen Valley is a textbook example of a glacial valley in the Alps, drawings and photographs of its U-shaped valley sides, hanging valleys and waterfalls being found in any learned tome about alpine geography. It is also beautiful and offers an easy and interesting day's cycling, even though you follow the same route out and back. After Lauterbrunnen itself, the valley opens out, with wonderfully convoluted rocks in steep cliffs and long, thin waterfalls jetting from caves and springs about two thirds of the way to the top.

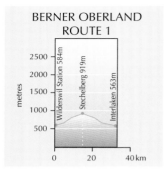

Above rears a stupendous line-up of snowy crags: Monch, Jungfrau, Gletscherhorn and Breithorn. Farms, fruit trees, meadows and pleasant camp sites follow with few vehicles to disturb you. On the east wall south of Lauterbrunnen, Trummelbach Falls offer a lift into the mountain to see cascades of glacial water draining from the Eiger – very noisy, very dramatic, wonderful water-carved sluices, with much spray and distinctly chilly.

ITINERARY		
Distance Location (km)		**Directions**
0	Wilderswil Station (584m)	Cross the tracks by the level crossing and carry SO to cross the stream. TR and climb to Gsteigwiler following RR61 towards Grindelwald. The tarmac ends. Follow an unsurfaced track along the valley bottom to Zweilütschinen where RR6.1 goes on to Lauterbrunnen.
5	Zweilütschinen (655m)	Cross the line on a level crossing, over the river and up into the trees and shadows of the big truncated spurs. The path narrows and you need to walk 150m, past a steep drop to the river, shared with walkers, busy in the high season but empty in September. The trail goes up and down past flood controls and has a poor surface. The signposting is excellent all the way to Lauterbrunnen.
9	Lauterbrunnen (800m)	Short descent to the valley floor and RF onto a almost car-free road to Stechelberg.
15	Stechelberg (919m)	The road ends for wheeled traffic, except for daredevil mountain bikers. Return the same way.
33	Interlaken	

Route 2: Meiringen/Brienz via Grosse Scheidegg
76km; 1650m; strenuous

Up to Grindelwald

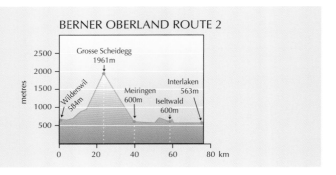

BERNER OBERLAND ROUTE 2

This is seriously difficult, but one can hop on a passing bus or train to ease the pain. It is well worth doing. The views are fantastic and there is a 16km downhill stretch after Grosse Scheidegg, where you almost touch the Eiger, Monch and Jungfrau stretching off in the distance. At the end of the long drop you pass close to the Reichenbach Falls where Sherlock Holmes met Professor Moriarty and his death. Meiringen is a pleasant little town with, unsurprisingly, connections to Sir Arthur Conan Doyle who went hill-walking there. There is a statue of Sherlock Holmes on the main square of the town and a replica of 221b Baker Street in the cellar of the English Church on the same square.

The less health-conscious rider may well be impressed by the cafés on the main street all of which feature meringues, reputedly named after the town, but probably even more so by the railway station which has a train every hour back to Interlaken. The floor of the valley down to the Brienzersee is occupied by a Swiss Air Force air-field. Progress can be blocked by aircraft taking off or landing. The hardy or fit can return to Interlaken on R8/9 along the heights above the lake. (There are two short sections of unsurfaced track.) Alternatively, you can carry on to Brienz and take a train or a ship back there. (You can always return to cycle the return leg in the opposite direction on another day, making use of the ship or train again.)

ITINERARY		
Distance (km)	Location	Directions
0	Wilderswil Station (584m)	Cross the tracks by the level crossing and carry SO to cross bridge by the church. TR and climb to Gsteigwiler following RR61 towards Grindelwald. The tarmac ends. Follow an unsurfaced track along the valley bottom to Zweilütschinen.
5	Zweilütschinen (655m)	TL towards Grindelwald through Lütschental. Cross the railway lines by Burglauenen Station and TL to follow a

		walkers' path along the river to reach Grindelwald Grund (943m). Grindelwald Dorf (village) lies 91m above.
16	Grindelwald (1034m)	Follow the narrow, steep, largely traffic-free road up to Grossescheidegg. Up above Grindelwald Postbuses have absolute right of way and so if you hear the post horn get off the road.
23.5	Grosse Scheidegg (1961m)	Dress up warmly and set off down through Schwarzwaldalp (1454m), Rosenlaui (1328m) and Willigen (621m) to Meiringen.
39.5	Meiringen (595m)	Follow R8/9 towards Interlaken. (TR for Brienz after about 11km.) Climb up past the back of the (very) Grand Hotel Giessbach. You are requested to push your bike through the grounds and may want to as it is a very steep unsurfaced section.
52.5	Giessbach (700m)	Another unsurfaced section. You drop towards Iseltwald on tarmac.
58.5	Iseltwald (600m)	One last short climb and you run along the lake shore through Bönigen into Interlaken near to Ost railway station.
76	Interlaken	

Route 3: Around Thunersee
75km; 1160m; difficult

This is an amusing day's cycling, mostly on quiet roads on tarmac. It offers you fantastic views into the mountains of the Berner Oberland and of Interlaken from above and has the advantage that halfway round the route, in Thun, you can throw in the towel and climb onto a ship or a train to be amazed that you climbed that high!

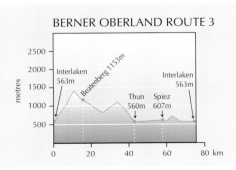

BERNER OBERLAND ROUTE 3

Thun is well worth visiting. The old town, off to the left as you ride into the town, has a medieval double decker shopping street (Oberhauptstrasse) and pleasant cafés around the Rathausplatz. The south side of the lake is much flatter. Spiez with its fine castle is another chance to climb onto the train or onto a lake ship. The route is described in an anticlockwise manner, but the other direction would mean that you get your legs into shape before hitting the hilly sections.

ITINERARY		
Distance (km)	**Location**	**Directions**
0	Interlaken West station	TL along the Bahnhofstrasse across the bridge at the northern end of the station. Follow signposting to Waldegg and then RF towards Habkern.
7	Habkern (1055m)	Follow signs to Waldegg. You pass signs exhorting you to pay a charge for road upkeep – these only apply to motorists.
14	Waldegg (1221m)	You climb over the highest point of the trip (1408m) and drop into Waldegg.
16	Beatenberg (1153m)	You descend further into Beatenberg. You could take a funicular down to Beatenbucht and a ship across the lake to Spiez. The road drops through tunnels to Sigriswil.
26	Sigriswil (807m)	Long climb to Heiligenschwendi (1002m) before dropping through Goldiwil (905m) into Thun.
43	Thun (560m)	TR before the railway station under the underpass towards Allmendingen (574m), where you follow R8 and then R8/9 to Spiez.
58	Spiez (607m)	From railway station downhill out of town on busy road, then death-defying LT across traffic (use crossing) and along quieter lakeside roads parallel to railway and main road to Därligen.
70	Därligen (562m)	Follow cycleway perched over lake, finally underneath major highway. About 3km on wide hard shoulder before exit on signposted road to traffic lights. Cross with traffic lights to security of cycleway and descend into the quiet of the delta farms. Follow route into Unterseen and Interlaken.
75	Interlaken	

Route 4: Wattenwil
70km; 380m; moderate

This is a trip on mainly surfaced cycle tracks and quiet roads into the low-lying hills on the south side of the Thunersee and offers superb views of the Berner Oberland mountains from a distance. This description starts and ends in Interlaken but you could take a train or a ship from or to Spiez.

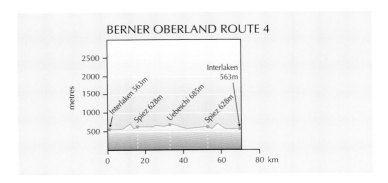

ITINERARY		
Distance (km)	Location	Directions
0	Interlaken (563m)	R8/9 through Unterseen, Därligen, Leissigen and Faulensee to Spiez.
17	Spiez (628m)	TO on railway station platform. TL down hill and veer left through traffic lights. TL at roundabout to go under railway towards Spiezmoos. Follow R9 to Wimmis.
22	Wimmis (629m)	TR to follow RR64/74 up Zwieselberg to Amsoldingen.
30	Amsoldingen (640m)	Follow RR74 towards Wattenwil, but RT at Dittligen on R4 towards Thun to Allmendingen and R8.
42	Allmendingen (574m)	Follow R8 towards Spiezmoos, unsurfaced and surfaced. Some of the surfaced route is on minor roads. Take care!
53	Spiez (628m)	Follow R8/9 to Interlaken.
70	Interlaken	

Route 5: Luzern
82km; 970m; difficult

This is a one-way trip returning by train. You could also consider taking a train to the top of the Brünigpass from Interlaken. You have a choice of routes over the pass. The official route (R9) from Meiringen up the Brünigpass is steep and rough. Alternatively, the minor road from Meiringen through Brünigen climbs steeply on the busy main road from Brienz for about a kilometre over the pass.

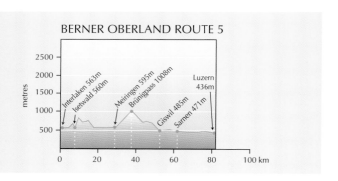

BERNER OBERLAND ROUTE 5

	ITINERARY	
Distance Location (km)		**Directions**
0	Interlaken (563m)	**RB** Take bridge over Aare to Goldswil and along road north of Lake Brienz to Brienz and RT onto R9 at end of lake. **T** Pick up R9 by station and ride out, passing under autobahn, to Bönigen, then along quiet lakeside road. Then steep, rough, dramatic unfenced section to road junction at Giessbach (smart hotel, waterfalls).
14	Giessbach (758m)	Take downhill plunge on road to delta flats at Stägmatten. Continue to Meiringen on rural roads, across military airfield (controlled when planes cross, very noisy).
27	Meiringen (595m)	**RB** Use road to Brünigen and continue on road over pass and down to Lungern. **T** Either use road to pass top or R9 rough route through woods above road. R9 trail beyond pass is almost unrideable at first, later very pleasant.
40	Lungern (752m)	**RB** Continue on road to Giswil. Tourists follow R9 along rough track on west of Lungerer See, then back to tarmac and rejoin road into Giswil.

53	Giswil (485m)	Take R4/9 signs along west side of lake to Sarnen, pleasantly up and down.
61	Sarnen (471m)	RB Stay on R4 to Stansstad, avoiding rough trail. T RT onto R9 by VSIB out of town, some rough trails through the woods. Use road to Stansstad with care.
66	Stansstad (435m)	LT onto R9 then interesting narrow section under autobahn and along through Hergiswil and climb to Horw. RT on R9 along lake edge, through villages to outskirts of Luzern. Follow R9 to station, beware trams and other cyclists.
82	Luzern (436m)	

Route 6: Frutigen and Kandersteg
94km; 940m; difficult

This route follows quiet, mainly asphalted roads offering good views of the mountains. It would also be paradise for railway freaks. The rolling climb along the sides of the Kander Valley offers good views of the BLS line to Brig through the Lötschberg Tunnel. Masochists could also follow a very steep minor road up through Elsigbach to reach Adelboden, but it is a long climb followed by an unspectacular descent. The scenery on that route out towards Adelboden is pleasant. South and west of Adelboden there are awesome mountain views and interesting trails for mountain bikers.

En route to Adelboden

Farmhouse in Ringgenberg (Route 1)

ITINERARY		
Distance Location (km)		**Directions**
0	Interlaken (563m)	R8/9 through Unterseen, Därligen, Leissigen and Faulensee to Spiez.
17	Spiez (628m)	TO on railway station platform. TL down hill and veer left through traffic lights. TL at roundabout to go under railway towards Spiezmoos. Follow R9 to Wimmis.
22	Wimmis (629m)	Join RR64 across the fields followed by a minor climb and descent through Reichenbach-im-Kandertal to Frutigen.
35	Frutigen (780m)	Follow RR64 for a steep climb in part unsurfaced to Kandersteg.
47	Kandersteg (1207m)	Return to Interlaken by the same route or take a train from Kandersteg.
94	Interlaken	

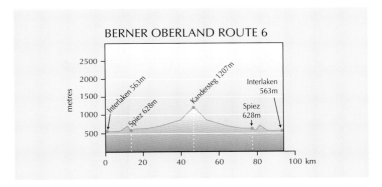

BERNER OBERLAND ROUTE 6

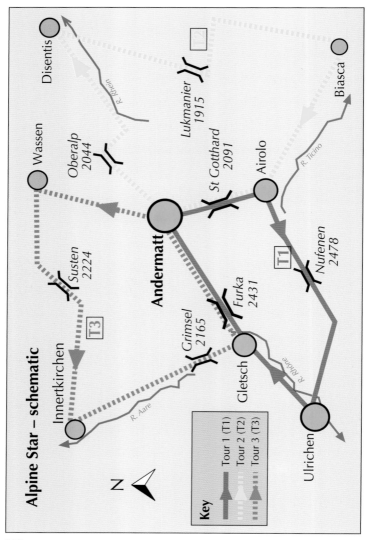

Alpine Star – schematic

Disentis

Wassen

R. Rhein

Lukmanier
1915

*Oberalp
2044*

*St Gotthard
2091*

Biasca

Airolo

R. Ticino

Andermatt

*Nufenen
2478*

T1

*Susten
2224*

*Furka
2431*

T3

*Grimsel
2165*

Innertkirchen

Gletsch

R. Rhône

R. Aare

Ulrichen

N

Key
Tour 1 (T1)
Tour 2 (T2)
Tour 3 (T3)

11 THE ALPINE STAR

These routes look more like a butterfly than a star but they are known as the Alpenstern (Alpine Star). Andermatt is surrounded by high passes with the Rhein, Rhône and Ticino rivers all rising in mountains nearby. There are three circular routes from Andermatt that are supposedly manageable in one day but graded here as 'exceedingly strenuous'. The mass cycling event known as The Alpen Brevet takes place along these routes each summer in August and there is information about it available in English on the web: www.alpenbrevet.ch. The Brevet has been modified drastically at very short notice in the past, because of snow-blocked passes – even in August – so make sure you have enough food and adequate clothing before you set off on one of these trips.

Naturally, you can split these routes and stop at the bottom of a pass overnight. Information about facilities can be found in chapters 1, 2 and 3. Do check at a tourist office that the passes on your chosen route are open before you set off. Andermatt and Wassen are in Canton Uri, and Innertkirchen is in Canton Bern, where German is the official language. Disentis is in Graubünden where Romansh is spoken. Biasca and Bellinzona are in Ticino where Italian is spoken.

Lukmanier summit reservoir (Tour 2)

TOURIST INFORMATION			
From/to	Name	Address	Telephone/Website
Andermatt, Wassen, Realp	Tourist Info Uri	Tellspielhaus Schützengasse 11 Postfach CH-6460 Altdorf	+41 (0)41 872 0450 www.uri.info
Sustenpass, Grimselpass	alpenregion.ch	Bahnhofstrasse 22 CH-3860 Meiringen	+41 (0)33 972 5050 www.alpenregion.ch
Ulrichen, Furkapass	Valais Tourism	Rue Pré Fleuri 6 PO Box 1469 CH-1951 Sion	+41 (0)27 327 3570 www.wallis.ch
Passo di Lucomagno (Lukmanierpass), Biasca	Ticino Tourismo	Casa postale 1441 Via Lugano 12 CH-6501 Bellinzona	+41 (0)91 825 7056 www.ticino-tourism.ch

Tour 1: The Alpine Circuit Gotthard–Nufenen–Furka
106km; 3020m; exceedingly strenuous

This trip climbs over the Gotthard Pass the easy way from the north. Once across the border into Ticino, R3 swings right and follows *pavé* (cobblestone road surface) that never seems to get shorter, but is almost traffic free. You do finally arrive at the summit area by the hospice and park your bike by the sausage and souvenir stall along with several hundred motorists – a scruffy area and disappointing for such a historic spot. The Gotthard National Museum and the fort are excellent and well worth visiting, but it's time to go down the cobbled hairpins (a Swiss national monument) of the Val

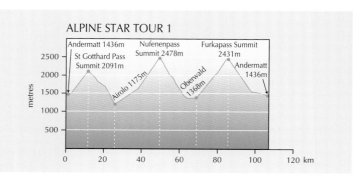

Tremola road. This is the kind of road that Fausto Coppi cut his teeth on in the days when racing cyclists survived on spaghetti, brandy and black coffee. The *pavé* is bumpy, but the alternative, modern road features tunnels, snowsheds and motorists with unknown skills. Cheer up – you will be able to contemplate the cobbles more slowly climbing up on Tour 2.

The Nufenenpass/Passo di Novena is modern and not very scenic. However, it is high and once down below in Ulrichen you may well prefer to take a train back rather than tackle the Furkapass. If you do manage it, it's a fast run down the Furka back to Andermatt from the top.

ITINERARY		
Distance Location (km)		Directions
0	Andermatt (1436m)	TO near station. Stay on R1/3 through village centre to road to Hospental. Take any RT across railway line to follow a much quieter road left to Hospental station.
3	Hospental (1452m)	LT at roundabout signposted Airolo, St Gotthard Pass (R3).
13	St Gotthard summit (2091m)	Small TO in museum building. R3 (pavé) to Airolo runs down between the Ospizio and Museum.
26	Airolo (1175m)	TO opposite station. Climb road towards Ulrichen, Oberwald and Passo d Novena.
48	Nufenenpass summit (2478m)	Descend thankfully.
62	Ulrichen (1346m)	Over the level crossing and take a RT on to a minor road parallel to R1 towards Oberwald and Furkapass. (It is a better quality road.) You pick up R1 later. Stay on the R1 cycleways to Oberwald where the surface quality is good to avoid a major tunnel. Climb over Furkapass on R1.
83	Furkapass summit (2431m)	Descend through Realp to Andermatt.
106	Andermatt (1436m)	

Tour 2: The Three Language Tour: Oberalp–Lukmanier–Gotthard

161km; 3300m; exceedingly strenuous

Whether this or Tour 3 is tougher is debatable. This has ten per cent less climbing than Tour 3, but is the longest by far.

It starts with a quick run up the Oberalppass, which is not too strenuous. There is then a spectacular drop to Disentis with its fine abbey church before the climb over the

The abbey in Disentis at the junction of the Lukmanierpass and Oberalppass roads

Lukmanierpass/Passo del Lucomagno. It is advisable to avoid this route at weekends and there are tunnels and snowsheds on the way up so do not forget your lights.

Once you are over the Lukmanier enjoy the stunning descent to Biasca. Then turn north and follow the old St Gotthard road up to Airolo, an 875m climb. The scenery, the railway and even the autobahn make for an interesting trip. Most of the traffic is on the autobahn, droning above you. In Airolo you are only 27km from Andermatt, but it includes a 15km, 1000m climb over the pavé of the Val Tremolo. From the summit Andermatt is only 13km downhill.

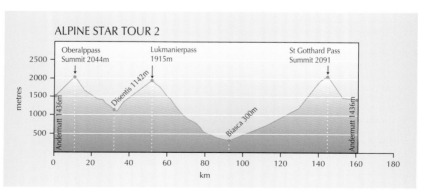

ALPINE STAR TOUR 2

Oberalppass Summit 2044m — Lukmanierpass 1915m — St Gotthard Pass Summit 2091

Disentis 1142m — Biasca 300m

Andermatt 1436m — Andermatt 1436m

metres: 2500, 2000, 1500, 1000, 500

km: 0, 20, 40, 60, 80, 100, 120, 140, 160, 180

ITINERARY		
Distance (km)	**Location**	**Directions**
0	Andermatt (1436m)	TO near station. TR by TO to follow R1/R2/R3 then TL to follow R2 on road over Oberalppass. Dark snowshed near summit.
11	Oberalppass (2044m)	Follow R2 on road through Sedrun.
34	Disentis (1142m)	RT to follow RR36 towards the Lukmanier summit.
54	Lukmanierpass summit (1915m) in tunnel.	Follow road downhill.
58	Acquacalda (1700m)	Ignore first RR36 left as this is rough in parts.
63	Campra (1410m)	Shortly after Campra follow the RR36 signpost right to follow an almost unused section of old road. Similarly take the very quiet surfaced road off right at the peak of the left turn hairpin through Largario, Ponte Valentino, Marolta, Prugiasco, Acquarossa, Dongio and Ludiano to Biasca.
96	Biasca (300m)	RT on R3 towards Airolo.
130	Airolo (1175m)	R3 towards Andermatt.
148	St Gotthard Pass summit (2091m)	Descend R3 to Andermatt
161	Andermatt (1436m)	

Tour 3: The Alpen Brevet Junior Route
120km; 3520m; exceedingly strenuous

There are even tougher routes available for participants in the Alpen Brevet, but the description here is of the Junior event, which is hard enough!

The route leaves Andermatt and takes the road through Göschenen to Wassen. This route is less dangerous in this direction, cycling downhill rather than cycling uphill, but care is still needed. In Wassen the climb over the eastern approach to the Sustenpass starts, easier than approaching from the west but still strenuous. After the summit there is a nice long drop in and out of tunnels (lights on, sunglasses off) into Innertkirchen, where you turn left to climb over 1500m to the Grimselpass summit. This road too has several tunnels, which can often be bypassed by taking the old road, which has somewhat variable surface quality but may be preferable.

When you get there, the Grimselpass summit is tidier than the St Gotthard summit and is followed by a 400m drop to reach Gletsch, where you turn left for Andermatt, climbing 674m over the Furkapass on the way. As you go up you pass the Hotel

Above the Aareschlucht on the Grimselpass road

Belvedere with good views of the rapidly melting Rhône Glacier. Take a break for a look. The glacier won't be there much longer. The summit café on the Furka provides a welcome break after which you probably won't need to pedal much until Realp. Then the route is level into Hospental with a final downhill cruise into Andermatt for that long-awaited shower, food and a drink.

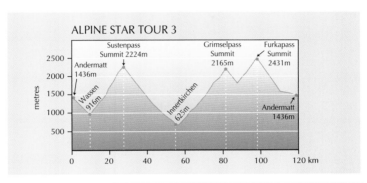

ITINERARY		
Distance Location (km)		**Directions**
0	Andermatt (1436m)	Follow R3 down through Göschenen to Wassen.
10	Wassen (916m)	LT follow road over Sustenpass towards Innertkirchen.
28	Sustenpass summit (2224m)	Downhill towards Innertkirchen.
56	Innertkirchen (625m)	TL to ascend Grimselpass on R8.
82	Grimselpass summit (2165m)	Descend to Gletsch on R8.
88	Gletsch (1757m)	TL to ascend Furkapass on R1 towards Andermatt.
99	Furkapass summit (2431m)	R1 towards Realp (1538m), Hospental (1452m) and Andermatt.
120	Andermatt	

APPENDIX 1:

Useful websites and information sources

USEFUL WEBSITES AND INFORMATION SOURCES		
Name	**Description**	**Website/postal address**
Bed and Breakfast Switzerland		www.bnb.ch
Bike and Sleep	Bike hotels	www.velotel.ch
DB	German Railways	www.bahn.co.uk
SBB/CFF/FFS	Swiss Railways	www.sbb.ch
Swiss Budget Hotels		www.rooms.ch
Swiss Tourism		www.myswitzerland.com Schweiz Tourismus Postfach 695 CH-8027 Zürich
Swiss Youth Hostel Association		www.youthhostel.ch
Veloland Schweiz	Cycling coordination/ Route planning	www.veloland.ch
Ostschweiz Tourismus	Regional Tourist Authority Eastern Switzerland	www.ostschweiz.ch Ostschweiz Tourismus Bahnhofplatz 1a CH-9001 St Gallen
Berner Oberland Tourism	Regional Tourist Authority Berner Oberland	www.berneroberland.ch Destinationen Berner Oberland Postfach CH-3800 Interlaken
Berner Mittelland Tourism	Regional Tourist Authority Berner Mittelland	www.smit.ch Schweizer Mittelland Tourismus c/o Bern Tourismus Amthausgasse 4 Postfach 169 CH-3000 Bern 7
Watch Valley Tourism	Regional Tourist Authority Jura	www.watchvalley.ch Watch Valley Coordination Route de Sorvilier 21 CH-2735 Bévilard

USEFUL WEBSITES AND INFORMATION SOURCES		
Name	Description	Website/postal address
Regional Tourist Authority Baden Württemberg	North bank of Rhein between Konstanz and Basel	www.tourismus-bw.de Tourismus Marketing GmbH Baden-Württemberg Esslinger Strasse 8 D-70182 Stuttgart
International Bodensee Tourist Authority	Regional Tourist Authority for the Bodensee	www.bodensee-tourismus.com Internationale Bodensee Tourismus GmbH Hafenstrasse 6 D-78462 Konstanz

Have you thought about choosing somewhere flat next time?

APPENDIX 2:

Recommended accommodation

To find B&Bs visit www.bnb.ch and to find youth hostels, visit www.youthhostel.ch.

Rhône Route
- Fiesch YH – Good sport and leisure facilities. Ideal for sporty families for a few days.
- Sion – B&B Ms Liberek, very romantic in the old town.
- Lausanne YH – No evening meals at weekends. Popular with school groups.

Rhein Route
- Andermatt B&Bs – Check www.andermatt.ch (in German).
  B&B Verena Kumli-Regli (Mariahilfsgasse 6, tel: +41 41 887 1965, kumli-regli@bluewin.ch) can be recommended.
- Oberalp Pass Gasthaus – Piz Calmot, piz.calmut@bluewin.ch
- Bonaduz – H Weisses Kreuz, Versamerstrasse 5, tel: +41 81 6411174
- Schaan (Liechtenstein) – Youth hostel
- Oberriet – B&B Rohner, very modern rooms, rightly very popular.
- Winden – Familie Manser, Täschliberg, www.taeschliberg.ch, near Egnach. Lullaby in the evenings on the Alpenhorn.
- Gailingen B&Bs – Check www.gailingen.de.
- Unterlauchringen – Gasthaus Adler, www.adler-lauchringen.de, in German.
- Basel YH – Basic hostel near SBB station.

North–South Route
- Basel – See above
- Luzern – H Tourist, St Kaliquai 12
- Lukmanier Pass – Hospezi S Maria
- Acquacalda – Centro Ecologico UomoNatura, www.uomonatura.ch. An almost carbon neutral hotel.
- Locarno – Youth hostel

Alpine Panorama Route
- Sörenberg – B&B Bauernhof Salwideli. Evening meals can be taken in the nearby mountain inn (Gasthof Salwideli) or you can cook in a well-equipped kitchen; Gasthof Salwideli specialises in locally grown food.
- Thun – Zunfthaus zu Metzgern, Rathausplatz, www.zumetzgern.ch
- Burgistein – Stauffenbühl, B&B, excellent evening meal provided on prior request. Fantastic views of the Berner Oberland, tel: +41 (0)33 3562301.

Mittelland Route
- Hauptwil – B&B, Fam Volz, erwvolz@bluewin.ch
- Bargen (8km off route on Aare Route) – B&B Mühlthaler. Interesting house for solar power fans.
- Neuchâtel – La Colinière, Ms Martine Colin, www.neuchateltourisme.ch. Small but comfortable former groom's room in the stable block.
- Champagne – B&B, Ms Georgette Banderet, Logis le Cédre, logislecedre@hotmail.com
- Lausanne – See above

Engadine Circuit
- Splügen – Hôtel Bodenhaus, www.hotel-bodenhaus.ch. Historic inn, with good food.
- Davos – Youth hostel, half board only
- St Moritz – Youth hostel, half board only
- Nauders – Gasthof zum Goldenen Löwen, Postplatz. Immense evening meals, very good value for money, tel: +43 5473 87208.

Jura Route
- Basel – See above
- Mariastein-Rotberg – Youth hostel, mock castle
- Courgenay – Hotel du Boeuf, www.boeuf-courgenay.ch. Serious food, superb rösti.
- Le Bémont – Youth hostel
- Travers – Hotel Cret de l'Anneau

Aare Route
- Unterlauchringen – See above
- Bargen – See above
- Thun – See above
- Leissigen – Youth hostel, Swiss chalet par excellence.
- Interlaken – B&B Fankhauser. The decor is something else.

Lakes Route
- Chateau d'Oex – Hotel de Ville
- Zweisimmen – Hotel Post
- Interlaken – See above
- Rapperswil – Youth hostel
- Schaan (Liechtenstein) – See above

APPENDIX 3:
Glossary of cycling terms

GLOSSARY OF CYCLING TERMS			
English	French	German	Italian
Air pressure, low	Trop peu de pression	Luftdruck, zu Wenig	Poca aria
Allen key	Clé Allen	Inbus	Chiave a brugola
Axle	Essieu	Achse	Asse
Bearing, Ball bearing	Roulement, Roulement à billes	Lager, Kugellager	Cuscinetti
Bell	Sonette	Glocke	Campanello
Bicycle/Bike	Vélo	Fahrad/Rad/Velo	Bicicletta, Bici
Bolt	Boulon	Bolzen	Bullone
Bottle	Bouteille à boire	Trinkflasche	Bottiglie
Bottle holder	Porte-bidon	Flaschenhalter	Porteborraccia
Brake	Frein	Bremse	Freno
Brake blocks	Patin de frein	Bremsgummi	Ceppo
Brake cable	Câble de frein	Bremszüge	Cavi freno
Cable	Cable	Draht/Kabel	Cavo
Cable casing	Gain de conduite	Zughülle	Guaina per fili
Chain	Chaine	Kette	Catena
Chain link	Maillon de chaine	Kettenglied	Maglia della catena
Chain link pin		Kettenniet	
Chain ring/ Chainwheel	Plateau de pedalier	Kettenblatt	Corona moltipliga
Chain tool	Chasse-rivets, Dérive chaine	Kettennieter	Smonta catena
Cogs/Sprocket	Pignon	Ritzel	Pignone
Crank	Pedalier	Tretkurbel/Kurbel	Pedivella
Derailleur	Dérailleur	Kettenschaltung	Cambio, Deragliatore
Dynamo	Dynamo	Dynamo	Dinamo
Fork	Fourche	Gabel,	Forcella
Frame	Cadre	Rahmen	Telaio
Free wheel	Roue libre	Freilaufrad	Ruota libera
Front derailleur	Dérailleur avant	Umwerfer	Deragliatore
Front light	Feu avant/phare	Vorderlicht	
Gear cable	Câble de dérailleur	Schaltzüge	
Gloves	Gants	Handschuhe	Guanti
Handlebars (broken)	Guidon (cassé, fissuré)	Lenker (Kaputt)	Manubrio
Helmet	Casque	Helm	Caschi

English	French	German	Italian
Hub	Moyeu	Nabe	Mozzo
Inner tube	Chambre a air	Schlauch	Camera d'aria
Lock	Cadenas	Schloss	Antifurti per bicicletta
Lubricant/Grease/Oil	Lubrifrifiant/Graisse/Huile	Schmiermittel/Fett/Öl	Lubrificante/Grasso/Olio
Luggage carrier, rack	Porte bagage	Gepäckträger	
Mudguard/Fender	Garde boue	Schutzblech	Parafanghi
Nipple	Douille	Nippel	Nipple
Nut	Écrou	Mutter	Dado
Pannier	Sacoche	Packtasche/Tasche	Borse per bicicletta
Pedal	Pedale	Pedal	Pedale
Phillips screwdriver	Tournevis cruciforme	Kreuzschlitz-Schraubenzieher	Cacciavite a croce
Pliers	Pinces	Zange	Pinza/Pinze
Pump	Pompe	Pumpe/Luftpumpe	Pumpa
Puncture/Flat tyre	Crevasion	Platten, Plattfuss	Foratura
Puncture repair kit	Rustines	Flickzeug	Pachchetto/Kit riparazioni
Rear light	Feu arriere	Rücklicht	
Rim	Jante	Felge	Cerchione
Rim tape	Fond de jante	Felgenband	
Saddle	Selle	Sattel	Sella
Screw	Vis	Schraube	Vite
Screwdriver	Tournevis	Schraubenzieher	Cacciavite
Spanner, adjustable	Clé Anglaise	Schraubenschlüssel/Engländer	Chiave Inglese
Spanner, wrench	Clé hexagonale	Schlüssel	Chiave
Spoke	Rayon	Speiche	Raggio
Spoke key	Clé à rayon	Speichenschlüssel/Nippelspanner	Tiraraggi
Spring, Oil/Air	Ressort, Air/Huile	Feder, Öl/Luft	
Sunglasses	Lunette	Sonnenbrille	Occhiati
Suspension fork	Fourche à suspension	Federgabel	Forcella Ammortizzata
Thread	Filet/Filetage	Gewinde	Filetto
Tyre	Pneu	Mantel/Reifen	Copertoncino
Tyre Lever/Tire Iron	Démonte-pneu	Reifenheber	
Valve	Valve	Ventil	Valvola
Valve, Schrader	Valve Schrader	Autoventil	Valvola Schrader
Valve, Presta	Valve	Ventil, Französisches	Valvola
Wheel	Roue	Rad	Ruota
Wheel trueing	Centrage des roues	Rad Zentrieren	Centare le ruote

NOTES

NOTES

NOTES

NOTES

LISTING OF CICERONE GUIDES

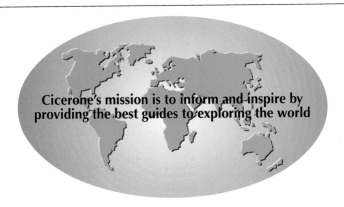

Cicerone's mission is to inform and inspire by providing the best guides to exploring the world

Since its foundation over 30 years ago, Cicerone has specialised in publishing guidebooks and has built a reputation for quality and reliability. It now publishes nearly 300 guides to the major destinations for outdoor enthusiasts, including Europe, UK and the rest of the world.

Written by leading and committed specialists, Cicerone guides are recognised as the most authoritative. They are full of information, maps and illustrations so that the user can plan and complete a successful and safe trip or expedition – be it a long face climb, a walk over Lakeland fells, an alpine traverse, a Himalayan trek or a ramble in the countryside.

With a thorough introduction to assist planning, clear diagrams, maps and colour photographs to illustrate the terrain and route, and accurate and detailed text, Cicerone guides are designed for ease of use and access to the information.

If the facts on the ground change, or there is any aspect of a guide that you think we can improve, we are always delighted to hear from you.

Cicerone Press
2 Police Square Milnthorpe Cumbria LA7 7PY
Tel:01539 562 069   Fax:01539 563 417
e-mail:info@cicerone.co.uk   web:www.cicerone.co.uk